MW01054225

THE PRISON BEFORE THE PANOPTICON

The

PRISON

before the

PANOPTICON

*Incarceration in Ancient and Modern
Political Philosophy*

JACOB ABOLAFIA

HARVARD UNIVERSITY PRESS

Cambridge, Massachusetts & London, England

2024

First printing

Library of Congress Cataloging-in-Publication Data
Names: Abolafia, Jacob, author.
Title: The prison before the Panopticon : incarceration in ancient and
modern political philosophy / Jacob Abolafia.
Description: Cambridge, Massachusetts ; London, England : Harvard
University Press, 2024. | Includes bibliographical references and
index. | English; words and phrases in Greek or Latin.
Identifiers: LCCN 2023040684 | ISBN 9780674290631 (cloth)
Subjects: LCSH: Imprisonment—Philosophy. | Punishment—Philosophy. |
Imprisonment—Early works to 1800. | Punishment—Early
works to 1800. | Prisons—Philosophy. | Prisons—History.
Classification: LCC HV8529 .A35 2024 | DDC 365.01—dc23/eng/20231212
LC record available at https://lccn.loc.gov/2023040684

For Ima and Abba

CONTENTS

Introduction   *1*

1. The Paradox of Incarceration in Democratic Athens   *25*

2. Plato's Theory of Incarceration   *45*

3. Incarceration in Thomas More's *Utopia*   *75*

4. "All Restraint of Motion"—Incarceration in Hobbes   *102*

5. Bentham's Panopticon—between Plato and the Carceral State   *126*

Conclusion   *157*

Notes   165

Acknowledgments   227

Index   231

THE PRISON BEFORE THE PANOPTICON

INTRODUCTION

BEFORE THERE WERE prisons, there was the idea of the prison. Incarceration as a penal practice, and certainly as a widespread penal practice, is relatively new—only a bit older than the United States.[1] The prison has been a topic of interest to political philosophers, however, for much longer than that. In the case of the prison, the idea precedes the institution.

Some of these early ideas were entirely detached from any prison in the real world, while others were intimately linked to emerging practices of penal incarceration. But taken together, they make up a long and largely unnoticed history of thinking about the prison. Theoretical traditions that begin with Demosthenes's *Against Timocrates* and Plato's *Laws* pass through some of the touchstones of modern political thought, including Thomas More's *Utopia,* Thomas Hobbes's *Leviathan,* and Jeremy Bentham's *Panopticon Letters.* Early philosophical accounts of incarceration can help us to understand and contextualize the practice of incarceration today, when it has become hard to imagine a time before "doing time." We can even see the transformed traces of their ideas and arguments in some of the ways we still talk about prisons and penal confinement.

The early history of prison thinking is especially valuable at a time when prisons are not only ubiquitous but also profoundly broken. As many political scientists and activists have observed, the scale, cruelty, and discriminatory character of mass incarceration in the United States poses a threat to the very legitimacy of democratic government.[2] While a philosophical history of the prison's beginning cannot save us from our present failure to punish our fellow citizens well or justly, it can help us to better understand how and why a democratic society might use the terrible power of penal confinement. This history also offers a basis for assessing the extent to which our own justifications for imprisonment stand up to scrutiny.

This book tells the story of two philosophical approaches to incarceration and, secondarily, of their assimilation into the more familiar theories of the prison that characterize the modern era of incarceration. The first of these approaches emerges from the contentious relationship between imprisonment and popularly authorized forms of government. Democratically minded thinkers have long been drawn to the egalitarian possibilities of the prison as a single form of punishment for rich and poor, weak and powerful alike. But they have also recognized the potential challenge to the equal status of citizen rulers posed by penal confinement: a citizen in prison is deprived of their right and ability to rule.

The second theoretical approach is that of the prison as the site of penal rehabilitation or reform, especially as formulated by Plato and his followers. Throughout much of the early history of thinking about the prison, the idea of incarceration as a method of improvement—for both the prisoner and the community at large—was inseparable from the idea of the prison itself. On the page, at least, theories of incarceration frequently expressed an aspiration for social cohesion by affirming the civic membership of criminals and reintegrating them into the social whole. In this vein, the prison was distinctly associated with reform and deterrence and thought to be incompatible with, or at least orthogonal to, other theories of punishment, such as retribution. In this respect, the long history of thinking about the prison is at odds with recent trends in the theory and practice of penal incarceration toward retributivism, incapacitation, and segregation.[3]

These unnoticed origins of prison thinking are significant because, like electoral democracy and market capitalism, prisons have emerged over the past two centuries as one of the signature features of modern liberal societies. No longer merely one form of punishment among many, imprisonment has gained an effective monopoly as the only civilized way to carry out the demands of justice in cases of serious crime, displacing expulsion and corporal and capital punishment. The almost unquestioned legitimacy of the prison since the Enlightenment has rested largely on its claim (however transparently false) to be a product of scientific progress, a sign of the humanity of contemporary society, and a socially beneficial means of rehabilitation. To speak about the modern prison is to speak euphemistically of "correctional systems," "penitentiaries," and "reformatories."

To be sure, there is good reason to consider the prison distinctly modern. The jails and dungeons mentioned in the Bible, Greek histories, and other ancient and early modern texts were almost always intended only to hold prisoners, often before their sentencing or until a sentence was carried out—never primarily to punish them.[4] But what sort of modern institution is the prison? Is it, to return to our initial comparison, a phenomenon like market capitalism—a concept that has no real parallel from before the modern period? Or is incarceration more like electoral democracy, an institution with deep roots in the European tradition, an idea that has appeared, disappeared, and reappeared in many various guises since its inception in ancient Athens?

The answer is that the prison is both thoroughly modern and deeply rooted in European political thought. This duality arises from a slipperiness in how we define the term *prison*. The term *prison* most precisely refers to *punitive incarceration*—the use of confinement as a penalty rather than as a form of pre- or posttrial custody, torture, coercion, or temporary detention. Given this definition, it is generally true that concrete evidence of punitive incarceration, what we might call "the prison in the strict sense," is exceedingly rare in the premodern historical record, making the brief moments of theoretical invention that I aim to trace in this book all the more exceptional.[5] But prisons in the broad sense—defined as sites of confinement, dungeons, keeps, and stockades—played roles across the history of human civilization. The idea of the prison as an institution without premodern precedent, then, turns on what I will call the prison/jail distinction—the idea that incarceration as a punishment differs essentially from the mere act of chaining someone up.

Some version of this prison/jail distinction is fundamental to the self-understanding of prison theorists since the eighteenth century, who generally aimed to inaugurate a new era of "reformatories" and "penitentiaries" different from the prisons and workhouses that had characterized early modern Europe.[6] The contemporary reality of American jails—where those convicted of crimes languish together with those awaiting trial, where pretrial custody can be every bit as painful as punishment, and where a supposedly limited period of confinement can stretch on indefinitely—has led some to point out that today, at least, the prison/jail distinction has become merely ideological.[7] Confinement, this view purports, is confinement, no matter what the purported reason for it. To make punitive incarceration a special or privileged form of imprisonment, then, is to operate within an ideological world constructed by prison theorists that only obscures how real incarceration functions.

To this critique, we can only respond that the analysis of ideologies is one of the chief tasks of social and political philosophy. No matter the social reality under which they wrote, the philosophers and theorists this book will examine all relied on some version of the prison/jail distinction in making a case for punitive incarceration. Demosthenes struggled to walk a rhetorical line between a practice his audience agreed with, custodial incarceration, and a controversial one, punitive incarceration. Plato distinguished between the custody of the body and the reform of the soul. Thomas More differentiated his version of penal servitude from the slave camps and work dungeons of Roman history on which it was based. And Bentham helped to construct the penitentiary/jail distinction in its modern form with one hand while slyly erasing it with the other. Each of these theorists of incarceration introduced some version of the division that would become a central ideological hallmark of modern punishment.

This focus on the conceptual construction rather than the material reality of incarceration is also a function of the method of this book. I treat punitive incarceration as a discursive site rather than an archaeological site.[8] In other words, I approach the prison as a thing that was imagined, taken up, and talked and written about—even if the object of discussion itself, the actual spaces or legal practices of confinement, remained elusive or ambiguous. This orientation toward moments of discursive interest in incarceration has also guided the selection of the texts at hand. The readings that form the backbone of this book constitute a series of interlocking moments in the history of political philosophy, moments where perennial concerns about autonomy, community, and punishment temporarily crystalized around the idea of incarceration. These are not the only points when prisons, in the broad sense, have served as discursive sites. They are, however, some of the clearest examples of the prison in the strict sense as an object of philosophical analysis.[9]

This study is motivated by the conviction that the history of the philosophy of incarceration is connected to the political ideas that structure our world today. The crisis of mass incarceration makes the passages in Plato, Hobbes, and others of pressing interest to a contemporary reader. And it is my hope that a deeper understanding of early ideas about imprisonment may help us to understand why the conceptual foundations of the modern prison have reached their own moment of extreme crisis. In the wake of mass incarceration, the idea of the prison itself has come under increasing critical and philosophical pressure.[10]

THINKING ABOUT IMPRISONMENT BEFORE THE PRISON

If the prison as a penal institution did not find much political purchase before the social, cultural, and economic conditions of the late eighteenth century, the *idea* of punitive incarceration—and especially of reformatory incarceration—nevertheless has a rich and largely unnoticed legacy in the history of political philosophy. Discussions of the prison can be found amid the heady intellectual foment of the Athenian democracy of the fifth and fourth centuries BCE. These ideas reappear, both independently and in conversation with one another, across a variety of texts and contexts, including Jewish and Christian Hellenism, Renaissance Platonism, and some of the foundational thinkers of early modern liberalism.

Philosophy is not written in a vacuum. Just as the changing conditions of modern society over the past fifty years have had a clear impact on the possibilities of thinking about the prison, so too every earlier theory of incarceration has rested on the changeable nature of a particular social world. Different theories of incarceration therefore rely on varied and even contradictory assumptions about the importance of citizenship, the seat of human behavior in the body or the soul, the form of the state, the relationship between masses and elites, and the foundations of political association in reason, passion, or interest. These different social and moral theories also interacted with the radically different material conditions under which different philosophers wrote and, equally importantly, under which their understandings of crime and punishment were formed. The prison emerges as a discursive site again and again, but the form the discourse takes and the nature of its themes are deeply historically contingent.

To track the various theories of incarceration as they emerge, each chapter will focus on specific arguments for imprisonment: those made by Athenian democrats, Plato, Thomas More, Thomas Hobbes, and Jeremy Bentham respectively. While the chapters are arranged chronologically, the organizing principle of this book is the conceptual distinction between what I will call the popular authorization approach and the Platonic correctional (or reformative) approach. These two approaches are conceptually independent, meaning that neither relies on the other for its plausibility. While the two theories interacted in Athens and again in early modernity, it was not until the modern era of the "Birth of the Prison," to use Michel Foucault's felicitous phrase, that these two ways of explaining why it is right to punish by confinement were ultimately assimilated into modern prison theory.

The bulk of this study characterizes these two competing ways of justifying incarceration on their own terms and in their historical contexts. The first theoretical family, the popular authorization theory of incarceration, begins in the Athenian democracy of the fourth and fifth centuries BCE and reappears—albeit transformed—in the work of Thomas Hobbes. Despite their different political environments, material conditions, and theoretical assumptions, both Hobbes and the Athenian democrats place a premium on the formal equality between citizens. Both also envision the involvement of citizens in punishment, whether through direct participation in Athens, or by means of Hobbes's "social contract." Consequently, their theories each confront the possibility of citizens being asked to punish their political equals, thereby authorizing their own possible future punishment. In popularly authorized regimes, whether the small-scale direct democracy of Athens or the centralized states of modernity, locking up our fellow citizens poses considerable ideological and practical contradictions. The content of these tensions may vary, but their paradoxical form is strikingly similar—citizens *can* imprison one another, but to do so might undermine the formal relationships that underlie the foundation of the regime. I call this problem *the paradox of popularly authorized punishment*. As we will see, the violation of physical liberty required by incarceration proves to be a special case of this paradox.[11]

The second family of thinking about incarceration emerges first in the philosophy of Plato and was adapted from him (directly or indirectly) by later authors including Thomas More and Jeremy Bentham. The key tenet for both Plato himself and for subsequent theories in the Platonic tradition is that incarceration can change the minds of criminals, returning them to the political community in a better state than when they were removed from it. This second family of theories is more closely interested in the technique of incarceration. It justifies the confinement of criminals by means of a set of assumptions about the psychological foundations of human behavior. These Platonic theories try to explain how the human mind works, how physical confinement affects psychic function, and how confining criminals will make them better citizens.

The Paradox of Popularly Authorized Imprisonment

Arguments over incarceration in Athens must be understood in relation to democracy and its limits. On the one side of the debate, imprisonment, with its constraints on the body of the imprisoned (in the jail at Athens, prisoners remained chained up, even inside), was clearly in tension with democratic norms around bodily integrity. Yet there was also a democratic case to be made for the egalitarian nature of imprisonment—the wealthy are as pained by prison as the poor are. And incarceration—unlike exile, ostracism, or execution—keeps citizens within the boundaries of the state, preserving a sense of civic unity, even within the context of punishment. But the strongest case for imprisonment in the face of its uncomfortable associations with the treatment of slaves comes from the very power of the jury to impose it. The speechwriter and politician

Demosthenes, for instance, advocated for incarceration by urging citizens to imprison a powerful political figure as a demonstration of democratic power. By enacting a punishment that skirts the boundaries of what is democratically viable, the citizen jury reminds itself and its potential enemies of what democratic bodies might be willing to do to defend their authority.[12]

The prison, in this Athenian-democratic context, is just another tool in the democratic arsenal. But, given its conflict with other democratic values, the prison is a relatively ineffective tool, especially compared with other juridical practices like the "suit against illegal legislation" (*graphē paranomōn*). The Athenian justification of penal incarceration grapples with the contradiction between democracy as a set of ideological commitments (to the inviolable bodies of citizens or to a principle of gentleness) and democracy as a set of power relations. Ultimately, Demosthenes argues, this is a knot that only the members of the demos, in their capacity as officeholders (in this case, specifically as jurors) can untangle. Democratic punishment is whatever is best for popular rule, even if that punishment seems, on its face, to be undemocratic. This is the first instance of a paradox around the popular authorization of imprisonment.

The second main example of the tendency toward a paradox in popularly authorized incarceration can be found in the philosophy of Thomas Hobbes. Hobbes, an accomplished classical scholar, was keenly aware of Athenian practices of punishment.[13] But Hobbes's theory of punishment (and thus, his theory of incarceration) was grounded in an intellectual framework far removed from that of ancient direct democracy. Against the Greeks and Romans who, according to Hobbes, were concerned with the freedom of states to act as collective bodies, Hobbes insisted that both the source and the limits of liberty lie in the contract between individual subjects and a sovereign. This contract forms the conceptual foundations of a state or commonwealth. Given that the fundamental point of the contract is to preserve the security of one's life, "a man cannot lay down the right of resisting them that assault him by force to take away his life. . . . The same may be said of wounds, and chains, and imprisonment."[14] Incarceration appears at the very center of Hobbes's theory. On his account, prisons, and indeed almost every form of corporal or capital punishment, immediately sever the social contract between the citizen and the state.

This power of the prison to sever the covenant between a subject and a sovereign, while keeping the subject quite literally *bound* to the will of the sovereign, also presents a special opportunity for returning the subject to the body of the commonwealth. A prisoner will only leave prison if one has consented to the sovereign's laws of one's own so-called free will, though while in prison, one is under no obligation to the sovereign at all. Hobbesian incarceration can consequently be thought of as the suspension of freedom with the aim of forcing the prisoner to make the same choice one would to exit the state of nature—by once again accepting the sovereign's will in return for one's physical liberty. By producing the conditions for a new contract between sovereign and citizens, the prison is ideally situated to serve the goal of punishment, which is, according to Hobbes, to "form" the criminal's will and to serve as an example to others.[15]

Despite many important differences between their wider political theories, in both democratic Athens and Hobbes incarceration exists in a paradoxical tension with the structure of the regime. The prison, moreover, brushes up against an essential boundary condition—that of the status of free citizens in Athens and that of the conditions under which it is rational to consent to the authority of a sovereign, according to Hobbes. In calling this shared contradiction a paradox of "popularly authorized" incarceration, this book identifies a recurring tension between the freedoms promised by political theories grounded in popular consent and the punishments that ensure the necessary conditions for those freedoms.[16]

The Athenian and the Hobbesian cases also share a certain negative feature, one that helps to distinguish them from the other family of prison theories examined by this book: the two "popular" theories decline to posit an explicit theory of *how* or *why* the prison works. This unanswered question of the technical requirements of confinement, what goes on in the prison and why, is taken up by the second major tendency in early prison theory: the tradition of thinking about the prison as a means of reforming the soul (or mind) of the criminal.

The Platonic Tradition

The tendency to view prisons as a place to correct errant souls has its origin, like the paradox of popularly authorized imprisonment, in ancient

Athens. Unlike the democratic discussions of the prison however, this theory emerged not from the exigencies of political life but rather from a philosophical problem recognized by Plato. Given that they believed that punishment is only justified if it improves its recipient, Plato and other Athenian intellectuals were left to question what sort of punishment might really change a criminal for the better. Plato offered incarceration as a possible solution to this problem, using the prison both as a dramatic setting and as a literary or mythical image of correct punishment. In his dialogue the *Laws*, Plato even went as far as to detail how a reformatory prison would work in practice.

Plato identified two guiding questions that structure this imagined prison. The first of these is about the moral psychology of crime: What goes wrong in the mind of a criminal (and how might it be fixed)? The second is about a socially situated theory of practical reason: How do the actions of individuals relate to a broader set of communal norms and practices (and what is the concordant relationship between psychology and law)? In the *Laws*, Plato presents a version of incarceration that considers both how criminals think and how these thoughts fit into the complicated social fabric of an ancient city-state. The *Laws'* moral psychology of crime leans heavily on the metaphor of punishment as education and healing. Plato suggests that, just as in learning, punishment is accomplished by changing the soul of the criminal; and, as in medicine, crime is a sort of mental disease, and punishment is a cure. In support of this psychological, reformative theory of punishment, Plato advances an extensive theory of how the soul works and how punishment can regulate psychic functions: the prison, with its closed environment for learning and convalescence, is Plato's ideal institution for punishing crimes that are caused by a disorder in the rational soul.

The prison in Plato's *Laws* may not be the most memorable or influential political institution to have emerged from Plato's political thought, but it did have a long and surprisingly successful afterlife. The story of the reformative tendency in prison thinking, then, is also a story about Plato's reception by later thinkers. Jewish and Christian Platonists found a model for their own communal aspirations in Plato's description of an enclosed, therapeutic house for damaged souls. They also took the language of temperance and reason that had characterized Plato's social and moral psychology of incarceration and adapted it to the ascetic spiritual practices of monastic communities, which aspired to serve as sites of reform and recuperation for those fleeing the temptations of the wider world.[17] This modified Platonic project of reformatory confinement survived and indeed thrived for some thousand years, until Plato's own texts were once again taken up directly during the European Renaissance.

The best example of prison thinking in the New Learning of the Renaissance can be found in the work of Thomas More. In his *Utopia*, More explicitly appealed to arguments and ideas from Plato's *Laws* in constructing a fictional island polity, which practices a platonically inflected form of future-directed incarceration and penal labor. More's role in reinstating incarceration as a secular political practice is also a return to a particularly Platonic way of thinking about the moral psychology of crime and the connection between criminals and society. But More's attention to the laboring masses rather than to philosophical and political elites points to a somewhat different social theory than that of the Platonic model. For More, the prison is to be used to ward off the widespread ills of poverty and laziness rather than to dialectically instruct wayward intellectuals and politicians.

It was not until the work of More's countryman Jeremy Bentham that labor finally took its place as the central reformative agent of punishment and incarceration. It might seem strange to identify Bentham, a famous materialist and the founder of utilitarianism, with the idealist Plato, but Bentham saw himself in continuity (and in competition) with More's *Utopia*—and, by extension, with its Platonic model. Bentham thought that More's use of labor to punish and reform did not sufficiently explain how hard work could improve criminals and society. Bentham himself, on the other hand, was confident that the moral psychology of pleasure and pain and the normative principle of the "greatest happiness of the greatest number" could help design institutions that accomplished what earlier theorists had only ever fantasized about: the efficient and reliable inculcation of prosocial behavior.

Part of what makes Bentham's prison so attractive as an analytic device is his clear-eyed explanation of the rationale (and the rationality) of incarceration. Bentham calculated that it would be possible to use a precise knowledge of human interests and motivations—based on pleasures and pains—to both control the behavior of inmates and to make that behavior profitable. The Panopticon was to be a prison built on the principle of "inspection"—the actions of every inmate would be visible to a central authority, which would itself remain unseen. Bentham's prison is not only a place for hard labor; it is also a factory, and the central watchman who observes the prisoners also oversees their efficiency as workers. The business structure of the Panopticon is as important as its circular architecture. Each Panopticon could be funded by a joint stock company, whose investors would ensure that it operated with the utmost efficiency.[18] But the Panopticon was conceived as both a penal institution and a more general institutional scheme, which Bentham hoped to apply to social welfare (a "Pauper Panopticon") and even to schooling.

With Bentham, the Platonic, Utopian theory of a rationalized form of punishment reaches both an end and an apex. Bentham's idea of the prison is no less rationalized than Plato's or More's, and his ideal of a society ordered by the same principles that determine correctional punishment is no less total. Bentham viewed the Panopticon as a tool for inculcating a set of rational behaviors like cost-benefit analysis and delayed gratification, behaviors that characterize the middle class, the class that is most adept in producing utility for society as a whole. While Bentham is known for professing that individuals are the best judges of their own interest, his prison theory shows that he was not averse to using penal institutions for interest formation, aiming to inculcate the lower classes with the values of the idealized industrious middle class. Bentham marks the Platonic tradition's arrival to a social and political world much like our own.

I have chosen Bentham and his Panopticon as the endpoint of this study because he was, in many ways, the final philosopher of prisons to precede widespread real-world incarceration. By the time Bentham wrote, prisons had definitively begun to move off the page and into the cities and suburbs of the industrializing world. Thinking about the prison against the background of incarceration as practiced is an entirely separate project from an abstract examination of the early history of prison thinking. In fact, mapping the growth and development of ideologies of incarceration in the nineteenth and twentieth centuries has become a major research agenda in history, sociology, and political science.[19] We cannot do justice to the story of the modern prison in its entirety, but I will try to show, if only briefly, how the early history of prison thinking can be an illuminating complement to discussions of modern incarceration.

FROM EARLY PRISON THINKING TO THE MODERN THEORY OF INCARCERATION

It is only a slight oversimplification to say that the two early traditions of thinking about the prison—popular authorization and the Platonic theory of reform—were recombined by the penal theories of the Enlightenment into a new general theory of incarceration. For the theorists of the modern penitentiary, the legitimacy of penal incarceration as a liberal or democratic institution (something akin to the theory of popular authorization) was now dependent on its ability to change wayward ("delinquent") souls through psychic reform. The two early theories of incarceration thus ceased to function independently at more or less the same moment that modern reformatories and penitentiaries achieved their hegemonic position in modern societies.

For much of the nineteenth and twentieth centuries, the prison was widely understood to be a distinctly enlightened and democratic form of punishment.[20] Part of the penitentiary's strongest claim to legitimacy was its apparent compatibility with modern theories of self-rule. Alexis de Tocqueville traveled to America to study its newfangled ways of punishing and found instead the subject of modern democracy writ large.[21] Benjamin Rush, signatory to the Declaration of Independence, made an influential case for the prison in republican terms, describing the United States as "an infant commonwealth" rejecting "the manners of ancient and corrupted monarchies" through the use of incarceration.[22] One hundred years later, Zebulon Brockway, another leading voice of American prison reform, introduced his plan for an ideal prison system with the axiom that "not only should there be unity of spirit in the general government and the prison system of the state, but *identity of aim*."[23] Brockway went as far as to identify "executive" and "legislative" aspects to prison administration.[24] The prison was the republic writ small. But as Rush, Brockway, and many others made clear, it was precisely the power of the penitentiary to *reform*, to restore the convict to the community, that made incarceration indispensable to democracy.[25] They solved the paradox of popularly authorized punishment by treating the reform of fellow citizens an expression of civic equality. Self-rule and soul craft were both elements of the modern idea of the penitentiary.

This psychic-political doublet at the heart of modern prison thinking was taken up and expanded upon by scholars in the 1970s. Michel Foucault's analysis of the birth of the prison takes as one of its main themes the intertwining of psychological science and the political legitimacy of punishment. In Foucault's words, the history of the prison is the history of "the scientifico-legal complex from which the power to punish derives its bases, justifications, and rules."[26] According to Foucault, the justifications for punishment—justifications that, in the era of the modern liberal-democratic state, are assumed to come from the ideological wellsprings of popular self-rule—are really grounded in the efficacious technique of punishment. Incarceration is democratic (or republican) *because* it works to reform and rehabilitate. The form of modern penal justification is the popular authorization theory, but the content is that of the Platonic tradition, with its emphasis on the psychological conditions for soul craft. Even Foucault's ironical claim that modern prisons are the reverse of Platonism because they use the knowledge of the soul to control the criminal body suggests the way in which Platonic ideas about punishment were taken up and transformed by modern theories of punishment.[27] As with incarceration in democratic Athens, arguments for the legitimacy of the prison emerged in tandem with liberal societies' concerns over their own legitimacy.[28] But unlike in Athens, in modern prison theory political legitimacy and the power to change minds became interdependent.[29]

But at the very time Foucault and others were painstakingly uncovering the ideological matrixes of "penal modernism" (to use David Garland's phrase), the justificatory framework for incarceration in the United States was undergoing a seismic shift. American prison populations, rather than decreasing as predicted by the "decarceration" movements of the 1960s and 1970s, instead doubled, tripled, quadrupled, and then some. Prison construction boomed across the continent, with private prisons and "super-maxes" springing up alongside superannuated reformatories and penitentiaries. America was plunging headlong into the age of mass incarceration.[30]

The rapid and unexpected transformation of the American prison system did not accord with the theories of disciplinary control and the industrializing liberal social order that had emerged from the first generation of revisionist scholarship on the prison. The new, "postmodern" justifications for prisons in the age of mass incarceration, and penal practices themselves, were different in kind from the modern theory of incarceration described by Foucault and his contemporaries.[31]

Even before the demographic shifts that characterized American prison growth in the late twentieth century, an intellectual shift had started to take place in discussions of punishment. In the wake of the critical scholarship of the 1960s and 1970s, reform and rehabilitation began to be seen as dehumanizing, paternalistic, and undemocratic.[32] In place of reform, philosophers offered a new account of retribution and responsibility. By treating punishment as recompense for the crime, the thinking went, the criminal would be fully respected as a moral agent rather than "treated" by an all-knowing scientific-legal authority.[33] The turn to retribution dovetailed with a shift in focus across the criminological disciplines, from the reformative power of confinement to the deterrent power of sentencing.[34] Penal sentences, it was thought, should be guided not by how long it might take for the soul to be crafted; rather, they should reflect both the dictates of moral proportionality and the supposed science of criminal deterrence.[35]

The social and political conditions that encouraged the American prison boom were not, of course, caused by abstract considerations about retribution and moral autonomy. Changes like mandatory sentencing guidelines, three-strikes laws, and racialized patterns in policing and prosecution all had more to do with the electoral winds of "penal populism" and politically motivated "wars on crime" than with political philosophy.[36] But the theory and the practice of contemporary incarceration did ultimately converge on a sort of new justification for the prison, one very different from both the classic modernist account of Foucault and the early history chronicled here.

The contemporary American prison has become first and foremost a warehouse, a site of incapacitation and segregation. Penal confinement is carried out with an eye to removing the offender from society for as long as possible rather than with any pretense to "reform" or "correct."

This justification for imprisonment may be considered popularly authorized, insofar as many of the recent innovations in American imprisonment have come with an electoral mandate. But there is no longer even an ideological pretense that incarceration is rehabilitative, let alone that it is intrinsically democratic.[37] Proponents of the prison support such punishment not because of its unique virtues but because it fits within a broader strategy of being "tough on crime" that has its own distinct historical and political roots.[38] The loudest critics of the prison, for their part, no longer aim to reform it or return it to a healthy function. Rather, they increasingly call for abolishing incarceration entirely.[39]

This introduction has traced the transformation of two ancient families of prison theory—the popular authorization approach and the Platonic theory of reform and rehabilitation—into the modern era of the prison as a hegemonic penal form. For a time, these early theoretical tendencies comingled in the reform-minded justifications of the prison that flourished in liberal democracies throughout the nineteenth century. At some point, however, both these arguments lost their hold on the penal imagination.[40] The sorts of reasons given for the prison at the very moment of its greatest expansion in the late twentieth century—from fear of "super-predators" to "wars" on drugs and crime—grew increasingly distant from the communal-republican ideas coinciding with the birth of the modern prison. The final pages of this introduction will take up the contemporary legitimation crisis of the prison, primarily in the United States, to illustrate what prison thinking from before the Panopticon might be able to tell us about the legitimacy of the prison today.

BEFORE THE PANOPTICON AND AFTER
MASS INCARCERATION

The legitimacy of the modern practice of punitive incarceration (after Bentham but before the intellectual and political upheavals of the 1970s) was built on a double foundation—scientific theories of reform combined with civic-republican commitments to the return of the criminal to the community. Each part of this doublet was a necessary part of modern polities' justifications of incarceration, and together, they were sufficient to render punitive imprisonment an almost unquestioned form of punishment in developed democracies.

With this conceptual framework in mind, we can see the fate of theories of the prison since the 1970s in a new light. Independently of the shifting social conditions that caused the population-level expansion of mass incarceration, intellectuals across the political spectrum came to criticize one or both constituent parts of the argument for the prison's legitimacy. On the left, the pronouncements of the French Groupe d'information sur les prisons (of which Foucault was a member) and an influential report by the American Friends Service Committee, *Struggle for Justice*, both denounced incarceration as a paternalistic and discriminatory system of punishment. According to these and other radical voices, the language of reform only served to mask a penal reality of racist and classist oppression.[41] In addition to radical arguments that reform was inherently paternalistic, voices from the center and the right attacked reform for the purely pragmatic reason that "nothing works" to rehabilitate criminals.[42] For the first time in its two-hundred-year history, criminology began to lose faith in the technical possibility of the sort of soul craft that the concept of the penitentiary had taken as its major premise.[43]

The collapse of reform, one necessary premise in the argument for punitive incarceration, would probably have been enough to occasion some sort of legitimation crisis for the modern prison. But as it turned out, the second necessary premise—that reformed citizens are important parts of the civic community—also came under assault, at least in the United States. The story of mass incarceration is fundamentally a story about the redrawing of citizen boundaries around criminals and criminality in America. Part of this story concerns racial backlash, as Black people in the process of winning their formal civil rights were subjected to increasing criminalization and ghettoization by drug policy, redlining, zoning, and housing exclusion.[44] At the same time, the victims' rights movements and even civil rights movements focused political and public attention on the pain and identity of victims, often to the exclusion of the humanity of criminals—or those who were perceived to be criminals.[45] As intensive policing and high incarceration rates led to an increasing sense of political exclusion and anomie in marginalized communities, mass incarceration silently redefined who counted as a full member of the political community.[46] The idea that the criminal was someone of value to the democratic community or that the community should care when and how the criminal would return to it came under attack from every direction.

The prevailing social and intellectual winds in the late twentieth-century United States were thus against both necessary premises in the modern argument for the prison. And yet it took some time before a political philosopher formulated the proposition that prison in its late modern form had become obsolete.[47] Angela Davis made a powerful case, based on some of the social and historical factors discussed here and others, that the practice of penal incarceration could no longer be morally or practically justified.[48] Equally important was Davis's solution to the penal dysfunction of mass incarceration: prison abolition.

A full evaluation of the philosophical case for (or against) prison abolition is beyond the scope of this project. The theoretical history undertaken by this book, however, suggests an additional reason why Davis's claim that the prison is no longer legitimate has resonated so powerfully with scholars and activists alike. Neither of the intellectual resources on which the modern theory of the prison initially relied—the idea of reform and the value of incarceration for popular self-rule—can be plausibly endorsed in the United States in the age of mass incarceration.

This study also helps us to see that the combination of these earlier theories into the premises of another (now falsified) argument is itself historically contingent. Premodern theories of the prison, as each chapter will show, tended to stay within one of the two families of prison argument, *either* the popular authorization of incarceration *or* the Platonic theory of reform. Each argument seemed to its proponents to be sufficient on its own. Even if the modern idea of the prison is no longer philosophically attractive, might one of the early theories of the prison provide at least theoretical grounds for justifying some form of incarceration?[49] The following sections will revisit each early theory of the prison to determine whether, taken separately, either approach might help advance the debate between those who imagine a future for the prison and those who want to do away with it altogether.

THE FUTURE OF PLATONIC REFORM

The family of Platonic theories of reform has a few distinctive conditions for justified imprisonment. First among these is an attention to future-directed punishment, through reform of the criminal and deterrence of both the criminal and others. Second is the idea that the punishment should benefit the individual person being punished. The final and most demanding criterion for Platonic reformative theories is an interest in the specificity of penal technique—the insistence that a punishment must plausibly do what it is meant to do. Despite their differing visions of a successful form of penal confinement, the authors of the Platonic tradition all thought that punitive incarceration must and could pass these conceptual tests.

Almost no prison today, in the United States or elsewhere, meets Plato's philosophical conditions for just punishment. Many countries already violate the Platonic theory at the level of criminal law by stipulating that the purpose of punishment is retribution, a past-directed act. Most prisons, now and in the past, also violate the second condition of Platonic reform because they fail to imprison criminals in a way that makes them better. This has been a failure of the penitentiary since its earliest days. Every iteration of the reformatory becomes in turn a new "school of vice," as the Pennsylvania system of prison management gave way to the New York system, which became the Elmira system and then the Norfolk system, none ever quite managing to succeed in stamping out the causes of crime in the criminal mind.[50] The perpetual failure of incarceration to improve criminals in any meaningful way is related to the third element of Platonic reform: the idea that the technique of punishment (in this case, incarceration) must have a plausible mechanism for achieving its ends. Almost every technique for penal confinement—from solitary confinement to prison labor to psychological counseling—has failed to reform or make penitent, at least in any empirically verifiable way.[51]

Defenders of incarceration today often point to one apparent exception to this dismal conclusion. The case of so-called Nordic exceptionalism seems to provide an example of punitive incarceration that comes close to fulfilling the original purpose of the "reformatory": to break prisoners out of the cycle of crime and reintegrate them into society.[52] To Anglo-American eyes, the Nordic model of "open prisons," community-minded visitation, and generous job policies is often taken as the counterfactual for what prisons could be.[53] Leaving aside whether such characterizations of Nordic exceptionalism are in fact accurate, it remains unclear whether even Nordic prisons can clear the high bar that Plato (and Bentham) set: that penal institutions be able to trace their effects to "appropriate causes."[54] Much of the scholarship on the success of Nordic prisons points not to the prisons themselves but to the deep causes of a well-entrenched welfare state and a more egalitarian variety of capitalism. And even these causes are themselves possibly confounded by a history of social homogeneity.[55] When examined closely, the exemplar is not Nordic prisons but Nordic societies. It may be that *any* form of punishment could be made to function well in Scandinavia and that the Scandinavians themselves are as unjustified in their practice of incarceration as anyone else.

The standard for legitimate punishment demanded by Platonic reform does not in principle rule out the counterfactual possibility that some technique for reformative confinement will someday be found. Nevertheless, it is worth noting that any such future technique of reform would now have to contend with liberal norms around personal autonomy and civil rights, including the right to privacy—norms that were unfamiliar or unimportant to most of the authors of the Platonic tradition. The modern-day reformer must not only justify the technique of confinement technically; she or he must also justify it against a standard for the dignified treatment of equals that rules out many of the suggestions canvassed in this book, as well as many of the techniques of "improvement" put into practice in the prisons of the nineteenth and twentieth centuries. The idea of Platonic reform is a standard that no prison, and certainly no American prison today, can meet.

THE FUTURE OF POPULAR AUTHORIZATION

Popular authorization theories begin from the observation that imprisonment is inherently at odds with a government grounded in the self-rule of equals. For the Athenians, incarceration is a problem for democracy because it is degrading and redolent of slavery. For Thomas Hobbes, imprisonment violates the bodily security that grounds the social contract between subject and sovereign and negates the authorization that the subject gives to the sovereign to use coercive force. But both versions of the theory agree that despite the contradictions between self-rule and imprisonment, governments are justified in using punitive confinement if it is necessary to secure the popularly authorized regime. In Athens, Demosthenes argued, the many could (and should) vote to imprison if it made their rule over the few more secure. For Hobbes, it is rational for a subject to authorize the sovereign to use imprisonment to protect the goods secured by a well-ordered state, even if when one suffers imprisonment, it may also be rational for one to resist.

The first observation of early popular authorization theories—that incarceration is at odds with important elements of popular self-rule—seems truer than ever, at least in the United States. After all, scholars and activists have the same concerns about mass incarceration that Athenians seem to have had about their much more limited use of incarceration: that it is reminiscent of slavery.[56] And, as we have already noted, mass incarceration has discrete and measurable antidemocratic effects on political participation and equal voice.[57] One of the most direct ways in which incarceration is at odds with democracy is through the exclusion of prisoners from civic life. The American practice of felon disenfranchisement is even more directly at odds with democracy.[58] More abstractly, we might observe the harshness of mass incarceration, the mandatory minimum sentences, the aggressive policing tactics, and the relish with which politicians claim to be (and are rewarded for seeming) "tough on crime" and say, as George Kateb does, that American punishment today violates the very spirit of democracy and democratic community.[59]

But the way in which the American electoral system seems to reward the advocates of harsh punishment also points to an apparent problem. This is the "popular" aspect of the phenomenon known as "penal populism." Harsh penal policies, including those that contribute to mass incarceration, are often deeply popular with electorates. The more punishment is brought to the fore of electoral politics, and the more control over punishment is placed in the hands of elected officials, the harsher punishment seems to get.[60] And indeed, the popular authorization theory of incarceration holds that the people, the demos, can choose to punish however it likes, even if it chooses to do so in ways that are unegalitarian. The popularly authorized sovereign *can* do whatever it wants—but that does not mean it *should*. The history of Athens gives us examples of the people making undemocratic punitive mistakes and later regretting it.[61] Hobbes, too, is clear-sighted on this point, noting that there will be more and less prudent ways for the sovereign to use its power to punish.[62] Again, drawing from Kateb, we must make a distinction between the aspect of the popular authorization approach that appeals to "sovereign authority" and that which is grounded in the democratic "spirit of the laws."[63] The former traces the right to punish to the fact of popular sovereignty and is therefore powerless against the penal populist claim that just punishment is whatever the democratic sovereign wants. The "spirit of the laws" behind popularly authorized punishment, however, can help us to understand precisely what form of incarceration could nevertheless be justified in the service of self-rule.

The early versions of the popular authorization approach studied in this book agree on two basic points. The first is that incarceration is justified if it preserves the basis of popular self-rule. The second is that popular self-rule is best preserved by leniency for the many and penal harshness for the powerful few. Crucially, this second point provides the content for what a democratic "spirit of the laws" should mean. The idea that democracy requires leniency, as the Athenians understood, follows almost trivially from the good of political equality. Equal respect for citizens as fellow rulers encourages norms of gentleness and forgiveness, at least for the citizen in-group.[64] And despite his reputation as a dour pessimist about human nature, Thomas Hobbes reached similar conclusions about leniency, at least when it comes to most crimes. For Hobbes, gentleness is to be preferred not on egalitarian grounds but on practical ones. The poor and the many are often forced into crime by their extreme need, and they are not usually capable of doing harm on a societal scale.[65] It is not worth rupturing the social contract by punishing them harshly.

Contemporary theorists of democratic incarceration seem poised to join this philosophical tradition of clemency.[66] But Hobbes and his Athenian predecessors also agreed on another major aim of popularly authorized punishment—the restraint of the wealthy and the powerful. Demosthenes asks his audience forthrightly: What is the point of the prison if it cannot keep a wealthy criminal in check? When he urges the citizen jury to punish or imprison, it is quite literally "to make an example for the others," and there is no doubt that "the others" he means are the oligarchical few.[67] Hobbes too focuses on punishment as a means to subdue the great and the proud, who by dint of wealth, connections, and self-conceit "are the first movers in the disturbance of commonwealth."[68] For these thinkers, the spirit of popularly authorized incarceration meant using it to neutralize the enemies of the regime. Contemporary scholars agree that economic inequality and a concentration of political and social power in the hands of fewer and fewer people have some correlation with penal populism and mass incarceration. But curiously, very few modern voices have taken up the early theoretical position that popularly authorized regimes should prioritize punishing the powerful.[69]

There are good reasons why contemporary theorists might be squeamish about prioritizing the punishment of the powerful. As a preliminary matter, it goes against the bedrock principles of liberal jurisprudence to combine political considerations with the criminal law. What's more, there has always been a bit of confusion surrounding the status of the powerful in a popular regime. Are the wealthy few part of the demos? Are they an external threat to its rule? In a mixed constitution like that of the United States, the rule of elites is a legal feature that seems almost inescapable.

And yet, in the face of the evidence that the current structure of criminal law serves in effect to "punish the poor," the voices of the early popular authorization approach to incarceration urge us to consider if it might not be possible to be harsh to the socially and politically powerful and lenient to the weak. Perhaps we ought to punish the crimes of the great—financial crimes, tax crimes, political crimes, and crimes of corruption—with greater severity, while responding to the crimes of necessity committed by the disadvantaged with gentleness.

One of the greatest similarities between the contemporary, postmodern critique of incarceration and the early approaches canvassed in this book is that—in contrast with the nineteenth- and twentieth-century modern theory of the prison—both recognize the prison as a uniquely harsh form of punishment, to be used sparingly. Popular authorization theorists conclude, perhaps shockingly, that harsh penalties like incarceration should be reserved for the great and powerful, because their crimes are the greatest threats to the good of all. What's more, there is also reason to hope that a polity committed to punishing the powerful is more likely to treat the average criminal with the respect due to a person of note. If the wealthy find their way to prison more often, prison sentences would perhaps be less unduly harsh and humiliating.[70] The popular authorization approach is in the end agnostic about incarceration as a particular technique—and therefore silent in the debate over reform or abolition. Rather, it suggests to both camps that the way toward a more humane and democratic penal system lies in paying as much attention to whom the law aims to punish as to how.

Let us conclude with the voice of an early advocate for a democratic theory of punishment. Protagoras, Plato's democratic mouthpiece, points our attention to the way in which punishments are "audits" performed by the polity on itself.[71] These audits reflect not only the actions of an individual but the wider fabric of the society against which those actions must be interpreted. In a community riven by something like mass incarceration, imprisonment cannot serve as an appropriate form of "auditing" because the prison is itself implicated in the rending of that social fabric.

This is the lesson of the early tradition in thinking about incarceration—a lesson that we should not let the last two hundred years of modern prison history obscure: techniques of punishment must still be justified against the ends of punishment. The ends of punishment in a democracy are equal respect for the dignity of every citizen and the protection of the popular regime against all threats to it. And finally, when the state punishes, it must look to the future of all concerned, including the criminal, only and always. The prison in its current form may no longer be a suitable technique for these ends, but the history of thinking about the prison should remain as a conceptual resource for as long as democratic communities still struggle to punish better.

THE PARADOX OF INCARCERATION IN DEMOCRATIC ATHENS

WE BEGIN WITH two wooden ships, set against the expanse of the Mediterranean Sea. One sits low in the deep blue water, its single sail taut in the stiff breeze. The second is much larger, with three banks of oars moving in measured unison as if to an unheard rhythm. The larger ship quickly overtakes the smaller. Long grappling hooks are thrown out from the side of the warship, holding the heavy-laden merchant boat from Egyptian Naucratis fast, as a group of armed men quickly overpower its small crew and set about searching for plunder. We do not know exactly what they found, but we know that it was worth some five hundred fifty pounds of silver.[1]

The warship was an Athenian trireme, sent off on state business to the coast of Asia Minor in the summer of 355 BCE. The captains of the ship were two trierarchs, Archebius and Lysitheides, from the wealthiest class in Athens. Their passengers, ambassadors to the Court of Mausolus, were themselves the well-off sons of generals and tax collectors. These privileged pirates hoped to hoard their winnings, but back in

Athens, word got out. A man named Euctemon denounced the captains to a committee appointed to investigate missing public funds. After a series of suits and countersuits, the three ambassadors found themselves in danger of being imprisoned for stealing state property.

A looted ship and a simmering legal feud might seem like an unlikely start for the history of the philosophy of incarceration, but the speechwriter for Euctemon's prosecution also happened to be one of the most eloquent exponents of Athens and its democracy, Demosthenes. In his courtroom attempt to explain why it was right that three distinguished citizens should remain in prison, Demosthenes ended up providing the clearest picture of the democratic theory of incarceration to reach us from antiquity.

Incarceration, according to Demosthenes, has some characteristics that are deeply consonant with Athenian democracy. Imprisonment, unlike financial punishments, affects rich and poor citizens alike, and prisons, unlike exile or capital punishment, keep criminals within the community rather than excising them temporarily or permanently. But incarceration runs counter to other equally important democratic principles, including the sacrosanct character of citizen bodies and the clear demarcation of members of the demos from nonmembers. On which side of the "democratic boundary" do prisoners fall?

Demosthenes proposed a conceptual solution to these tensions by distinguishing crimes between citizens qua equals ("horizontal" punishment) and crimes committed by elite actors that threaten the regime ("vertical" punishment). This solution foregrounds the political nature of incarceration for Athenians, because by identifying incarceration as a "vertical punishment," Demosthenes was insisting that imprisonment is only suitable when it advances the interests of the demos. The idea that imprisonment can be at once both a challenge and a boon to democratic rule forms one of the main themes of this book—the paradox of popularly authorized incarceration. In the case of Athens, the key paradox is between the apparent privileges of citizenship—physical safety and freedom—and the absolute authority of the people to rule, and to protect their rule, by any means necessary.

Most histories of the prison (and theories of the prison) have skipped right over ancient Athens, assuming that penal incarceration did not exist before the dawn of the penitentiary in the eighteenth century.[2] A casual perusal of the literature on Athenian criminal law would not necessarily change anyone's mind. At first glance it seems like incarceration simply did not exist as a criminal punishment in the premodern Mediterranean world.[3] There had always been a need to detain prisoners of war,[4] and every ancient culture had a mode of detaining those awaiting trial, execution, or under remand for some other reason,[5] but the evidence for the use of the prison as a regular penalty is less than certain.[6]

One possible origin for legal imprisonment is in the evolving relation between debtors and creditors in Athenian society. The lawgiver Solon abolished the practice of selling Athenian citizens into slavery,[7] though various forms of debt bondage may have persisted into the fourth century BCE.[8] In the fifth and fourth centuries, a debtor could be imprisoned until repayment of the debt, and, later, merchants could be imprisoned over defaults on loans.[9] Whether or not incarceration replaced debt bondage, a resemblance between imprisonment and enslavement was clear to many Athenians (as our reading of Demosthenes below shows). The meaning of that resemblance, however, was less than obvious. The prison as a substitute for enslavement could be read as a democratic victory, linked to the revered Solonic reforms, but it could also serve as a reminder of the symbolic place of slavery, a nether state to which citizens might be subjected, unfree, if not totally enslaved.

The transition between the use of imprisonment in private suits as a substitution for slavery or bond servitude and the use of incarceration as a standard penalty (timēma) is also murky. There is reason to believe that by the end of the Peloponnesian War, those in debt to the city could be imprisoned,[10] but many of the remaining examples from the fifth century consist in extraordinary or political uses of the prison: a man offers himself up for imprisonment instead of paying a fine;[11] a speaker calls prison more powerful than ostracism, just as ostracism is itself falling into disuse.[12]

The increased use of the prison, whatever the cause, appears to have come into its own by the most catastrophic break in the democratic regime—the reign of the Thirty Tyrants, a group of oligarchs who ruled Athens after its final defeat by Sparta in 405 BCE.[13] The Thirty used the prison as a place to conduct political confinement and executions out of the public eye.[14] As opposed to the many forms of Athenian social control that were about the viewing of bodies and the reaffirmation of social knowledge, the prison was an "undisplayed" form of corporal punishment, taking place between the state and the criminal, without the mediation of the community.[15] This "hiddenness" might seem to paint the prison as oligarchic rather than democratic, but, as contemporary work on the state capacity to punish suggests, once the state apparatus acquires a certain punitive capability, it is more likely that its use will persist and even expand than that it will disappear, even if the political rationales governing that use eventually change.[16] This seems to be the case with the Athenian prison, where the wartime practice was continued under the restored democracy. The first pieces of evidence that imprisonment could in fact be used as a sentence in a non-debt-related case date from just after the restoration, while the strongest pieces of evidence date from some decades later.

One such early piece of direct evidence for imprisonment as judicial punishment purports to be from 399 BCE. It is the account of Socrates's trial immortalized in Plato's *Apology,* where the philosopher considers imprisonment as an alternative to the death penalty requested by the prosecution.[17] In fact, as we explore in the next chapter, Plato took a special interest in the prison, setting two of his most memorable dialogues there and giving his own theory of incarceration in the *Laws.*[18] With the exception of Demosthenes, however, no other Athenian author wrote in any sustained way about incarceration, and the paucity of such evidence has fed the scholarly confusion over the prevalence and importance of incarceration in Athens. In the case of the prison, even the sum of all extant evidence cannot provide us with an "objective" account of an historical institution.[19] What this contentious evidence does provide, however, is the evidence of contention. Consequently, this chapter looks for the meaning of the prison by diving into the Athenian debate rather than by canvassing every source.

Demosthenes's speech *Against Timocrates,* written for a litigant in a court case in the mid-fourth century, offers the most comprehensive view that has survived of the form and content of Athenian deliberation about imprisonment. Demosthenes was intensely engaged in the political/ideological discourse of democracy, its practices, and its values.[20] His speech integrates the question of incarceration into existing political conflicts and shows how competing actors with competing interests (and competing visions of democracy) fought over the correct interpretation of the set of practices, rituals, and buildings that we can call the "institution" of incarceration. Demosthenes's treatment of the prison against this ideological background suggests that punitive imprisonment had symbolic significance, even if it did not have a definitive constitutional status. This will allow us to treat the prison, in Demetra Kasimis's words, "primarily as a discursive site, not exclusively as a historical referent within a juridical order."[21]

Marcus Folch has similarly approached the prison from a discursive/political direction. He notes that although the types of sentences and the exact position of incarceration cannot be established with certainty, a complete survey of every prisoner identified in the historical record results in a list populated wholly with names from the Athenian political elite. This suggests that whoever *actually* inhabited the prison (and we should assume that in the Athenian prison, through simple demographic logic, the poor were at least as likely to be subject to confinement as the elite), the prison was *written about* and remembered as an institution whose significance was as much about elite political behavior as criminal/juridical procedure.[22] The prison was familiar *to elites,* in this account, as a tool for controlling elites. According to Folch, researchers have been so punctilious about not importing modern notions of incarceration into the ancient world that they may have unwittingly imposed a later (Roman) juridical frame onto one of the most political institutions of Athenian democracy.[23] This is not to say that all, or even most, of the prisoners in the Athenian jail were elites—again, it is probable that they were not. What the surviving literary evidence (written by elites) allows us to do, however, is pinpoint the position of the prison within the debates taking place between intellectuals and politicians in democratic Athens.

We can use Demosthenes's speech *Against Timocrates* as a window into the concerns and anxieties of Athenian political life, anxieties that were refracted through approval of and opposition to incarceration. A careful reading of the rhetoric used by Demosthenes (and the views he imputes to his opponents) reveals that penal practices were a symbolic and discursive touchstone for some of the issues at the heart of what democratic citizenship meant for Athenians.

Against Timocrates is the second of a pair of speeches (the first is *Against Androtion*) dating from a very early moment in Demosthenes's career, while he was still a *logographos*—a speechwriter for hire. Both were written for a man named Diodorus, whose identity and connection to Demosthenes are uncertain, and both speeches are directed against the same rival clique of wealthy politicians, a group that may have been connected to the rhetorician and intellectual Isocrates. Our copy of *Against Timocrates* is a draft of a text that was not delivered—perhaps because the defendants settled out of court. The structure of the speech as we have it thus presents an argument in its not quite final form and includes, for instance, both a defense of imprisonment and Demosthenes's prediction of what Timocrates will say against it. This rhetorical situation has the effect of giving insight into the prison's democratic critics as well as its proponents and of allowing the reader to see both sides of the argument on a number of topics, including whether the prison was oligarchical or democratic, whether it was fitting for free men or slaves, and whether it was an egalitarian institution or tool of rough justice.

A colorful passage from the earlier of the two speeches, *Against Androtion,* can serve as a starting point as we try to understand how to read *Against Timocrates*. One of the themes Demosthenes deploys in *Against Androtion* is that of the wealthy politician Androtion as a malicious and humiliating tax collector, prone to "dragging people off to prison" (Dem. 22.53, 56).[24] From a legal perspective, it is incontestable that Androtion had the right to arrest people in arrears. Demosthenes, however, insists that Androtion's use of imprisonment, though not illegal, was *undemocratic.*

Demosthenes supports his accusation by appealing to historical memory, suggesting that this "dragging people off" is reminiscent of the Thirty Tyrants (22.52) and contrary to the "gentler way" in punishment that characterizes democratic life.[25] It is not only the physical act of dragging but the invasion of personal space that conjures up tyranny. Androtion turned the houses of private citizens into prisons while acting as a public servant (*en dēmokratiai politeuomenos*).[26] By this, Demosthenes does not mean that Androtion put people under house arrest; he means that the physical violation of invading a man's home is equivalent to the physical violation of touching his body (by chaining him up) and is therefore an act of violence against the citizen. "For if," Demosthenes argues, "you want to examine in what way a slave is different than a free person, it is that for slaves, on the one hand, the body is made responsible for quite all crimes committed, for free persons, on the other, even having suffered the greatest misfortune, they are preserved from [bodily harm]."[27]

Demosthenes's appeal to the historical memory of tyranny is a good example of the need to understand incarceration against the background of particularly democratic features of Athenian life. Imprisonment, or at least Androtion's use of it, violates Athenian norms about the body of the citizen and, what's more, seems to be an "uncivilized"—that is, undemocratic— way to treat free Athenians.[28] Building to a climax, Demosthenes says that even a city of slaves would not tolerate Androtion's outrageous behavior (*hubris*), let alone a proud democracy. Demosthenes baits the jury, describing how Androtion dragged citizens off in public, called free people slaves, and gleefully asked "if the prison had been built for no purpose" since "the criminals" (from Androtion's oligarchic perspective this is supposed to mean "the people") are not in it (22.68).

This rhetorical question gives an insight into the way Demosthenes is implying that aristocrats like Androtion see incarceration. The prison is, in the tradition of the Thirty Tyrants, Androtion's oligarchic tool for enslaving the city and brazenly assaulting citizens' bodies. Demosthenes emphatically responds to this with a rhetorical statement of his own— perhaps the prison *does* have no purpose, having failed to hold Androtion's father, a rich debtor.[29] In *Against Androtion*, Demosthenes uses the historically antidemocratic origins of imprisonment to tar an opponent, but he also implicitly proposes a possible democratic theory of the prison as a form of egalitarian punishment—it is the perfect tool for locking up dangerous oligarchs.

This brief look at the *Androtionea* provides some idea of the scope of "democratic" punishment and some of the anxieties around incarceration that will return more forcefully in *Against Timocrates*. Athenian democracy affirms equality through a painstaking awareness of the citizen body and a (theoretically absolute) distinction between citizen and slave concerning bodily integrity. If the citizen body is bounded from below by slaves, it is bounded from above by the aristocracy, who, somewhat paradoxically, are nevertheless still citizens.[30] Democracy is defined by the rule of the demos over and against various elites, and punishment can be an important threat against the rich, whose status and power threaten the presumption of equality. Also important is the implicit determination that the same legal institution can be democratic or undemocratic, depending on how, or by whom, it is used.

The idea of "democratic punishment" as a political practice distinct from and indeed opposed to oligarchic punishment gains additional plausibility in light of Matthew Simonton's work on oligarchy in the classical Greek world. Oligarchs recognized the need to punish for their own reasons—rather than the equality and respect over which democrats obsessed, the watchwords of minority rule were stability (between the rulers and the ruled) and consensus (within the ruling class). Oligarchs worried about crimes that might cause resentment among the people (the nonoligarchic demos), and they feared behavior that threatened agreement among their own clique.[31]

This means that oligarchic punishment takes two forms. When directed within the aristocratic class (horizontally), punishment is exemplary and public but respectful. Exile is the prime example of such punishments, as it preserves bodily integrity, avoids cause for retaliation, holds out the possibility of reintegration, and removes the threat to political order. But when Greek oligarchs were worried about the restive underclass (vertical punishment), they either punished in secret (like the Thirty in the Athenian jail) or staged a public spectacle, to make an example.[32]

To speak proleptically about a theme that will become clearer in Demosthenes's *Against Timocrates,* democratic punishment exists along these same fundamental axes as oligarchic punishment but with a very different order of priorities. Democracy is interested in maintaining citizen equality (horizontally) and maintaining the hierarchies of demos over elites and citizens over noncitizens, respectively (vertically). The prison's historically oligarchic history and the uncomfortable associations it brings with it thus pose a problem for democratic politics. There are two possible solutions—to challenge the democratic legitimacy of the prison or to assimilate incarceration to the available democratic ideologies. Both strategies were tried out in democratic Athens. We know this because both strategies are preserved in *Against Timocrates.*

Demosthenes's client Diodorus probably lost the case in *Against Androtion,*[33] but Didorus was happy enough with Demosthenes to hire him again shortly thereafter, for a second case involving Androtion's posse.[34] It is here that we return to the privileged pirates with which we began the chapter, for it was Androtion and his companions who were the ambassadors on the mission to Mausolus, and it was the same litigant, Diodorus, who sued them along with Euctemon for having kept the spoils for themselves. Amid the suits and countersuits, a confederate of Androtion's named Timocrates proposed a law that would allow debtors to remain free from prison after their conviction but before they repaid the debt, if they provided sufficient collateral for bond. In a sense, Timocrates is appealing to the reality of a world before the prison/jail distinction: it should not be Athenian practice to punish by imprisonment (what we are calling "prison in the strict sense"), and there is no reason to keep people in jail if they provide sureties.

This puts Demosthenes in the position of articulating a version of the prison/jail distinction—that is, articulating a reason for why imprisonment as a punishment, over and against the traditional uses of the jail, is appropriate for Athens. If *Against Androtion* treated Androtion's use of the prison as oligarchic and merely wondered about an alternate, democratic practice of incarceration, *Against Timocrates* reverses the argument, avoiding the oligarchical overtones of some aspects of imprisonment in favor of a case for how the prison works (or should work) in a democracy. While according to the facts of the matter this would seem to be a case about coercive rather than punitive incarceration, the speech does not recognize a difference and uses the language of punishment, simply. What seems to be a bit of conceptual elision helps to directs our attention to incarceration as a discursive site. As important for Demosthenes as the question of whether imprisonment is appropriate *according to law* is what a democratic law of imprisonment *should mean*.[35]

Demosthenes sketches out Timocrates's assault on imprisonment along three fronts:[36] first, imprisonment itself is illegal; second, even if it is technically legal to imprison someone, it may not be fitting (*kalos*) to do so; and third, the technique of imprisonment is specifically unsuitable for the habits of a democracy (it is not *gentle* or *philanthropic*). Demosthenes may be especially worried about these arguments given that he used some version of the second and third himself in the earlier case against Androtion, when he repeatedly reminded jurors of the connection between Androtion's penchant for imprisoning debtors and the oligarchic behavior of the Thirty.

On the first question, that of legality, Demosthenes thinks Timocrates might cite at least two pieces of evidence to convince the jury that imprisonment is eo ipso illegal. One is the law permitting people to remain free before their trial with the provision of sufficient sureties (24.144–45). The second is the oath that members of the *boulē* swore not to imprison citizens. These pieces of evidence could suggest that it is not ever possible (that is to say, legal) to imprison. Demosthenes must show that it is both possible and fitting.[37]

Precedent seems to be squarely on Demosthenes's side (even Timocrates's own legislation, in seeking to allow some people to avoid prison, implicitly admits that others will stay there). But, as Demosthenes knew, in the political arena of the court, "law" is always open to reinterpretation, and he must show that the law of prison (an area of law that was comparatively recent) is of a piece with the democratic values held in common by the jurors. To counter Timocrates, Demosthenes makes an attempt, common enough among fourth-century orators, to link his argument for imprisonment to the memory of the sixth-century Solonic code.[38] Given Demosthenes's own failure to cite any concrete examples of imprisonment before 403 BCE, this might seem an unlikely move, but by exploiting the ambiguity between "being chained up" in prison and being chained in the stocks (*podokakkē*), Demosthenes is able to cite well-established laws that require "locking up" (*desmoi/to dedesthai*) thieves, malefactors, and traitors (24.103).[39] The balance of the evidence surely points to confining criminals as a possible legal sanction—but by calling attention to the connection between the prison and the stocks, Demosthenes has created a new problem for his argument.

The association of the prison and the stocks introduces an inconvenient fact—the prisoners in the Athenian prison were also continually chained up.[40] By conceding the corporal nature of imprisonment, Demosthenes has moved the discussion toward one of most sensitive issues in Athenian democracy, slavery. The image of free citizens subjected to chains (*desmoi*) could not but conjure thoughts of enslavement, but as Demosthenes himself had noted in *Against Androtion*, punishments that touch the body are only given to slaves, while other ways are found to punish free people.[41] The form of punishment was one of the defining characteristics of what it meant to be free or slave, as is confirmed by a phrase of Plato's, who has Socrates describe imprisonment as "being enslaved" (*douleuonta, Apol.* 37c).[42]

The clear demarcation of the difference between slave and free was essential in a society where slaves were ever present in public spaces but legally excluded from public life. In fact, in reminding the jury about the crimes and misbehavior of Androtion, Demosthenes repeats nearly verbatim the description of the distinction between slaves and free persons he had used in his earlier speech.[43] Now, however, this distinction is forced to sit uneasily with the fact that Demosthenes is *defending* the use of a corporal punishment (chained imprisonment) on the delinquent debtors.[44]

Demosthenes does not address this contradiction head on. Instead, he focuses on the right of the jury to assign whatever penalty it sees fit. Shrewdly, he reminds the jurymen of the extreme crimes where they would have no problem inflicting harm on the bodies of the criminals— "thieves, temple-robbers, parricides, murderers, draft-dodgers and deserters." By throwing into doubt the legal right or the moral imperative of a jury to use the corporal punishment of imprisonment, Timocrates is throwing *all* corporal punishment into doubt.[45] This neat little sophism shows imprisonment's liminal position. On the one hand, there is a strong cultural reason for a juryman to feel uncomfortable with imprisonment; on the other, the juryman is reminded that he is not only within his rights to violate citizen bodies; sometimes it is the very thing the law demands. At least some of the varied arguments running through this disorganized speech are not as separate as it might have seemed at first— Demosthenes needs to stress the importance of the "rule of law" to convince jurors who are being made squeamish by corporal punishment that it is necessary for them to fulfill what the law requires (24.116–17).

This anxiety around the body is reminiscent of but structurally different from the repudiation of corporal punishment in modernity. If liberal states view citizen bodies as rights bearing and inviolable, for the Athenians, the body represents a citizen/noncitizen divide, the very boundary of the demos and of political life itself.[46] Freemen and slaves were often physically indistinguishable, making this legal distinction even more fraught and important.[47]

The discomfiting nature of imprisonment not only stems from a blurring of the line between slaves and free persons; it also has to do with the structure of social identity that accompanied the inviolate body of the citizen. As early as Homer, being "low status" (*aischros*) is associated with being vulnerable to bodily assault, and it is well known that the roots of the Athenian sense of justice are to be found buried in the archaic conceptual economy of honor (*timē*) damaged and repaid.[48] The party of Androtion and his friends, it must be remembered, was a wealthy and illustrious group, including the son of the general Laches, and each of the defendants had a long career of public service behind him.[49] Was it appropriate (*kalos*) to treat such men like slaves, or would doing so itself be shameful (*aischros*, 24.125)?

Once again, Demosthenes does not provide a clean or conceptually tidy answer. He first attempts to show that it is Androtion and his like who have already forfeited their honor through their crimes and have thus opened themselves to the demands of justice (*labein dikēn*). He brings up the same story he told in the *Against Androtion*, noting that it was Androtion himself who had violated social expectations by unjustly imprisoning sober and respectable citizens (*hoi sōphronōs bebiōkotes*, 24.126). He goes out of his way to make the money owed a matter of cash stolen directly from the army and the goddess Athena herself, painting the defendants as treacherous, impious (24.177), and, crucially, shameless (especially around money, 24.182–83), thus undermining their claims to good treatment.

Hedging his bets, however, Demosthenes also provides an argument that prison is a form of punishment that is *not* shameful at all, "for the city deemed it right not to trust [the defendants] . . . but [thought it necessary for] them to remain there where many other citizens have also remained. For, as well you know [*kaitoi kai*], some are imprisoned on account of fines and some on account of sentencing, but either way they bear it without complaint" (24.132). Even if Androtion is as respectable as he claims to be, many other respectable people have obeyed the wishes of the people and spent time in prison. The social meaning of the prison has not yet entirely been decided, so Demosthenes prepared arguments to appeal to both possibilities—that in a democracy every citizen is too high status to be corporally punished unless he has committed a serious crime, and the opposite argument, that imprisonment, as a democratic form of punishment, should not be thought to violate the social expectations of honor and status accorded to free persons.

The position of the prison within the social economy of shame is equally ambiguous in other sources. There is good evidence to suggest the prison developed a reputation for housing a certain type of infamous or "low" character.[50] On the other hand, the complaints that are heard from high-status figures about their time in chains highlight the physical harm one suffers by being chained up.[51] It is not entirely clear whether the reproach (*oneidos*) such elite actors feel at being imprisoned is merely due to the fact of being punished or has some special relation to the particularly demeaning nature of physical confinement.

The prison touched on a set of (sometimes contradictory) anxieties that were central to Athenians' idea of their democracy. The presence of chains was a reminder of slavery and simultaneously a reminder of the ability of the people to punish and restrain wealthy elites. No citizen deserved to be shamed, but rich criminals should not be shamed any less than poor ones would be. Given that there are good arguments on both sides of these questions, both proponents and critics of democratic incarceration had to find a stronger way of making the case for or against the use of the prison in a democracy. Ultimately the plausibility of the prison had to be decided according to what we might call the "civic ethos" of Athenian punishment, the stock of assumptions, beliefs, and values to which Athenian citizens and statesmen had shared recourse in their attempts to define what was fitting for a democracy.[52]

One element of this ethos was the way that Athens, rightly or wrongly, considered itself exceptional among Greek states for the "civilized" or "gentle" way its laws functioned.[53] For Demosthenes, this gentleness comes from the reciprocal respect citizens feel for one another as a result of social capital built up through repeated interactions.[54] It is thus desirable, and indeed possible, to punish gently (*praōs*) because of the prevailing state of concord (*homonoia*) found in a democracy.[55] But once again, the ambiguous status of incarceration creates what Demosthenes fears is an opening for Timocrates to claim that his legislation was designed to curtail a harsh (*deinos*) form of punishment (24.77) and that getting rid of imprisonment is a benefaction to the democracy (24.170). Demosthenes even expects that Timocrates will protest harsh punishment for himself given that he was proposing a form of prison abolition, an act that would have been "gentle and moderate" and to the benefit of the powerless.[56] Timocrates seems to have good democratic values on his side.

In response to this, Demosthenes makes what may be his most inspired contribution to the theory of democratic incarceration.[57] He begins by returning to the distinction he began to develop in the *Androtionea* between punishments that are used against "the people" (those "respectable citizens" whom he associates with the jurymen by using the plural "you") and punishments that are used to put the great and the powerful (*hoi politeuomenoi*) in their place.[58] There are two forms (*eidē*) of law that correspond to these two forms of punishment. The first governs the horizontal relationships between citizens, those relationships where the social capital that accrues among equals is most in evidence; the second concerns the vertical relations between "the people" and "the politicians."

The first sort of law is the sphere of softness, clemency, and civility, ensuring goodwill among citizen equals. The second is the place to be harsh and decisive, to keep the oligarchic tendencies of the political class in check.[59] Getting rid of incarceration would only be "civilized" (*philanthropōs*) if it obtained in the first sphere of law (just as it is the first sphere that Androtion violated when he dragged "respectable men" out of their homes). Demosthenes cannot deny that prison is harsh, but it is altogether appropriate for the second sphere: public criminals and public crimes (such as robbing the public treasury).

In positing a conceptual distinction between two reasons for imprisonment, Demosthenes is groping toward a more explicit theory of how the justification of a particular form of punishment relates to a broader theory of punishment. Extrapolating out from Timocrates's argument (or, in fact, Demosthenes's own approach in *Against Androtion*), one sees a line of argument that stresses the attenuation of harshness—not because democracies are "soft on crime" (the dependence of Athenian justice on righteous anger is well studied) but because democracies should focus on what is necessary to maintain democratic concord rather than on relitigating the past.[60]

To justify incarceration in this context, Demosthenes needs to redirect the attention of the jurors from the past (the harm done) to the future (the effect of punishments on democratic behavior). Legislators and law itself are concerned with the future—"how people should behave, and how things should go" (24.116). Getting rid of imprisonment is not only a threat to the rule of law, Demosthenes argues, it decreases the ability of the democracy (in this case, the institution of the courts) to "make things go better [for the people]" in the future (24.209).[61] This point is given a place of honor in the peroration, where the jury is urged to get angry (*orgisthēnai*) and to correct (*kolasai*) criminals by making an example of them, for the purpose of punishment in a court is to habituate (*ethizein*) and to teach (*prodidaskein*, 24.218) the many.[62]

The question of imprisonment caused Demosthenes to enter a series of paradoxes and entanglements that it is not clear he was able (or intended) to solve. Chief among these is tension between the potential of the prison to be an instrument of democratic equality (keeping elites in check) and the problem that, by subjecting citizens to chains, uncomfortable boundaries between slavery and freedom are necessarily breached. In this way, the prison butts up against the great "unthought thought" of Athenian democracy—equality can only proceed so far in a society founded on a central fact of inequality.

Demosthenes's contortions show the ambiguous status of incarceration for Athenians—was it a leveling down, where all citizens suffered the degrading experience of chains, or was it a normal experience of democratic life, one of which no citizen should feel particularly ashamed? In Timocrates's (perhaps disingenuous) vision of democracy, incarceration is bad because it always encroaches on the social categories of shame and social identities maintained through an economy of esteem.[63] But in Demosthenes's version of democracy, prison is one of the resources available for constructing a new and different sort of social order beyond the old assumptions about shame and honor. Equality and gentleness are temporarily sacrificed in favor of asserting the authority of the people over the power of the rich and the few.

It is worth noting, though Demosthenes himself does not do this directly, the way in which incarceration differs from other possible vertical punishments like exile or ostracism (which, although not technically a juridical process, is nevertheless analogous): imprisonment keeps the criminal within the ambit of Athenian society. As the vicissitudes of fifth-century politics showed, sending wealthy citizens with social and political connections away from the city could give them an opportunity to appeal to an alternative power base and perhaps even to take sides against the very Athenian state that had pronounced the punishment.[64] The democratic prison, by confining all criminals at the heart of the civic space, reflects an attitude toward crime as something that needs to be addressed and contained within the polity rather than banished or expelled from it. This reflects the value that self-ruling forms of government tend to place on their citizens. This democratic care for citizens in punishment is also suggested by the *cost* that incarceration incurs, especially compared to other forms of punishment.[65] Equality requires a regime of punishment where the wealthy and powerful remain physically and symbolically under the eye of the demos.[66]

DEMOCRATIC VALUES AND THE THEORY OF PUNISHMENT

Demosthenes's speech walks a tightrope between admitting that the prison is a harsh practice unbefitting free citizens and entertaining the possibly that it is precisely this harshness that, if turned against the oligarchic class, can make the prison supremely democratic. When modern prison reformers praised the connection between incarceration and democracy, however, it was neither gentleness nor the power of the people that was foremost on their minds. As we stressed in the introduction, it was the power of the penitentiary to *reform*, to restore the convict to the community, that made incarceration indispensable to modern liberal states.[67] Given that the reformative theory of punishment also originated in ancient Athens, we might expect a relationship between reform and the prison to be found in Athenian democratic theory as well.[68]

Plato hints at a connection between rehabilitation and democracy by placing a version of the reformative theory of punishment in the mouth of a speaker with impeccable democratic credentials. Protagoras of Abdera was a sophist and associate of Pericles and who dabbled in both political theory and political practice.[69] According to Plato's depiction, Protagoras claimed that political virtues are tied to education and that unvirtuous behavior, "injustice and impiety—collectively the opposite of the political art," is met by "anger [*thumos*], correction [*kolasis*], and chastisement [*nouthetēsis*]," in short, by reform (Plato, *Prot.* 324a1, 324e2). Because punishment of political crimes aims to correct past behavior, the practice itself assumes that the virtues whose deficit it aims to fix can be learned, indeed *will* be learned by the criminal *and* others. For

> no one corrects the unjust with only the crime in mind and for the sake of that crime, as long as they're not imposing penalties irrationally [*timōreitai alogistōs*][70] like a wild beast. But the one who undertakes to correct according to reason [*meta logou*] doesn't penalize for the sake of the past crime—for "what's done cannot be undone"—but for the sake of the future, so that neither the doer himself not anyone else will do wrong again, seeing him punished. (324a6–b5)

In some ways, this sounds like the same sort of future-directed language used by Demosthenes when he urged the jury to "make things go better [for the people]" (24.209). But Protagoras is offering a new account of *rational* punishment. The fulcrum of Protagoras's reasoning is this: only punishment that aims at the future can be justified, for what is done is done (as proverbial for Plato as it was for Shakespeare). Protagoras is prosecuting what Nietzsche called "the spirit of revenge." There is no gain for the state or for the criminal in obtaining retribution for a past deed; in fact, revenge is primitive, beastly, inhuman. The context for this passage is a broader theory of education, and indeed Protagoras makes clear that the criminal is to be punished so that he might *become better* (*beltiōn genētai,* 325a7), the same phrase the sophist used to advertise his own services as educator.

There is some evidence to suggest that Protagoras's arguments, or others like them, made their way into the wider democratic discourse in Athens. Pericles's claim in the Thucydidean funeral oration that Athens is "a lesson [*paideusis*] for Greece" has a distinctly Protagorean echo.[71] And Plato has Socrates respond to Protagoras's great speech with the observation "someone could probably hear a very similar speech from Pericles, or another of the ones capable at speaking" (329a1–2).

In fact, in the famous debate recorded (or invented) by Thucydides over the fate of the rebellious Lesbian city of Mytilene, one of the speakers, the otherwise unknown Diodotus, takes a stand on punishment that is strikingly Protagorean.[72] He begins by praising the idea of democratic debate itself, both for its usefulness for good deliberation (*euboulia*) and its instructiveness for action. The opposite is "uneducated" anger (*meta apaideusias*). The Protagorean theme of *euboulia* appears throughout the speech, but it is in his dismissal of the retributive theory of punishment that Diodotus's similarity to Protagoras is clearest.[73] "Our dispute, if we are sensible, will concern not their injustice to us, but our good deliberation (*euboulia*) about what is best. . . . In my opinion what we are discussing concerns the future more than the present."[74] Here, once again, is the idea that democratic deliberation goes hand in hand with a rejection of retribution and opens itself to the possibility of instruction.[75] Diodotus is in a struggle for the legacy of Periclean democracy against the demagogic party of Cleon (who seeks to punish according to wrath, *orgē*). Taken together, these sources give a sense of at least one influential elite Athenian attitude about what makes popular government work and how education and punishment fit into a cohesive democratic worldview.[76]

None of these discussions of democratic punishment as future directed and reformative makes any mention, however, of incarceration as the technique or the prison as the site of rehabilitation. Each seems to take for granted that any punishment, whether extreme violence in the case of Mytilene or the unnamed punishments in the case of Protagoras, can do the work of teaching, in a generalized sense.[77] These arguments are all guilty of an error that M. M. McCabe called "institution begging"—that is, assuming the institutions of punishment as they exist can fulfill the philosophical role assigned to them.[78] Even Protagoras does not explain in any detail, at least in Plato's version of his speech, which sort of punishment will improve the punished and how. In the *Laws*, as we discuss in the next chapter, Plato tries to provide a solution to this problem, giving an account of the prison that is fully integrated with both a theory of reform and a moral psychology of how carceral rehabilitation works. But the prison in the *Laws* is run by a secretive council of philosophers and not answerable to any popular scrutiny; it is, in short, no longer a democratic institution.

With the notable exception of Plato, no Athenian seems to have considered the means of punishment to be a determinant factor in discerning just punishment. Perhaps this is because the attention of Athenian penology was more often directed to the end of punishment than the means. From the early retributive idea of the demos exercising its righteous rage to Demosthenes's later appeals to the demos as a body of sensible, civilized jurors with their eyes to the future, what remains constant is the interests of the democracy (and the demos) above all else.[79]

CONCLUSION: FROM THE PARADOX OF POPULARLY AUTHORIZED IMPRISONMENT TO THE PLATONIC SOLUTION

The practice of penal incarceration seems to have died out along with the Athenian democracy. The fine-grained distinctions that motivated Athenian debates about the merits of future-directed punishment versus revenge and concerns about the differences between citizens and noncitizens would have gradually lost their importance in a world where the arbiter of punishment was a king rather than a jury, and the civic unit of "the people" began to lose its effectual power within the larger empires of the Hellenistic age. No significant textual or historical discussion of penal incarceration survives from Hellenistic or Roman antiquity, and it was only during the rise of late-antique Christianity, with its stories of imprisoned martyrs and ascetic confinement, that incarceration once again became a matter of wide interest among theorists of politics and society.[80]

It is therefore understandably difficult to identify any continuous tradition of thinking about the prison along the lines that Demosthenes or other Athenian democrats explored, but it is nevertheless possible to isolate a theoretical problem that they faced, a problem that would return in different forms in later theories of the prison. The Athenians were challenged by incarceration in two ways: One was the historical memory of the prison as something bound up with antidemocratic moments, whether the tumults of the Peloponnesian War or, more immediately, with the practices of the oligarchical Thirty Tyrants. The other was the unique ideological challenge of the prison as a corporal punishment for citizens that did not sever them from the city (like capital punishment or exile) but kept them around in a sort of civic limbo, both part of and apart from the civic body.

These problems suggest the structure of a more general "paradox of popularly authorized imprisonment," the challenge that incarceration poses to forms of political regime that base themselves on popular consent. Advocates of popular rule, such as Demosthenes, may have good reasons for using incarceration as a form of punishment (in Demosthenes's case, the prison is depicted as harsh enough to be deterrent while still somehow being acceptable for citizens), but they will always run up against the fact that incarceration challenges the very categories that make democracy possible. In the case of Athens, these categories include the distinctions between slavery and freedom and between citizens and noncitizens (i.e., between rulers and nonrulers). In other systems of popular rule, as we see from the discussion of Hobbes in Chapter 4, the precise categories in question might shift, but the structure of the problem remains. By its very nature, carceral confinement places citizenship, the building block of popular government, in an unstable, in-between position.

There are a few possible solutions to this paradox. One was offered by the optimistic American voices canvassed in the introduction—the prison can prove itself to be democratic but only if it has the right organizational structure or produces the right sort of relationship between the criminal and the community. Another unfortunate American solution is to incarcerate precisely those citizens whose civic membership has already been called into question because of race, class, or some other disqualifying factor. But one of the most influential solutions to this paradox was already suggested in fourth-century Athens itself.

Plato, as keen an observer of Athenian politics as the city ever produced, wanted to preserve the value of improving the one being punished, as well as to keep the prison as a means of punishment. To do so, he dispensed with the democratic priority of the citizen and with the democratic procedure of punishing. If the prison is going to work, Plato thought, it needs to be entrusted not to the people but to the experts, the people who know what treatments can improve criminals and how to administer them. The next chapter tries to understand what Plato thought a prison run by these experts would do and how he thought it would do it.

2

PLATO'S THEORY OF INCARCERATION

AN UGLY MAN, with a bulbous nose and a beard like that of a raunchy woodland demon, sits on a low stone bench, rubbing the places on his legs that have recently been in fetters. The room is big enough to hold at least a few of his many friends and admirers, who look on anxiously. In the man's hand is a cup, filled to the brim with a bitter draught of poison hemlock, but he seems unperturbed, indeed unperturbable. We know this image from paintings, plays, and most of all from Plato's *Phaedo*. The death of Socrates is the most famous moment in the history of the Athenian prison.

Plato therefore had good reasons to play close attention to the prevailing ideas about crime and punishment in Athens. His teacher Socrates was executed in the jail after being accused by democratic politicians of having "corrupted the youth."[1] In a bit of political-philosophical irony, Plato's repeated engagement with the philosophy of punishment in general and the technique of incarceration in particular would provide a solution to the problem Athenian democrats had set themselves about how to simultaneously punish and improve.

Plato's penal theory is extensive and complex, integrating the technique of punishment, the justification for punishment, and the theory of human behavior. This theory both echoes the ambition of Athenian intellectuals to punish by improving and goes far beyond any existing Athenian penal practices. Plato's ideas about confinement as a plausible technique of psychic reformation set a pattern for the theory of imprisonment that would survive, in various forms, until the eighteenth-century "birth of the prison."

Plato based his argument on premises that would have been familiar and even attractive to readers steeped in democratic ideas about citizenship and punishment, but he extracted from these premises a set of conclusions about incarceration that kicked away the democratic ladder on which it had climbed up, so to speak, and entrusted punishment to a new form of institution, one which answered not to the sovereign demos but to the "divine" force of reason (*nous*). We can recognize a version of Plato's idea, that punishment requires the assistance of the rational science of understanding souls (criminal psychology), behind almost every later theory of penitentiary or reformatory prisons as sites of soul craft or improvement. In view of the foundational nature of Plato's prison theory, we will study his work on punishment and incarceration in detail, from its Athenian roots, through its psychological components, and on to its social and philosophical aims. Plato's intricately designed theory of how incarceration works, which has a close affinity with the discourse of democratic punishment without itself being committed to democracy, is a good illustration of the conceptual independence of the two early theories of incarceration, even when they were in clear conversation with one another.

The prison that Demosthenes, Timocrates, and the other figures from Athenian history argued over in Chapter 1 was a building somewhere near the Athenian marketplace. It may not have been a purpose-built structure and is unlikely to have had much differentiation between the types of people being held within.[2] The difference between this simple structure, whatever it looked like, and the prison system that Plato ultimately proposed in the *Laws* is the difference between incarceration as a piecemeal development in Athenian jurisprudence and the fully imagined institution, cut from whole cloth, that appears as part of Plato's philosophical-political experimentation.

In the *Laws*, Plato provides us with not one novel prison building but three. The first of these is something between a prison proper and a city jail. It is common to all sorts of criminals and located near the central marketplace. In some respects, this building is rather like the Athenian jail where Socrates drank his hemlock—the building Timocrates and his associates so wanted to avoid. The Athenian Stranger's[3] explanation that this jail is "for the sake of securing the bodies of the many" (908a) has a distinctly demotic ring to it and suggests that he is distinguishing the use of incarceration for punishing and remanding bodies from the use of incarceration for soul craft. This first prison represents something close to incarceration as a corporal punishment (much as it was treated in the sources from Chapter 1).[4] The jail, which in the *Laws* is usually referred to by the term "bonds" (*desmoi*), is to be the site of a different sort of incarceration than goes on in the other prisons. Chains aim at the body—the other prisons aim at the criminal soul.

Perhaps to separate them from the jail, Plato gives each of the other two prisons a proper name. The first is called the *sōphronistērion* ("Right-Think Tank"),[5] and it is located "near where the Nocturnal Council meets." This casual aside is the first mention in the *Laws* of the Nocturnal Council, ultimately the supreme constitutional body of the state. The introduction of the council alongside the *sōphronistērion* is no coincidence— as we will see, the roles of the two institutions are intimately intertwined. The third prison is to be built in the middle of nowhere, in a place as desolate and wild as possible. It is to be called "a name suggestive of punishment." Some have, rather literally, thought that this means its name *is* "punishment," but they miss a characteristic bit of Platonic subtlety.[6] The Athenian Stranger had already discussed what names are most effective in causing the fear of punishment—"Hades and the like" (904d2).[7] This last prison will be called "Hell" or "Tartarus."[8]

In contradistinction to the jail, which serves many functions (including but not limited to penal incarceration), the two prisons exist in relation to a single family of crimes—impiety in word or in deed. There are three forms of atheistic impiety, all punished by imprisonment—not believing the gods to exist (henceforth just "atheism"); believing that the gods exist but do not intervene in human affairs (henceforth "deism");

and believing that the gods can be bribed through prayer or sacrifice (henceforth "traditionalism").

These three prisons of Plato's *Laws,* perhaps the most detailed theoretical discussion of penal incarceration that survives from antiquity, present us with a series of riddles. How did the prison, a liminal and underused aspect of Athenian penal law, become an integral part of one of Plato's most intricate mediations on political philosophy? How did Plato solve the problem of "institution begging" that we identified in Athenian penal thought—that is, how can incarceration "improve" criminals, or, more simply, how do prisons work? This chapter tries to answer these questions in some detail. It presents the conceptual basis of Plato's prison theory, including his engagement with Athenian democratic culture and the picture of human psychology that informs the argument in the *Laws.* This will allow us to better understand the complex set of moral and psychological assumptions that underlie Plato's penal theory, as well as his use of incarceration.

Plato's theory of incarceration is part of his general justification for punishment, the basic tenets of which can be summed up by two Socratic paradoxes: (1) "It is better to be punished justly than to escape punishment" (because "being punished is being improved"); and (2) "No one does wrong willingly."[9] The tendentious relationship between these paradoxes and the day-to-day beliefs of Athenian citizens is explored most clearly in Plato's *Gorgias,* during the character Socrates's examination of the orator Polus.

If punishing a criminal is deemed good by the people, and the criminal identifies with the aims of the community, Socrates insists that Polus must admit that a good thing is being done to the person who is punished. If being punished is good, then "one who is punished is benefited" (*Gorg.* 477a2–3). Leaving aside whether the argument is valid, it makes clever use of a contemporary Athenian civic-democratic norm.[10] Socrates appeals to Polus's sense of shame and identification with the community and elicits his agreement that if the community (in the guise, for instance, of a jury) decides that a good thing is being done *to* him, then he must agree that it is also good *for* him (to be punished accordingly).

This communitarian-democratic notion of punishment, which relies on the identification of the individual with the political whole, falls apart in the face of the dialogue's final interlocutor, Callicles. Callicles is an aspiring democratic (demagogic?) politician who thinks of himself as an elite "lion" among the democratic sheep. While he agrees that it is important to discipline the masses, Callicles insists that it is the prerogative of a superior person to remain undisciplined and allow his desires to run rampant (*mē kolazein*, 491e–492a1). A Calliclean "lion" feels no shame in the face of his fellow citizens and thus need not agree with the community that his punishment is "good." For Callicles, wanton or criminal behavior is the consequence of pursuing urges and desires motivated by pleasure, urges that everyone would indulge if they could be sure of getting away with them.

If Callicles's psychological account of crime is true, then discipline and correction should focus on counteracting the allure of pleasure and getting these unruly desires under control. Socrates now introduces the language of "structure and order" (*taxis kai kosmēsis*) to define "law and what is lawful" to Callicles (504c2, 504d1–2). By analogy with medical patients, whose appetites and intakes are closely monitored and controlled by the doctor, "it is necessary to restrain [the soul] from its appetites and not leave it to do anything except that from which it will become better" (505b2–4). Punishing (*kolasis*, "disciplining") in its purest form is nothing other than keeping the soul away from the bad things that it desires.

Socrates does not draw the obvious conclusion from this, that the form of punishment best suited to disciplining desire would be isolation from harmful stimuli and watchful regimentation of life's necessities. Rather, he suggests that it is discussion itself that should serve as punishment. Socrates is disappointed that Callicles "won't undergo improving" by continuing the argument "and [with it] undergoing the thing which the discussion is about, being disciplined [*kolazomenos*]" (505c3–4), as if being refuted intellectually about pleasure would be enough to discipline Callicles.

Perhaps, under ideal conditions, Socrates could show anyone the truth of the idea that doing injustice is worse than suffering it and being justly disciplined is better than escaping punishment (cf. 527bc). In convincing them of something that is true (and, less obviously, by reordering their souls), Socrates would have made them better. But, as Callicles's stubbornness demonstrates, it is not clear whether an "undisciplined" person would ever voluntarily stick around to be improved through philosophical discussion. More importantly, it is unclear why the reader should believe that discussion will in fact make such a person well-behaved. Like Callicles, a criminal can always walk away.[11]

This incomplete argument about the form and technique of punishment may help to explain one of the most outstanding features of the *Gorgias,* the "eschatological myth" that takes up its final pages.[12] The most important element in the myth is the stripping away of the corporeal and political context for punishment. Plato shows that, without bodies, without juries, without mobs and demagogues, it is easy to imagine a system where "those punished rightly by another, either become better and improve, or become examples to the others" (525b3–4).[13] The souls of the dead are brought before divine judges and sentenced to some sort of pain and suffering before being allowed to proceed to the Isle of the Blessed. The precise nature of the process is left unclear (cf. 525bc, 526bc), but, as the souls are disembodied, these must be cognitive pains like those suffered by Polus and Callicles above—being shamed or being shown to be wrong. This image of true, fair punishment as an examination of the soul seems modeled on Socrates's own brand of dialectical examination.[14]

Plato's description of the geography of the afterlife contains another clue to the meaning of the myth. Plato posits two possible destinations for souls, the Isle of the Blessed and "Hades" or "Tartarus"—the pit. Plato calls the latter of these "the prison of retribution and justice" (*to tēs tiseōs te kai dikēs desmōtērion,* 523c).[15] By using the image of a prison, Plato suggests that the afterlife is more akin to a civic institution than to the cosmic order of the poets. The myth is thus also an answer to Callicles's stubborn refusal to be "improved." If Socratic soul treatment fails to complete the task of ordering on the individual level, then perhaps the solution lies at a higher level of social organization, with an institution designed to do the same sort of work on recalcitrant souls that the judges of the myth perform on the scarred and scabby shades of the dead. If the myth of the afterlife is effectively describing a prison, then perhaps the prison can do the work of the afterlife.

If the myth of the *Gorgias* can be read as an allegory for the conditions necessary for true, fair punishment (including psychic investigation, punishment that improves, an institution that has coercive power over souls unwilling to be bettered), can similar lessons be gleaned from other Platonic myths? As it turns out, penological and carceral elements are not unique to the *Gorgias* myth.[16] One of the major themes of the myth that concludes the *Phaedo* (a dialogue that takes place entirely within the Athenian *desmōtērion*) is what precisely it might mean for the soul to separate from the body—how and why it may be possible to conceive of a disembodied soul. This is an exploration, in other words, of the idea in the *Gorgias* that souls in the afterlife are examined "naked." A soul goes down to the underworld, says Socrates, "possessing nothing except for its education [*paideia*] and upbringing" (*Phaedo* 107d2–3). Even here, in a dialogue apparently removed from the questions of civic education and politics that motivate the *Gorgias,* the state of the soul is a consequence of the very issues that Socrates, Gorgias, Polus, and Callicles fought over—what it means to educate and be educated. What goes on in the "underworld" is an extension—indeed, an outcome—of civic education.

The mechanisms for sorting the souls in the *Phaedo* are, it must be said, different from the mythical judges of the *Gorgias.* Here the soul's own character and its past actions determine whether it finds an easy way through the tortuous subterranean geography Socrates describes or whether it gets lost and wanders through a sort of purgatory (108ac). There is a judgment (113d3), and souls either pay the penalty (are punished) for their deeds in life or gain honor for them. Some souls are incurable, and some have a further stage of punishment, after which they must persuade other souls to receive them back into the society of shades. Pious souls are set free and fly from these regions "as if from a prison [*desmōtērion*]" (114c1) to return to the surface of the earth, where they are reincarnated. Good souls, adequately educated ones, have no need of prison to make them better.

The general structure of Socratic punishment is readily identifiable in the prison/underworld of the *Phaedo*—souls are rehabilitated through punishments. After these punishments, the souls join other souls who led better lives than they did, suggesting that they themselves have "become better." As with the *Gorgias* myth, at least two interpretive strategies are available to the reader. The first is to take the Pythagorean geography of the underworld at least in some measure seriously, as a sort of "likely story" of how the reincarnation of immortal souls theorized in the dialogue (e.g., at 78d and following) functions in the physical cosmos. The second is to focus on Socrates's recommendation that this tale serve as an "incantation" and ask what lessons can be drawn from it.[17] Aside from its decisive contribution to the "consolation of philosophy" genre, the myth also highlights the social context of punishment. Souls find their way (or do not) based on the approbation or condemnation of their fellow souls (107bc). A key criterion for when punishment has ended is whether a soul is ready to be readmitted to the company of better souls, and indeed, those who bypass punishment altogether are, it seems, readmitted into the company of living humans.

This adds a layer of complexity to the picture of what the institution of punishment must do that was absent from the *Gorgias*. In the *Gorgias*, the social context of punishment was present, but the idea that punishment exists in part to return the criminal to the society that punishes him was not. The finality of the Isle of the Blessed as a destination for adequately punished souls is therefore a less precise analog for the relationship between the criminal and the society that punishes him than the metempsychosis of the *Phaedo* and, indeed, the *Republic*. Without delving into the Myth of Er, the extravagantly complex and fantastical passage that concludes Plato's masterwork, it is worth noting certain important continuities there with the *Gorgias* and *Phaedo*. Here too Plato is explicit about the ability of punishment to make people better (619d, where those who have undergone punishment make wiser choices than those who have not); and here too reincarnation is the crucial metaphor for expressing the iterative nature of punishment. A successful punishment does not fix the event of the past; it prepares the criminal for the future. It is worth pausing here to note that, as with Dante, his successor in mythographic penology, Plato's myths of punishment do not merely project the ordering of this world into the next. Rather, Plato manipulates the language of myth, and particularly myths of the afterlife, into a compelling picture of "true punishment," as applicable to this life as it is to the next one.

This link between carceral geography and mythography persists all the way to the *Laws*, which includes this striking passage: "It is necessary that the disciplining of these [criminals] here in their lifetime fall in no way short of that in Hades, as much as is possible" (881a8–b3). In the *Laws*, Plato says clearly what is only hinted at in the *Gorgias*, that social and political institutions must carry out the role usually assigned to divine punishment. The prison is the place where the scars that injustice leaves on the soul will be diagnosed and perhaps even be removed.

The idea that a brick-and-mortar prison might be able to accomplish something like the sort of psychic treatments proposed by the myth of the *Gorgias* is still not enough to defuse M. M. McCabe's cutting criticism of Plato's reformative theory—that punishment cannot truly improve people (and, therefore, it ought not be asked to do so, a criticism that has resurfaced in the modern criminological dictum that "nothing works" to rehabilitate criminals). The next section of this chapter will examine Plato's effort to answer this challenge by connecting the technique of punishment (and especially incarceration) to an element of penology that has been in the background—the moral psychology of the criminal.[18] This effort reaches its fullest expression in the same dialogue where Plato gives his clearest account of a working reformatory prison, the *Laws*.

THE MORAL PSYCHOLOGY OF INCARCERATION

The *Laws*, usually thought to be Plato's last work, is an investigation of an ideal state, its laws and institutions. Unlike the *Gorgias* (or the *Republic*), the *Laws*, set in Crete at an unspecified date sometime after the Persian Wars, self-consciously distances itself from any immediate Athenian context.[19] But, like those other dialogues, the work is as much about moral psychology as it is about political institutions; indeed, it assumes that the two must go hand in hand. The interlocutors, old men from Crete, Sparta, and Athens, begin their comparative inquiry into constitutional structure by comparing a city's struggle to maintain order and succeed against other cities to a person's inner struggle to be "better than himself" (626e–627a). The Athenian Stranger, who leads the discussion, expands upon this analogy by using the image of a puppet, pulled in one direction by the "golden and holy" string of "reasoning" (*logismos*, linked to the form of public reason that is called law at 644d–645a) and pulled in the other by pleasures and pains, as well as expectation, fear, boldness, and other passions (*pathoi*).

This image gives a structure for the role of both education and law in connecting the individual psyche with the political regime. The citizen must be educated to provide his reasoning the assistance it needs to overcome the pull of pain, pleasure, and passion on his behavior (645ab).[20] The legal framework of a polity, insofar as it is well designed, both aligns with reason (the link between human reason and political law is essential to the *Laws*)[21] and provides the content of the moral education the citizen will experience from childhood and throughout his life through contact with various social institutions (cf. 643e).[22] Becoming "weaker" or "stronger" than one's self is thus a question of not only the power of the mind's reasoning faculty but also of that faculty's assimilation of *generally correct principles* absorbed through contact with the civil law.[23] When a person's reasoning aligns with the objective demands of rational law, she can be said to have "overcome herself," or, to use another Platonic metaphor, she will reach a harmony (*sumphōnia*) between reason, pleasures, and desires (653b).[24] Such a citizen is well-educated (653c).

Given the role of education in aligning the reasoning faculty with civil law, the potential for utilizing education in punishment is clear. In fact, the *Laws* agrees with the Protagorean/Periclean project of creating a continuum between education and law. "Education is the training [*agōgē*] and guiding of children towards right reason according to law" (659d), and judges in the courts are teachers of the public (659b). This should also put us in mind of the instinctual agreement Polus felt for whatever the public deemed "good" in the *Gorgias*. When this social conditioning fails, when psychic harmony between communal law and individual desire has not been reached, when a person is not stronger than herself, then remedial education—punishment—becomes necessary.

In one of the rare moments of true disagreement between the characters in the *Laws,* the Cretan Clinias expresses some discomfort with Socratic doctrine as the basis for civil law: If "the unjust man is indeed bad, but he is unwillingly bad" (860d),[25] it will be impossible to distinguish the punishment for a great crime from that for a small one, given that all criminals are ignorant and therefore unwilling (857b). The apparent conflict between moral principle and the necessities of a penal code is important enough that the Athenian Stranger appeals to technical "philosophy" in an attempt to provide answer (*philosophein,* in one of only two appearances of the word in the *Laws*). In this case, "philosophy" provides the interlocutors (and the reader) with a more precise understanding of what goes on in the soul of the criminal.[26]

The Athenian proceeds analytically through the psychic causes of crime: There is something (1) in the nature of the soul that is connected to passionate impulse (*thumos*), and it "overturns many things through irrational force" (863b4). Presumably one of the things it can overturn is rational decision-making. There is a separate power in the soul that responds to pleasure (2), though it works differently, achieving its aim through "force of deceit" (863b8). Both elements, it is implied, can overcome the rational thought (*logismos*) or plan (*boulēsis*) of the actor, the first violently and immediately, the second slowly and corrosively. There is also a third cause of crime—ignorance (*agnoia*)—which can be further subdivided into a "simple" form (3) and a double form (4), where ignorance is compounded by the illusion of wisdom (*doxē sophias*), not knowing what one thinks one knows. This worst type of ignorance itself comes in two forms, the "great and savage" ignorance of the strong (4a) and the weaker errors of youth and old age (4b).

Using this scheme (reminiscent of but not identical to the tripartite theory of the soul in the *Republic*), the Athenian moves on to clarify what justice and injustice mean. Injustice is the tyranny (*turannis*) of passion and fear, pleasure and pain, and jealousy and desire in the soul. In short, it is the disordering of the soul, whatever the cause. If, however, "the [true] belief about the highest good, whether it is a city or a private person who thinks to aim at it, ... prevails in the soul and regulates every man, even if some error is made (*kan sphallētai ti*), everything done thus must be said to be just ... although most believe the damage to be an 'involuntary injustice'" (864a1–5).[27] True belief is thus both a necessary and sufficient condition for justice, while injustice always requires the absence of true belief. According to this strong intellectualist thesis, justice does not preclude *some* intellectual errors, but they are, apparently, relatively unserious.[28]

This division of the soul and its powers enables Plato to make a series of important distinctions concerning the causes of crime (and therefore allows him to answer Clinias's worry about differentiating between different degrees of criminal). He distinguishes between passion and pleasure, both of which act "tyrannically" to make a person "stronger" or "weaker" than herself; and ignorance, which is of a different species entirely yet still causes people to act against their best considered inclination (*boulēsis*).

This division is stated even more clearly in a parallel discussion of the definition of injustice in Plato's *Sophist*, which identifies two forms (*eidē*) of badness in the soul. The first is wickedness, which is a disease due to civil war (*stasis*) between beliefs, desires, anger, pleasures, reason, and pain in the soul (1 and 2 above). In the other, ignorance (3 and 4 above), which manifests as a sort of "shamefulness," the soul tries to aim itself toward the truth but misses the mark, due to some disproportion (*ametria*) in its faculties.[29] Again, when discussing the cure for ignorance, the interlocutors in the *Sophist* realize the category must be further divided. The larger, more serious sort is the recognizable genus of "not knowing what one thinks one knows" (4a), which is the cause of "when we err (*sphallometha*) during contemplation" (*Sophist* 229c5–6). This type of ignorance, it turns out, has a particular name ("foolishness"—*amathia*—the same word Plato will use to describe the honest impious criminals imprisoned in the reformatory prison of the *Laws*) and a unique solution—liberal education (*paideia,* the task carried out in that prison).[30] This seems to be the sort of ignorance that carries within it both the most dangerous sorts of crime *and,* apparently, the paradoxical example of the just criminal—the just man who makes some intellectual errors about important things.

The picture of criminal psychology that emerges from these passages has a great deal of significance for how punishments must work: The first two types of injustice are the result of some internal discord in the soul due to passion or pleasure and can be cured through discipline (*kolasis*), a technical reordering of the psychic elements into their correct arrangement. In such cases—an overpowering of rational thought (by passion) or an undercutting of rational thought (by pleasure)—the rational element in the soul is intact but silenced. The goal of corrective punishment in these cases, therefore, is not to act on or appeal to reason, it is to disencumber reason from these impediments.

In the *Gorgias,* Plato presented, via the exchange between Socrates and Callicles, a theory of how the pursuit of pleasure was the cause of crime and how the restriction of pleasure (or the dialectical proof that pleasures were not what the criminal thought they were) could serve as punishment. From the list of penal tools the Athenian gives in the laws—"deeds or words, or pleasures or pains, or honors or dishonors, or monetary fines or gifts" (862d)—it seems that corporal punishment, fines, and the threat of dishonor might all be used to temper the pleasure-seeking element that drove crime. Plato also assimilates crimes driven by anger/passion into this schema, calling passions "painful"[31] and suggesting that just as administering physical pains can counteract physical pleasure, administering psychic pains (through the loss of honor, for instance) might be the correct antidote to the psychic excitement of anger.

For this interpretation to cohere with the reformative, intellectualist core of Plato's thought, noneducative punishments must have some connection to the rational element that produces just behavior. Here, the language of the *Sophist* is helpful. Nonrational punishments (whether corporal or pecuniary) are able to suppress one of the parties in the "civil war of the soul."[32] This means the (possibly painful) "break-up of an existing pattern" of behavior that allows for the new habituation of the individual,[33] and Plato seems to include penal confinement (in its simplest sense of being chained up, *desmoi*) among other punishments that strike the necessary balance between the shock of nonrational punishment and the respect accorded to free citizens.[34] This is the form of incarceration practiced in the first prison (the "jail") "for the sake of securing the bodies of the many" (908a), confirming the distinction between the "corporal" use of incarceration for punishing and remanding bodies from the "reformative" use of incarceration for soul craft.

Habituation, or reeducation, is not an explicit part of the punishment for crimes originating in the nonrational elements of the soul (including "corporal" incarceration in the jail)—because the whole constitution of the *Laws* is designed to be a form of education. Once any pathologies have been removed through the shock therapy of nonrational punishment, the sort of society proposed by the *Laws* will ensure that the rational element is in control of practical reasoning within the individual soul and correctly oriented to the principles of the society outside of it.

Plato's description of the nonrational causes of crime allows him to admit of nonrational punishments that can fix the psychological deficit in the criminal and improve her to the satisfaction of society. Nonrational forces such as shame and financial (or even physical) pain can be especially effective in addressing criminals whose love of pleasure has overpowered their rational adherence to law or power of choice (*boulēsis*). By developing a place for nonrational punishment within the framework of a "rehabilitative" theory, Plato has made a concession to the commonsense view that conversation will simply not be enough for every sort of criminal and every sort of crime. Nevertheless, he has not given up on dialectic as an important technique of punishment—he has just reached a much more precise understanding of how and why dialectic improves the one who undergoes it. Dialectic is the cure for criminal ignorance, and its use is confined to the inmates of the *sōphronistērion,* or "reformatory" prison.

After these lengthy preliminaries, we are finally ready to address the role of penal confinement and how it can, according to Plato, successfully reform a criminal (as well as the additional puzzle of how philosophical argument can be a punishment). In addition to continuing the typology of criminals we began above (illustrated in table 2.1), we now examine more precisely what Plato thinks should go on in a prison, at least according to the *Laws.*

Incarceration is most closely connected to the last cause of crime in Plato's schema, ignorance (although, as we have noted, it also appears in the *Laws* as an additional form of corporal punishment). The major example of "ignorant" criminals in the context of the *Laws* is the phenomenon of impiety discussed in book 10. There, we learn that the three different types of impiety (atheism, deism, and traditionalism) are caused by different forms of ignorance, and consequently, they are to be treated by a variety of penal confinements.[35]

The first sort of ignorance is its most minor form (simply not knowing enough to do the right thing, type 3 above), but that is a rather uninteresting category, easily treatable, if we rely on the *Sophist,* through "technical training" (228d). More worrying is what the Athenian Stranger calls "a distinct and separate category, [which] is of expectations and opinion—it is a mere unsuccessful shot at the truth about the highest good" (*Laws* 864b6-7)—ignorance about ends.[36] This is the ignorance of those people who think they know what they do not—often elite criminals like Callicles (4a above). Both forms of ignorance share a distinct criminal pathology from passion or pleasure. They do not involve one psychic element overpowering the others (863d8). Rather, they point to an incompleteness within the reasoning element itself.

Within the second, more serious type of ignorance, Plato further distinguishes between two subtypes—ignorance combined with an "incontinence" toward pleasure and the ignorance of a fundamentally just person (with a basically well-ordered soul) who errs solely intellectually (864a). The first subtype, the criminals who also suffer from the "civil

TABLE 2.1. The moral psychology of crime in Plato's *Laws*

| Name | Irrational | | Rational Ignorance |
	Passion	Pleasure	
Cause	(1) Passionate elements in the soul overpower the rational faculty	(2) Desire for pleasure overpowers the rational faculty	Misshapen/ malformed rational faculty; covers both (3) "mindless" ignorance and (4) "unlearnedness"
Present in	Unpremeditated crimes	Premeditated crimes; devious atheists of all three types— scientific, deistic, and traditionalist (when combined with ignorance)	Honest atheists of all three types— scientific, deistic, and traditionalist
Treatment	Fines; corporal punishment, including corporal imprisonment, capital punishment, and exile—combined with socialization at the hands of the state's practices, laws, fellow citizens, etc.	For premeditated crimes: fines; corporal punishment, including corporal imprisonment, capital punishment, and exile—combined with socialization at the hands of the state's practices, laws, fellow citizens etc. For devious impious criminals: life imprisonment in the Tartarus prison	Chastisement (for mindlessness) or elenchus (for unlearnedness), both administered in the reformatory prison

war" with pleasure, will be dangerous and "dishonest."[37] On the one hand, such people have a defect in reasoning and so cannot be punished nonrationally, but on the other, they also have unbalanced psyches and so cannot be reformed only by dialectic (as the case of Callicles showed). In the city of the *Laws,* the Athenian decrees that they be given a sentence of life without parole in the prison called Tartarus, an isolated building on the border of the country (which shares a certain iconographic similarity to the mythological "prison of retribution" described in the *Gorgias*).[38] The double corruption of mistaken knowledge and a "civil war" with pleasure makes this the rare example of an "incurable" penological type, where reform defers entirely to deterrence.[39] Ignorance, or the weakness of the reasoning element, is still a chief cause of crime, but where pleasure combines with intellectual error, the rule of the rational element cannot be restored.

The second sort of seriously ignorant criminal is not under the dangerous sway of pleasure or passion and does not have a "civil war" in her soul. Her ignorance, unlike that of the pleasure-corrupted ignorant person, can be countered (and corrected) entirely with knowledge. In the context of the *Laws,* this correction will take place in the *sōphronistērion,* or reformatory prison, where she will be subject to instruction by the philosopher experts of the Nocturnal Council over the course of a five-year prison term (908e). Given that the psychological problem with this sort of criminal was "ignorance," instruction can plausibly be said to both reform her and "make her better."

At long last Plato has given us the site of the reformatory punishment he alluded to in the *Gorgias,* as well as a fuller psychological profile of the criminal who will be reformed. All that remains to uncover is the specific reformative technique that will be practiced within the reformatory prison. Here Plato makes yet another division within this subtype. Some cases of ignorance can be fixed by what the *Sophist* passage calls "chastisement" (*nouthetēsis*), one of the two tasks assigned to the reformatory prison (*Laws* 909a). This activity corresponds to a paternalistic form of scolding or encouraging and can be applied to any criminal exhibiting ignorance. Chastisement is a more active version of the process encouraged throughout society by the educative function of law itself. Of the three types of atheists in the *Laws,* two, the deists and the traditionalists, are said to be driven by a "lack of reasoning" (*alogia,* 900a) and have a certain intellectual weakness (*ou dunamenos*). We may surmise that they will be "chastised," given moral instruction meant to get the well-intentioned but weak-minded criminal back on track.

There now remains only the second half of this subtype, the last sort of ignorant criminal, a strong-minded but honest atheist, of the sort who does not believe in the gods because she "missed the mark" in understanding philosophical first principles. These criminals will also be imprisoned in the reformatory prison with their weak-witted colleagues, but the *Sophist* describes a more demanding form of education for "someone who thinks he's saying something though he's saying nothing" (230b, cf. *Laws* 881a): "[The punishers] collect his opinions together during the discussion, put them side by side, and show that they conflict with each other at the same time on the same subjects in relation to the same things and in the same respects. . . . Refutation (*elenchus*) is the principal and most important kind of cleansing" for this sort of person.[40] This penal regimen of dialectical, emphatically Socratic treatment is a punishment for those who are not disfigured by unruly passion, not incontinent regarding pleasure, and not simply foolish. Plato has created an institutional form of the very sort of dialectical punishment he proposed for Callicles in the *Gorgias* (though Callicles himself, corrupted as he is by pleasure, would presumably be sent straight to the Tartarus prison). With the prisons of the *Laws,* a psychiatric framework for penal soul craft has come fully into view.[41]

We have established, with a fair amount of precision, what happens inside the prison (restraint in the jail, deterrence through life without parole in the Tartarus prison, instructing the weak-minded and refuting the strong-minded in the reformatory), but that is not the same as knowing what the prison is for. Athenian punishment, for example, aimed variously at the protection of the democratic regime, the vindication of injuries against the demos, and the satisfaction of private citizens seeking to "take justice" from those who had injured or offended them. Plato never uses the language of satisfaction or revenge, and "making people better" is not an act of justice in the normal sense of the word.[42] To understand the political significance of the sort of well-ordered soul that emerges from Plato's prison (and from the other punishments proposed by the *Laws*), it is necessary to return to Plato's first discussion of reformatory punishment, in the *Protagoras.* In the Chapter 1, we examined the link the *Protagoras* draws between future-directed punishment and democracy. Now we will focus on another part of Protagoras's "Great Speech," his myth about the moral foundations of political life.

According to this myth, Zeus had the god Hermes give the tools for ruling a polis to all human beings in the same measure (in the background, of course, is the Athenian commitment to political equality). These tools, "justice and shame" (*dikē kai aidōs*, 322c), are identified as the "bonds of friendship" (*philias desmoi*) that maintain social order.[43] Accordingly, they provide the standard by which any violation of social concord is to be judged (322d). Shame and justice are thus both the origin and the measure of political virtue, and it is sometimes necessary to restore these virtues through the process of educational correction. As we saw in Chapter 1, the idea that these political tools belong to everyone and can be taught to those who seem to lack them forms the basis of an egalitarian, reformatory theory of punishment.

Most writing about politics focuses on what seems to be the more obvious political virtue, justice. It is justice that tells us what sort of punishment is fitting for whom, when, and why, just as it is justice that helps us identify the other principles of distribution in society. Shame would seem to be a decidedly junior member in this partnership. So why did Protagoras (and the earlier poetic tradition he was drawing from) identify shame as so important for political life? To be sure, shame plays a role in the philosophical dialectics of Plato's *Gorgias,* in relation to which it has received ample scholarly attention, but shame is rarely, if ever, placed at the center of Greek political thought.[44]

To understand why Plato had Protagoras say that shame deserves double billing with justice as the foundation of political life (and as the aim of punishment), it is necessary to get a handle on the semantic field that corresponds to the Greek word *aidōs,* a word that brings with it an exceptionally rich web of emotional and reactive meanings. The dictionary sense of shame, and its central meaning in Homer and other early poets, is something closer to respect or reverence "for the feeling or opinion of others or for one's own conscience." From this sense of awe or respect, *aidōs* can also refer to the sort of reverence a pious (*semnos, eusebēs*) person feels before a superior, especially a god (or perhaps a parent), and often connotes the sort of conduct that leads to approval by others—shameful and, especially, self-controlled (*sōphrōn*) behavior.[45]

This last sense, shame as self-control (or moderation), proves especially important in understanding the social, political, and moral importance of shame. The well-established connection between shame and a particular set of character traits (particularly continence around pleasures, especially sexual pleasures)[46] allowed the Greeks to use the word in one sense while hinting at and even depending on an echo of the other senses.[47] Plato associates shame with the *fear* of being shamed, like the fear Polus exhibited in the *Gorgias,* and Callicles refuses (unlike Polus) to be shamed, preferring to admit to any number of obscene or perverse preferences rather than to concede that he is vulnerable to the opinion of other people.[48] Shame and the threat of shamelessness plays an equally decisive and even more explicit role in the *Laws.*

SHAME, PLEASURE, AND LAW

The discussion of shame in the *Laws* is part of the complex and extensive theory of moral psychology that we began to unpack above. From its very first pages, the *Laws* is concerned with the sort of education (*paideia*) that makes people "eagerly desirous [*epithumētēs erastēs*]" of being good citizens (*Laws* 643e, reformative punishment, as we saw in the *Protagoras* and other dialogues, is one such form of "education"). If the dialogue's theory of anger, pleasure, and knowledge explained the types of criminality and their treatments, the role of shame in the soul is an equally important explanation of the "healthy" political psychology of the community to which reformed criminals are meant to return.

The Cretan Cleinias, the Spartan Megillus, and their Athenian acquaintance explore the psychology of the ideal political community through the warlike metaphor of being "stronger" than oneself (good) or "weaker" than oneself (bad). "Self-overcoming," it turns out, mostly means "overpowering" or being "overpowered by" one's inclination for pleasures or pains (633de).[49] The Athenian Stranger adapts this pleasure-focused language to discuss political virtue, which he defines as knowing how to "rule and be ruled according to justice [*meta dikēs*]."[50] From the beginning of the dialogue, the victory of self-control (*sōphrosunē*) over pleasure, which is connected verbally and conceptually to shame, is given a central role in political life as imagined by the *Laws.*[51]

According to the general model of political psychology proposed by the Athenian, each person contains two "foolish advisors," pleasure and pain, that are controlled by "opinions about the future," that is to say, by "expectation" (*elpis*). Expectation about pain is called "fear" (*phobos*), and expectation about pleasure is called "confidence" (*tharros*). Balancing between these is rational "calculation" (*logismos*) about the better and worse choice. This "calculation" is precisely what every law (the "public decree" of the state) aims to influence. All legislation, viewed from the aspect of moral psychology, is about swaying the expectation (and calculation) of future pleasure and pain.[52]

Shame (*aidōs*) is another name for this fearful expectation, because the fear of being recognized as "bad" produces the sense of shame. We can think back to the sort of psychological trait Socrates exploited when he convinced Polus that the latter did not want to be seen as "bad" and therefore would accept being justly punished. This shame-fear complex is of primary importance for the psychic struggle between law, pleasure, and pain. It is the task of legislation to "lead [citizens] into fear with the help of the law" (647c),[53] and the inculcation of shame/fear is accomplished "with the aid of justice" (*meta dikēs*), once again echoing the pairing of justice and shame proposed by Protagoras in his political myth.

Shame, especially the fear of social disapproval that it produces, plays a double role here. It is first and foremost a powerful tool to align the individual's interests with the demands of communal law and, thus, with virtuous, rational behavior.[54] But hidden within this "manipulative" use of shame is the emotion's natural role as a mediator of inter-subjective ethical life. The role of shame, and the correlative fear of the judgment of one's fellow citizens, shows that the working model of human psychology in the *Laws,* while based on pleasure and pain, is anything but solipsistic. Rather, it presumes that the individual's behavior must always be understood within a broader social context.

A good example of the social nature of this psycho-legal complex is the institution of public symposia proposed by the Athenian Stranger. These drinking parties, which revolve around a shared social experience while still offering the possibility of transgression and lawlessness, are the perfect testing ground for how a citizen will behave in the face of the temptations of civic life (649d).[55] For a person to behave well at a symposium confirms that shame still exerts some control over his behavior, even if other constraints are weakened. Institutionalized drinking becomes, in a sense, a practical variation on the myth of the Ring of Gyges from the second book of the *Republic*—it tests the goodness of the good man when the usual inhibitions are removed. Orderly drunkenness is evidence of good education.[56]

The symposium reveals whether shame has taken root in the soul of the citizen, but it does not explain how a person can be taught to be shameful. To understand the social production of shame,[57] it is necessary to turn to two of shame's close corollaries, honor (timē) and blame (psogos).[58] The Athenian introduces these two practices as primary tools for the transformation of the moral habits of a state (metabalein . . . poleōs ēthē, 711bc). Blame (like shame) is an external imposition on the behavior of the individual—but people are nevertheless convinced that they want to be worthy of praise (and not culpable for blame). In this way, the action of shame can be said to be both persuasive and voluntary, forced and unforced. To the reader familiar with the Laws, this combination of persuasion and coercion through the use of praise and blame mimics what Plato frequently emphasizes as one of the key elements in the Magnesian constitution—laws that not only act on the outside but also persuade citizens to obey through an appeal to reason (and, occasionally, emotion).[59]

Shame's ability to act externally and persuade internally makes it particularly useful for the legislative structure of the Laws. If a law must not only command but also seem plausible to the person it commands, the sense of shame that a potential transgressor feels in contemplating her deed goes some way to showing this rational/persuasive plausibility. Shame transcends the simple dichotomies of forbidden/permitted and society/individual to draw the opinions and habits of the social world into the soul of the citizen. The double design of law in the Laws, with a persuasive prologue (prooimion) joined to a "coercive" statute, appears itself to imitate the general structure of shame, acting simultaneously on the internal sense of identity and external sense of what is appropriate behavior.[60]

The importance of shame would have been familiar to a Greek reader of Plato's text, just as it would have been to someone listening to Protagoras's speech. What is surprising in Plato is the formal, institutional role that shame plays. Praise, blame, and the expression of shame were not usually thought to be part of law, stricto sensu.[61] In the Athenian's proposed law code, however, he includes not only the things that are normally "subject to law" (cf. 730b) but also the content necessary to "chastise and persuade" citizens about the right mode of conduct.[62] Praise, blame, and shame belong to the things that educate (paideueōn,

730b) citizens and make them more "well disposed" to the laws that are to be enacted.

The purpose of the constitution envisioned in the *Laws* is not only to produce self-controlled adults but also to produce citizens who are persuaded by the rightness of their own compliance. If, in Plato's *Republic*, the best city produces the possibility of the best life for the best person, and, in Aristotle's *Politics,* the good city is one where a good citizen is also a good man, then the *Laws* can be understood as proposing a regime where the consummate citizen (*akron politēn,* 823a) is the one most consistently persuaded by the legislator. This person will be virtuous, but her virtue will be a particular, law-governed sort—it is virtue gained "with the help of the laws" and, it should be said, with the shame inculcated by the prologues. The novel and exceptional use of shame can thus also be understood as a consequence of the particularly high premium placed on persuasion, *in foro interno,* as part of the constructional structure of the *Laws.* We might say, slightly fancifully, that the main difference between Plato's two great constitutional regimes is which one of Protagoras's two original political virtues they have at their center. The *Republic*'s philosopher kings aim at justice, while the Nocturnal Council and its prison are concerned with shame.[63] It is for this reason that moderation and responsiveness to shame become the final condition of release from Plato's prison. "When their time of imprisonment is up," if the inmates of the *sōphronistērion* "should seem to be reasonable" (*sōphronein*)—that is to say, if the prison has lived up to its name—"let them dwell among the right-thinking (*sōphrones*)" (909a5–7).

Plato's detailed and demanding theory of incarceration is even more striking when compared with the actual practice of incarceration as it existed in the Athens of his time. Incarceration, if we are to believe the texts we examined in Chapter 1, existed at the frontier of the democratic respect for the autonomy of free citizen bodies and the need of the citizen demos to control wealthy elites. For Demosthenes and his contemporaries, the prison was part of a political struggle over the meaning of "democracy"—the definition of membership in the demos and the limits to popular power.

The question that motivates Platonic punishment, on the other hand, is not who wields authority but rather what social and political structures are demanded by reason. At one point, Plato defines politics as the type of "knowledge" (*epistēmē*) that has power over "common life" (*to koinon, Statesman* 305e4–6). For Plato, it is not enough to have an end or value in mind, like the rule of the many (or even the rule of the few), and then to test political practices against it. Institutions, including techniques of punishment, must be justified by correct knowledge at every step and in every aspect. The lawgiver or the statesman must know (and predict) how different sorts of people will react to different sorts of laws and institutions, and each detail of the law, each element of each institution, must justify itself before the tribunal of reason.

Plato's ideal states are therefore sometimes called "epistocracies," because those who have knowledge of what is right should rule. But in the *Laws,* where political knowledge is embedded in statutes and institutional design as much as in any person, epistocracy must be understood more precisely as the rule *of* knowledge.[64] Correct knowledge of human souls is the principle according to which state power, including punishment, is to be applied. In the best system of laws, it is knowledge itself, knowledge of the criminal mind, knowledge of human nature, that can be said to be responsible for punishment rather than any public official.

I have intentionally framed this nexus of power and knowledge, of power distributed through the knowledge of human behavior, in a way meant to suggest Michel Foucault's conception of "power/knowledge." The exercise of power (in the form of coercive violence) in the *Laws* is as much about causing citizens to internalize knowledge (as the analogy of the soul as a puppet susceptible to the pull of reason illustrates) as it is about using knowledge to enable or effect state violence. This affinity between Plato and modern theories of incarceration deepens when one considers the close intersection between penology and psychology that Foucault identified in the modern "punishment-correction" of delinquency. The offenders in Plato's *Laws* are "delinquents" avant la lettre. Criminal behavior is explained by behavioral science rather than by the judicial processes of a court.

The Athenian use of incarceration described in Chapter 1, intertwined as it was with democratic values and the interests of the democratic jury system, seems to have lent itself to a more pragmatic, consequentialist theory of punishment. If keeping a person, especially a rich and powerful person, under lock and key benefited the demos more than it harmed it, then, according to Demosthenes, incarceration was justified. Plato, for his part, demanded a procedural transparency for his political institutions that even modern "technocratic" democracies still struggle to implement. The penal regime imagined by the *Laws* depends on a rationalized, technical process and the adherence of this process to an external, nonpolitically contingent standard of truth, as much as it does on the identity of the offender. Placing a criminal under confinement must conform to autonomous penological reason. A citizen jury is simply not fit to mete out such punishments.[65]

Despite these differences, the Athenian discourse around the prison and Plato's account of incarceration do share one striking detail—they are both focused on the punishment of elites. As Marcus Folch discusses, references to the prison in Athenian historiography are always in the context of elite personalities, male or female.[66] In the *Laws,* the reformatory prison is located on the acropolis, directly next to the seat of government (and is administered by its highest body, the Nocturnal Council). Even the Tartarus prison is filled with the sort of well-spoken personalities who sometimes become "tyrants and demagogues and generals," founders of mystery cults and sophists (908d).[67] This identification of political elites with heterodox unbelievers may seem rather exotic, but the supposition that the sources of social disorder come "from the top down," so to speak, is of a piece with fundamental suppositions in Athenian social theory, as we saw from Demosthenes's democratic exhortations against corrupt oligarchs. Plato and Demosthenes share a view of the social world divided into mass and elite. Demosthenes supports the political power of the many, and Plato opposes it, but both recognize that most powerful political actors will come from the elite class—the main question of politics is therefore whose side these actors will take and what interests they have at heart.[68]

The danger that intellectual elites pose to the civic order is a recurring theme in Plato's dialogues. Callicles is a demagogue willing to do anything to please his political "base." Thrasymachus, in the *Republic,* gives a classic version of the relativist argument that power provides its own justification. The misbelievers in the *Laws* seem, by comparison, distinctly unthreatening. But in the *Laws,* Plato is determined to show how even intellectuals who seem to bear no ill will can undermine the stability of an entire city.

The importance of impious intellectuals and other elites has to do with their social influence.[69] Even a "just" atheist "would be full of bold language [*parrhesia*] about the gods both at sacrifices and oaths (*horkoi*) and, and as he laughs at the others, makes others of this sort, as long as he goes unpunished" (908c6–d1). It is these novel beliefs that are the greatest threat to the social order (and social practices like oaths). Atheists (speaking, for the moment, of the "just" or uncorrupted atheists) do not themselves necessarily lack self-control (*sōphrosunē*) and the other political virtues at the heart of the *Laws*; rather, their intellectual commitments are a threat to the underlying conditions necessary for those political virtues. Cured of their intellectual errors, atheists might be among the most upstanding and virtuous of Magnesia's citizens.[70]

Under normal conditions, the Athenian Stranger's law code (including the penal code) contains the means to prevent (and even reverse) the threat of shamelessness that both he and Protagoras seem to have feared. For these shame mechanisms to work, however, certain prerequisites are necessary. The citizens must not have their own ideas about the gods or their worship (hence, in addition to the discussion of atheists, the ban on private cults at 910b–d). And similarly, they cannot have divergent ideas about virtue or the rational nature of ethics (like Callicles or Thrasymachus).[71] Incarceration and penal instruction can correct these intellectual and theological challenges to social solidarity.[72] Plato's Athenian Stranger expects the prison to teach the atheists, especially the temperate "just" atheists, that their "expectations . . . concerning the higher good" are incorrect (cf. 864b, 886ab).[73] In Athenian politics, challenges to social solidarity were often phrased in terms of challenges to popular rule, but for Plato, the threat was more abstract and diffuse, coming from politicians, orators, poets, musicians, and, finally, from unbelievers.

CONCLUSION

The Athenian democracy survived for only thirty years after Demosthenes delivered his speech *Against Timocrates*. No Greek philosopher after Plato seems to have been as concerned with the practicalities of how to punish well. And, for whatever reason, atheism did not stoke the fears of many political thinkers after the arrival of Alexander the Great.[74] The carceral moment in Athenian thought was a brief one. But this flash-in-a-pan aspect of the Athenian experiment in incarceration belies its intellectual importance.

Athenian thinkers pursued at least two independent ways of answering the question of what the prison is good for. As we saw in Chapter 1, some made the case that the prison could be good for democracy (or bad for it). And in Chapter 2, we followed Plato's developing ideas about confinement and incarceration as a possible form of soul crafting, education, or improvement. Both approaches reappear in later theories of the prison.

But Plato and his contemporaries also thought about penal confinement (and punishment more generally) in ways that are deeply foreign to modern sensibilities. For one, punishment in Athens was explicitly political. The texts examined in the first two chapters justified a punishment if it preserved the balance of power between mass and elite or protected an important foundational social practice (like belief in the gods). Incarceration, a new and potentially controversial form of punishment, was to be directed at the greatest political threats, which both Plato and Demosthenes agreed come from a few wealthy and ambitious men. Incarceration was not a routine sentence to be handed down in the name of an impersonal law. The prison was an ambiguous signifier, somewhere between a high-status replacement for the stocks and a low-status reminder that only slaves wear chains.

All of this should remind the contemporary reader than the ancient Athenian idea of incarceration bears a strong resemblance to the society that produced it. This society was one of small city-states, where, to a large degree, citizens knew one another by sight or reputation. As a result, relationships were mediated by social knowledge and by the fear of shame or humiliation in front of one's fellow citizens and equals. In Athens, the business of governing the city and judging criminals was carried out through the voting of large and sometimes boisterous citizen juries, a method not so different (as Plato sourly observed) from the collective approbation or disgust displayed in the city's theater.[75] In short, ideas like imprisoning a person for the good of the state or experiencing punishment as a moment of collective education for the punished and for the public bear traces of a particular world, one very different from the routinized and bureaucratized judicial processes that characterize our own mass society and its tendency to punish by class or demographic category.

All of this poses an important problem for a study of ancient and modern prison theories: To what extent can there or should there be a conversation between the world of antiquity and the modern world? In this conclusion, we will briefly take up this challenge and consider the possible advantages and barriers to making such comparisons.

The jail that stood somewhere near the central market square in fourth- and fifth-century Athens was not a super-max prison; nor was it a Panopticon. It was, truth be told, hardly even a prison. The internal layout, as far as can be determined, did not depend on individuated cells, and there was no definite custodial or psychiatric regime. Breaking out was, as Crito tells Socrates in Plato's *Crito,* not at all difficult. So even if it is true that, as we argued in Chapter 1, prison sentences were in principle available to an Athenian jury, it is still fundamentally necessary to draw a hard line between what went on in that low-slung building in the Agora and the hegemonic form of the prison as it began to develop in the late eighteenth-century Atlantic world.[76]

On the archaeological and architectural front then, there can be no comparison between the small building in Athens and the sprawling complexes of today. Ideologically and intellectually, however, the Athenian distaste of physical punishments for citizens, the democratic commitment to equality before the law, and the civic-republican interest in the educative function of punishment all make connections between Athens and modern liberal republics all but irresistible. Demosthenes, as we saw, argued that if incarceration was to be justified at all, it had to be justified in terms of popular rule, and when the first penitentiaries were constructed in England, North America, and postrevolutionary France, they were often described in just those terms, as the form of punishment befitting a free people.[77] Maybe we must treat the prison the way we treat other Athenian institutions—as a point of comparison with (and not as a precise parallel to) modern democracies.

If we choose this way of comparing the prison as it functioned in Athens with contemporary penal institutions, we are left with the same time-honored analogical tools that political theorists have used since Machiavelli.[78] We can note the analogy between the political repercussions of imprisoning a particular "class" (whether the oligarchs of Chapter 1 or the atheists of Chapter 2) with the late phenomenon of "mass incarceration"; we can observe how Athenian squeamishness about citizen bodies compares to the shift in sensibilities and retreat from corporal punishment as the ancien régime gave way to the liberal state. We can even use Demosthenes's arguments about horizontal and vertical equality under democracy to question the way punishment developed in modernity (all topics we take up in the second half of this book). But unlike the practices of Athenian democracy, the prison in Athens played almost no role in constituting the later Hellenophilic political tradition (excepting, perhaps, its fame as the site of Socrates's death). Athenian incarceration cannot be shown to have any direct relationship to the prisons that we know today, any more than the Athenian practice of voting can shed light on upcoming elections. While in some sense homologous, both are fundamentally different practices from our own.

At first glance, the comparative project is on firmer ground with Plato. Plato's theory of incarceration combined psychological expertise with a nascent understanding of a centralized legal order. This combination, applied to the differentiated penal regimes of his prisons in the *Laws,* seems much closer to the modern prison's roots in eighteenth-century ambitions for social control based on scientific knowledge. In addition, Plato's discussion of the causes of crime uses a hedonistic psychic model of expectation and aversion to map the behavioral incentives that should govern punishments. This is a departure from his moralized model of the mind in the *Republic* and a great deal closer to the materialist psychologies that informed the penal regimes of the Enlightenment.[79]

When we dig deeper, however, we find that, as with the Athenian prison, the disanalogies between Plato's political knowledge of the criminal soul and modern forms of criminology are as significant as the similarities. Foremost among these is the difference between Plato's reliance on universals to deduce the model of the soul and the empiricist foundations of the modern social sciences. Plato's epistemology relies on the existence of metaphysical categories. Sometimes this means a theory of "forms," but at other times Plato merely endorses the idea that nature can be carved at the joints and that dialectical inquiry can determine just where these joints lie (and thus, where each natural category begins). Plato's moral psychology of crime does not necessarily depend on the theory of the forms, but it does rely on the idea that the human mind is fully transparent to a priori rational inquiry.

The science of the soul that the Athenian Stranger proposes in the *Laws* is thus very different from the inductive, materialist approach to human behavior that characterizes modern psychology and criminology. Plato's jailers have no need to collect data to understand their prisoners. If the defining feature of modern "power/knowledge" is its drive to know every individual to the fullest extent possible, then Plato's idea of what it is necessary for the state apparatuses to know in order to "reform" the criminal is distant indeed. The mechanics of "teaching" or "reforming" for Plato adhere to a general rubric to which each case can be compared. This excludes both the disciplinary drive to analyze every inmate and the governmental drive to gather statistical information about populations. The foundation of knowledge for Plato is and remains pure reason, the purview of his Nocturnal Council.

If the relationship between Athenian ideas of incarceration and modern forms of punishment is not one of structural or functional parallels, we are left with two contrasting possibilities of how to understand the conversation about the prison in Athens. The first is that the ancient and modern phenomena are entirely independent of one another and that any similarities are strictly coincidental. According to this possibility, the idea of reformatory incarceration came into being twice, in different places and different times, and these two moments bare no more relation to each other than an instance of reformatory incarceration in any other civilization from any distant epoch might have to our own. The second option is that the link between the two institutions is not typological or functional but, rather, genealogical. It is true that reformatory incarceration in the city of Athens and in the minds of Athenian intellectuals looked very different from the modern penitentiary. But it is also true that modern penitentiaries were built according to a set of ideas about punishment and reform that, like all ideas, have a particular history. It is not implausible to hope to trace this history further than has been done before, perhaps all the way back to ancient Athens.

To tell the entire story of how the Athenian prison left its hereditary imprint on the modern institution both is and is not the task of the remainder of this book. It is, because the following chapters will try to tell precisely such a story. It is not, because to do so completely would require combing through two thousand years of penal history at a level of detail that would try both the expertise of the author and the patience of the reader. Rather than tracing every step of the journey between Plato and the Panopticon, we begin the next chapter with a likely story (*eikōs logos,* to use Plato's phrase) of how some Athenian ideas about reformatory incarceration were transmitted through the ancient world, before picking up the argument in detail with that great disciple of Plato, Thomas More.

3

INCARCERATION IN THOMAS MORE'S *UTOPIA*

AS HE SAT imprisoned in the Tower of London, awaiting his trial and eventually his execution, Thomas More's thoughts turned to confinement. More had considered joining the Carthusian order as a young man, and he confessed to his daughter that "if it had not been for my wife and you that be my children . . . I would not have failed long ere this to have closed myself in as strait a room, and straiter too."[1] More wrote two long theological treatises and a great deal of correspondence during his fifteen months of incarceration, and he seems to have noticed a parallel between his early hopes for spiritual succor in a monk's cell and this final period of reflection. In a bit of historical irony that might have pleased the subtle More, this meditative time in the Tower occurred some twenty years after he had made his own lasting contribution to the political philosophy of incarceration. In his *Utopia*, More drew upon both the Platonic tradition familiar to us from the previous chapter and the monastic tradition that he held in almost equal regard, to fashion a theory of confinement, labor, and soul craft that would prove to be a blueprint for the idea of the prison in the modern world.

Before we turn to More's theory of punishment and its context within the Renaissance recovery of Platonic thought, we must acknowledge the yawning historical gap between Plato's time and that of More, his devoted reader. We cannot do justice to what was nearly two thousand years of experiments in confinement and the (largely unrecorded) thinking about it, but we can say something about how the idea of the prison may have developed between Plato and More.

With the decline of democratic Athens, penal incarceration begins to slip through the cracks of the literary record (though there is scattered evidence of the continuing role of *desmotēria* in the various Hellenistic Greek poleis).[2] And with the rise of Roman rule in the Mediterranean world, penal slavery gradually began to take the place of many other non-capital punishments, at least for low-status criminals. High-status criminals, in turn, were banished through various forms of exile.[3] The vast penal machinery (and ever-growing demand for labor) of the expanding empire meant that at the height of the Roman Empire, it is likely that more people found themselves "behind bars" than ever before—whether in debtors' prisons, awaiting corporal or capital punishment, or toiling away in the mines and quarries of the imperial periphery.[4] But, paradoxically, the political idea of the prison grew ever less distinct over this period.

Whether the copious *carceres* (jails) across the Roman world were used for penal incarceration in the strict sense that this book is investigating, as a distinct and recognized form of punishment, is a matter of contention.[5] Aside from their important role in the self-understanding of Christian martyrology (many persecuted Christians lived, died, and reaffirmed their faith in Roman dungeons), prisons did not become the sort of discursive site that they had been in Athens and that they would become again in the early modern world.[6] Whatever the situation in the actual cities and towns of the empire may have been, the legal reformers and codifiers of the third and fourth centuries of the Common Era were inclined to minimize punitive incarceration as an acceptable Roman practice.[7]

The prevailing answer to the problem of the prison/jail distinction seems to have been to deny the legitimacy of the idea of the prison, in the strict sense. From an official perspective, at least from the time of Hadrian onward, custody was the central *legitimate* use of incarceration. This meant that Roman law, particularly imperial law, did not face the ideological paradoxes with which democratic Athens grappled. High-status prisoners could, in theory, be exiled, while low-status prisoners could be profitably put to work as penal slaves.[8] The conceptual illegitimacy of penal incarceration (as opposed to slavery) would have been small solace to the many people who undoubtedly found themselves locked up for periods (*temporaria vincula*) during the many centuries of Roman hegemony, but it does explain why Rome does not figure in the development of the idea of the prison as we have reconstructed it in this book.

The struggle over the civic significance of incarceration is not the only aspect of the Athenian debate to have fallen into abeyance during the Hellenistic and Roman periods. Plato's *Laws* continued to be read throughout the ancient world, but the prisons for unbelievers described in book 10 do not seem to have made much of a philosophical impact. There is, in fact, only one other literal use of Plato's word for a reformatory prison in the available corpus of ancient Greek texts,[9] in the Jewish philosopher Philo of Alexandria's first-century CE exegetical work *On Joseph (de Iosepho)*. This brief return of the idea of the "reformatory" provides an important clue as to the fate of Plato's theory of penal reform and hints at the mode and means by which Plato's discussion of incarceration was transmitted and transformed by Judaism and Christianity.

In *On Joseph*, Philo imports much of the structure of Plato's theory of incarceration, including the "medical" terminology for the soul of the criminal, as well as the use of education as both a metaphor for punishment and, even more strikingly, as the central technique of punishment. He does not, however, adopt the entire moral psychology that Plato used to justify incarceration and explain how it accomplished the aim of reform. Rather, Philo seems to rely on the simpler mechanism of acculturation. Interacting (*suneinai*) with good people can make a person good, and if corrupt jailers are replaced with upstanding and virtuous ones, the close quarters of prisons will force criminals to become like (*homiles-thai*) these role models (cf. *Ios.* 83).[10]

Elsewhere, Philo gives his readers a glimpse of what an institution of virtuous people influencing one another along the lines of Joseph's prison might look like in the real world. In the text, titled "On the Contemplative Life," Philo describes an isolated religious community living in the countryside near Alexandria.[11] The community's spiritual practice (askēsis, an old Cynic philosophical term here beginning the transformation into its modern cognate "ascetic") combines intense study of sacred texts with the simplest and most meager allowances for bodily needs. A clue to the ultimate significance of this text for the history of institutional soul craft and the practice and meaning of confinement can be found in the name Philo gives to the inner cell of each celebrant's house, the "holy place or monastery" (monastērion), the first appearance of this word in the written record.

This picture of Philo's spiritual ideal in action confirms the changes in the technique of soul craft that appeared in *On Joseph.* On the one hand, their isolated and communal lifestyle allows these "healers" to live their blessed life. On the other hand, their self-denial, the physical restraint of the appetites that Plato considered and rejected as soul craft in the *Gorgias,* heals their souls. Philo's new theory of ascetic community as a technique that lays souls open to instruction and healing began to find considerable favor among the growing adherents of ascetic Christianity.[12] There is some evidence that Philo's texts may have played a role in this process,[13] but even if it was not Philo himself who affected the shift from penal incarceration to monastic contemplation as the technique of Platonic soul craft, his adaptation of the Platonic theory of confinement is evidence of a process that may have been repeated dozens of times over the course of late antiquity. Elements of this process have been discussed by other scholars, including Julia Hillner's study of late Roman and early medieval practices of monastic incarceration.[14] In these cases, it is the Philonic techniques of shared ascetic practice and textual study that produce moderation (sōphrosunē) and reverence (aidōs), not Platonic dialectic or moral psychology.[15]

With the advent of monasticism, we have really arrived at an entirely new institution, one with its own history and internal logic, and thus a subject beyond the purview of our study. Nevertheless, this characteristic form of medieval confinement can be seen as a period of quiet metamorphosis for the theoretical problems and conceptual solutions we have found in the ancient discussion of penal incarceration. The late-antique and medieval monastery was often a site of voluntary self-confinement (though not always, especially in the Byzantine world), but its shared aims and historical link to Platonic theories of soul craft grant it both an analogical relationship to the prison and, perhaps, a genealogical one.[16]

It is in this genealogical spirit that we can connect the evolution of the idea of the Platonic prison back to Thomas More. More was part of a circle of Renaissance readers who aspired to view Plato more as a colleague than a predecessor. More himself read Plato's texts closely and in the original Greek. But More was also a devout Catholic, drawn to monastic asceticism and deeply familiar with the austere conditions of Carthusian monasteries and their distinct architectural reliance on individual cells, common property, and use of ecclesiastical prisons. This chapter argues that, thanks to his theoretical integration of both Plato and Platonizing Christian thought, More deserves considerable credit for reintroducing the Platonic theory of reformative confinement into the early modern world.

In *Utopia*, More draws on both Plato's theories and Platonizing monastic ideas about confinement to devise the central technique of punishment used by his ideal state: penal servitude. One of the major consequences of More's combination of Platonic theory with post-Platonic practice is the advent of a theory of psychic improvement that allows for the integration of punitive confinement and productive labor, a confluence with fateful consequences for the history and theory of incarceration. This chapter recovers how Platonic ideas about punishing were able to survive, and indeed to flourish, in early modern Europe by examining what More took from earlier Platonic thinking about incarceration and by identifying what is absolutely new in More's picture of imprisonment—most importantly, the soul-improving properties of labor.

READING MORE THROUGH PLATO

Thomas More's little "golden notebook" published in late 1516 introduced the word "utopia" to the world and provided the template for the many dozens of literary ideal societies that were to follow over the next five hundred years.[17] This is not to say that *Utopia* had no forerunners—indeed, the text of *Utopia* is insistently aware of earlier attempts to imagine ideal forms of government (most significantly in the work of

Plato and Aristotle), and earlier accounts of travel to foreign lands, imagined and semi-imagined, from the ancient world and More's own time (the text makes use of Lucian's *True History* and references reports of Vespucci's voyages). It is precisely this mixture of novelty and continuity that makes *Utopia* so fruitful for tracing out a pivotal moment in the history of punishment and incarceration.

In More's case, an awareness of the contemporary situation does not obviate the significance of ancient thought for his writing; rather, it enhances it. More was an important pioneer in the revival of Greek learning in northern Europe.[18] Along with his friend and colleague Desiderius Erasmus, More not only engaged in polemic around the importance of Greek thought; he was actively engaged in making Greek literature accessible to the Latinate world.[19] If, as some have argued, the Latinity of early decades of the Renaissance carried with it a series of political and philosophical propositions about freedom and republican mixed government, it should not surprise us that More's outspoken enthusiasm for Greek wisdom also had a distinct philosophical valence.[20]

This contextual background matches up with several passages in *Utopia* that develop the theme of Greek over Latin and the supremacy of Plato in particular. In his prefatory letter, More writes of the dialogue's main interlocutor, Raphael Hythloday, that he "is a man not so well versed in Latin as in Greek" (31).[21] Hythloday himself is described having made journeys like those of Plato, and even his name and demeanor have Platonic resonances (43–45).[22] Plato is described by the character More (henceforth "Morus") as Hythloday's "friend," toward whom the customs of Utopia made Hythloday more "sympathetic" (81, 101). The Utopians themselves are ravenous consumers of Greek philosophy, history, and grammar (including "most" of Plato), and More's earliest readers (his humanist friends) found frequent occasion to reference the relationship between More's text and Plato (whether they thought More had "outdone" and "gone far beyond" Plato or merely confirmed his theories).[23]

Both More's surroundings and the comments made in *Utopia*'s text and paratexts suggest that as More was drafting the book, the treatment of Plato was foremost in his own mind, as he knew it would be in the minds of his intended readers. There is another, material reason to highlight More's engagement with Plato's text—the new availability of the *corpus Platonicum* in the *editio maior* of Aldus (Venice, 1513). Aside from what may be an indirect reference to the edition in *Utopia*,[24] there is some reason to believe that More's use of Plato itself carries traces of the Greek text.[25] More was thus among the first modern political theorists to directly interact with Plato in the latter's own language.[26]

If an insistence on thematic continuity between Plato and More still looks unlikely, one rough contemporary parallel case may help clarify the practical context for More's adoption of Plato. Across the channel in the Netherlands, the burgher reformers and "leaders of opinion" who were responsible for the earliest efforts at penal incarceration on the Continent were themselves also deeply steeped in the classics. In Amsterdam and Leiden, as in London, humanism and politics went hand in hand. A passage from Seneca was inscribed over the lintel of one early Dutch "house of correction," and the language of reform, of "the right treatment" for wrongdoing (language that can, perhaps, be traced to Plato's *Gorgias*), was common currency.[27] Across the northern Renaissance, the texts of the classical curriculum were seen as tools to be applied directly to the problems of urbanization and the end of the feudal order.

Perhaps, as in our analysis of Philo, the combination of contemporary politics and ancient influences that we examine in More should be understood less as a "definitive" moment of transmission and more as a particularly accessible example of what may have been happening all over the lands of the northern Renaissance. More's *Utopia* emerged during and was inspired by this moment in the development of European letters, and it expressly addressed itself to a select readership of the moment's avant-garde, both in England and abroad. More was deeply conscious of the unique nature of his contemporaries' openness and orientation to the past, and he made this a central target of his text. To this end, More stitched into the fabric of the book at least two clues hinting at the link between the discovery of "Utopia" and the classical past.

As R. J. Schoeck demonstrated, the date given for the founding of Utopia, 1,760 years before the dramatic date of the dialogue, is a reference to reign of the Spartan king Agis IV in 244 BCE, an ambitious reformer who failed to carry out a planned redistribution of property among the Lacedemonians. As with all such details in *Utopia*, the meaning of this reference is equivocal, but it clearly situates More's literary work alongside the historical possibilities of reform in the ancient world (121).[28] The only other date mentioned in the island's history is the wreckage of a ship of Romans and Egyptians on the coast of Utopia "some twelve hundred years ago," meaning around the year 316 CE (107). More was surely thinking of the period around the Battle of the Milvian Bridge in 312, which, along with associated events, eventually led Constantine to adopt Christianity as the imperial religion. This means that the shipwreck and the form of Utopian wisdom that More is using it to illustrate reflect what was essentially the last moment of autonomous pagan culture in the Roman world. More wanted to stress the unmediated relationship between the Utopians and the non-Christian past, a relationship that hints at More's own unmediated attitude toward his sources. This evidence, both the Renaissance willingness to take the past as a guide to the present and More's chronological riddles, suggests that assuming a sort of continuity between Plato's thought and More's work is not only plausible—it is essential for understanding More's intentions.[29]

Before examining the traces of the Platonic tradition in punishing as they are visible in More, a few words are necessary about how to approach the literary and philosophical character of what is surely one of the slipperiest texts in the political-theoretical canon. As the radically divergent approaches to *Utopia* over the last hundred years attest, More's insistent irony and careful use of the dialogic form can lead to opposing (and equally plausible) interpretations of almost every aspect of his little book.[30] In making a limited case for *Utopia*'s role in the development of institutions of correction in the history of political thought, this chapter will largely sidestep the most difficult of these questions. The passages that most interest us all come from the mouth of Raphael Hythloday, who, even if he is not More's mouthpiece, is certainly a creation with clear and consistent Platonic tendencies. As in the Platonic and Ciceronian dialogues that served as More's model, the major characters, even when they disagree, can present plausible arguments and defend positions that the author finds important, even without his endorsement.[31] The remainder of this chapter is devoted to the analysis of one such "plausible position," one that perfectly illustrates the dual nature of More's adaptation of classical texts for his own novel purposes. The classical text in question is first and foremost Plato's *Laws,* and his purpose, as we will see, is the design of an institution to correct wayward behavior in the idealized state of the Utopians.

Much has been written about the reception of Plato in More's *Utopia*.[32] The most obvious comparison and the one that has flowed most easily from scholarly pens is between the communal federation of cities on More's island and the communistic polity of Plato's *Republic*.[33] It is true that several aspects of *Utopia* refer to Plato's masterwork. Aside from the propertyless society of the Utopians (which, unlike that of the *Republic*, does not involve the dissolution of the nuclear family), there is the adoption of metaphors such as "drones" for dysfunctional citizens and "disease" for political corruption in the city.[34] But despite the efforts of readers to see in Utopia a "new *Republic*," there are hints that, whatever the influence of that work, More intended his Utopia to function rather differently from Plato's masterpiece.[35]

Utopia's direct quotations of the *Republic* both come during the so-called dialogue of counsel, where Morus and Hythloday debate the merits of intellectuals giving advice to princes. Morus has recourse to Plato's idea that "until philosophers rule as kings or those who are now called kings and leading men genuinely and adequately philosophize . . . cities will have no rest from evils."[36] The placing of this sentiment in the mouth of the non-Platonic character of Morus suggests a certain distancing of the *Republic* from the Platonizing Hythloday. Indeed, Hythloday, in another direct quote, takes up an image from the *Republic* of a philosopher waiting out the storm of public life under the shelter of a wall. Hythloday does not note that this is a statement of Plato's concerning a non-ideal society different from that of the *Republic*—and he pushes the rule of philosophers decisively to the sidelines (101).[37]

For Hythloday, the key to a happy state is not the rule of the wise; it is the rule of wise institutions (*prudentissima instituta*) (100). Even the communism that seems so clearly to be a legacy of the *Republic* is, on closer inspection, rather un-*Republic*an. Instead of the limited lifestyle of shared property, meals, and erotic relationships meant to shape the guardian class in the *Republic*, Hythloday's account of the Utopians relates to a Plato who saw "that the one and only path to the public welfare lies through equal allocation of goods" (103). This wide-ranging communism is almost certainly a reference to the *Laws*, where Plato writes that "you find the ideal society and state . . . where the old saying 'friends' property is genuinely shared' is put into practice as widely as possible throughout the entire state."[38] More had possibly been put in mind of the passage from the *Laws* by its use in the recently published (1515) edition of Erasmus's *Adages,* where the first two proverbs are devoted to friendship as holding in common and friendship as radical equality, respectively.[39]

The direct citations of Plato come in book 1 of *Utopia,* which was probably written after most, if not all, of the second book was already completed.[40] If book 1 was written after book 2, with the intention of sharpening and reemphasizing certain aspects of the Utopian society and their relevance for contemporary political life, this means that More decided to frame Hythloday's travel narrative not only in a particularly Platonic way but also in a way that was distinctly different from the "paradigmatic" design of the *Republic.*[41] As More understood, the question, taken up in book 1, of whether to join public life as an adviser makes the stakes of the description of Utopia in book 2 rather different than they might otherwise be. The character Morus thinks of himself as a political realist, warning Hythloday against "out-of-the-way speeches" and "academic philosophy" (95).[42] By way of response, Hythloday stresses the difference between the "image" of the *Republic* and the "actual practice" of Utopia (104–5).[43] Hythloday is not, as many suppose, an idealist to More's realist. He is a political thinker dedicated to exploring the limits of what is actually possible, given the realities of human life.[44] For this reason, it should not surprise us that Plato's use of legal and penal institutions to shape and reshape moral psychology in the *Laws* proved to be a useful model for More's "actual" island.

Before examining the text of *Utopia* more closely, it might be useful to briefly recapitulate what might have been meant by a "wise institution" in More's time and in More's text. In contemporary social science, there are any number of ways to define or understand an institution.[45] Similarly, the Latin words *instituta* and *institutio* and their derivatives have a varied set of meanings, with roots in both classical and patristic usage.[46] Together, they appear more than forty times in *Utopia.* In the last pages of the work alone, *institutum* means variously "plans of living" (*instituta vitae*), "healthy institutions" (*salubribus institutis*), and "custom or practice" (*aliisque . . . eorum institutis*) (246–48).[47]

One very telling use comes in the work's peroration. Here the narrator Morus notes of the Utopians that the "chief foundation of their entire *institutio*" is communal living. And this "one thing alone" subverts everything that is true of normal states (246).[48] Morus is echoing an analogous passage a few pages earlier from what may have been the peroration of the initial version or "*Ur*-Utopia" (before the composition of book 1). There, reviewing the "form" of the Utopian commonwealth, it is Hythloday who focuses on the distinction between an economy of private wealth, which of necessity requires calculation (*rationem censere*) according to private interest and a system where there is no private property and therefore no private interest. The citizens themselves are not to be blamed for how they act (*certe utrobique merito*), for they are behaving in accordance with the dictates of whichever structure (*forma*) they live in (240).

This passage, which would have had an even more prominent position in the initial version, provides a key statement of More's attitude toward human behavior and how to change it. More assumes that citizens in every state act according to a calculation of their own interests. It is the institutional structure of their environment, however, that determines what the variables in this calculation are (for instance, the "cost" in pleasure or pain of a given action) and therefore what their behavior will actually be. Characteristically, More's position is both entirely novel and grounded in the classical tradition. In some sense, More has adapted the Ciceronian project of combining useful (*utile*) conduct with good (*bonum*) behavior. Rather than considering this as a moral duty (*officio*), however, More points to institutions as the alembic for transforming personal interests into prosocial behavior.

In the language of contemporary theory of institutions, More's understanding of the "structure" of the Utopian republic seems to echo the "rational choice" model of institutions as formal structures that affect the calculations of agents around their interests.[49] This should remind us of Plato's extensive use of educational institutions in the *Laws*. Scholars who have noticed this institutional affinity between the *Laws* and *Utopia* have addressed a number of the structures that More borrows from Plato, including strictures around sexual relations, the system of government on the island, the limitation of travel and financial dealings with foreigners, and especially the crucial role that education and schooling play in socialization.[50] As "culturalist" theorists of institutions would recognize, these symbols, practices, and moral frameworks also do the work of behavioral control on a level not easily assimilated to the process of strategic calculation.[51]

It is in the use of such diverse institutional and cultural tools to shape the decision matrix of the citizen that More seems closest to the institutionalism of Plato's *Laws*. The intimate link between shame, reform, and religious belief that undergirds the practice of punishment in the text of *Utopia* is both an example of the more general use of institutions to shape imperfect behavior, as can be seen elsewhere in the text, and a more particular case of the specific relationship we detected in the *Laws* between penal institutions, moral psychology, and the achievement of a well-planned social order.

CORRECTION AND PUNISHMENT IN *UTOPIA*

It is reasonable to assert that More is working in an intentionally Platonic and institutionalist mode in *Utopia*. But do the institutions imagined by More rise to the standard of explanation to which Plato held himself in the *Laws*? Plato, it will be recalled, made sure that the institutional forms concerned with the influence or modification of human behavior could be justified down to the precise technique and application of knowledge. Plato's penal system did not exist in isolation from the society in which it was designed to function, and elements of the system of confinement and technique of behavioral modification recurred throughout the social world. As we will see, each of these elements applies to More's project in *Utopia*.

The first characteristic of Plato's theory of punishment and incarceration was its relation to moral psychology.[52] More does not directly cite Plato's discussions of the soul, choice, and action (though he does indirectly reference a passage of the *Laws* from a few lines before the "puppet metaphor") (125n), but he understood the importance of a plausible account of moral psychology in discussions of political forms. One of the longest sustained passages in the text is the discussion of the hedonistic moral philosophy that predominates among the Utopians.[53] The main philosophical system on the island is a qualified Epicureanism. Qualified because, although its followers believe that pleasure is "all or the most important part of human happiness," they insist on finding support for this conclusion in their religion, "which is serious and strict, indeed almost stern and forbidding" (159, 161). Without religion, the Utopians declare that "no one would be so stupid as not to feel that he should seek pleasure, regardless of right and wrong" (161). This Epicureanism without atheism suggests that More is up to something more complex than merely recapitulating an eclectic mix of Hellenistic moral philosophy.

This passage provides, in a roundabout way, an account of moral psychology as it affects the ability of citizens to make decisions.[54] The Utopians "think that reason [ratio] by itself is weak and defective in its efforts to investigate true happiness."[55] Religious principles must act as an "aid" to reason, in some way tempering the rational discovery that the major factor in human judgment is the calculation of greater and lesser pain. More's account has predictably been called proto-utilitarian, but parts of it, and not only the theistic part, are decidedly at odds with later pleasure-guided moral theories. According to Hythloday, the Utopians distinguish not only between the "higher" and "lower" pleasures, as J. S. Mill would later do, but also between "genuine" and "false" pleasures (167, 173). This stress on a standard of truth against which pleasures can be judged places the moral psychology of the Utopians somewhere between the Epicurean revival of the late Renaissance and the much more ambivalent treatment of pleasure in Plato and Aristotle.

Plato, though by no means a hedonist, admits that pleasure is "especially human" and refers more than once to the image of pleasure and pain as a marionette's strings to describe the situation of "all mortal beings" bound up by pleasure and pain.[56] Aristotle, with remarkably similar language (pleasure is "closely connected to our species"), also finds reason to admit pleasure into his analysis of moral psychology.[57] Both are careful to distinguish between "true" and "false" pleasures (for Aristotle, the "natural" and "unnatural"), and for both, understanding pleasure is a necessary "prelude" to correctly designing the constitutional arrangement of the state.[58] More's Hythloday, while withholding judgment on the truth of the Utopian theories, insists that "whatever their principles are, there is not a more excellent people or a happier commonwealth anywhere in the world" (179). Regardless of the truth of these propositions about pleasure, they are exceptionally useful for political philosophy. This is another example of how More combines Platonic philosophical materials with a Ciceronian appeal to the "utility" of specific practices.

The approbation of "true" pleasure also lies behind *Utopia*'s boldest statement on moral psychology, the peroration on pride mentioned above. Utopian institutions, which provide "enough of what we really need," would long ago have been adopted everywhere "were it not for one single monster, the prime plague and begetter of all others—I mean Pride" (245–47). Pride is associated not only with wealth but with the "empty pleasures (*inanies voluptates*)" of the nobility and those who exist to serve them (243). Pride is the epitome of all that is antisocial, corrosive, and dangerous for a state. If pleasure and pain are the currency in which the institutions of Utopia trade, pride is the central threat to their correct valuation. It perverts a central element of practical reasoning— "every man's perception of where his true interest lies" (245). The moral psychology of social control in Utopia can thus be defined as the constraint of pride through the judicious appeal to pleasure.

The pursuit of true pleasure (and the maintenance of self-interest, correctly construed) is, Hylothoday says, produced by general good breeding (*educatio,* in the sense of the Greek *paideia*), as well as "instruction and good books" (155). As in Plato, the presence of education is a continuous and universal feature of the society. Not just those who will become scholars, but every child is introduced to "good literature (*literis imbuuntur*)" (155), and exposure to learning is by no means limited to the young or to the classroom. Intellectual pursuits are said to be the most common pastime during hours of leisure, and morning lectures given by the scholarly class are both frequent and widely attended (127). The educational system is omnipresent in Utopia, so much so that Utopia itself could be said to be an educational institution (in its common meals and morning lectures, it somewhat resembles More's own almae matres— Oxford and Lincoln's Inn). The whole island is constantly indoctrinating itself, and no citizen is ever very far from some form of instruction.[59]

The arguments about pleasure and pain that Utopians read in their books and hear in their lectures are not enough to guide rational behavior. Religion is the indispensable handmaiden of philosophy. But despite his later reputation for persecuting heretics with little remorse, More's presentation of the Utopian religion is notable for its tolerance.

What is dangerous in religion, according to the doctrine of Utopus, the mythical lawgiver of the country, is less any particular doctrine than a propensity for troubling the social order through zealotry and extremism (223). Two dogmas are excluded from this ecumenical broadmindedness—presumably the very doctrines necessary to buttress moral philosophy—the belief that "the soul perishes with the body" and that "the universe is ruled by blind chance, not divine providence" (225).

The connection between an immortal soul and the regulation of true pleasure operates in two ways. The first is the confidence in posthumous reward and punishment (an inheritance of philosophical religion that would survive through Kant). The second is the Utopian belief in ancestral specters, whose presence "keeps them from any secret dishonorable deed" (227). Both of these beliefs involve the existence of external checks on human action. Even if a citizen has somehow failed to be sufficiently socialized through education, the idea of ever-present surveillance—a watchful god and vigilant ghosts—will constrain her actions.[60]

This understanding of civil religion, and in particular the harsh treatment of psychic materialism and atheism, owes much to Plato's preoccupations in the *Laws*,[61] particularly to the Athenian Stranger's claim that "no one who believes that the Gods exist according to the laws ever comes to do an impious deed nor says an unlawful word."[62] Given that from time to time heterodox views reemerge, however, More also prepares for the possibility that the institutions of indoctrination—education and religion—might break down. Even Utopia needs a correctional system.

As in the *Laws*, punishment in *Utopia* forms a sort of continuum with education in governing behavior. Out-and-out punishments are few but harsh, because the "excellent upbringing (*educatio*)" and exceptional "moral training" given to citizens make any crime almost already a case of recidivism (185, cf. 195).[63] Only a handful of crimes receive an official punishment, usually enslavement (for adultery, assault, "heinous crimes," religious intolerance, and repeated unauthorized travel [191, 193, 223, 145]) and, more rarely, death (for recidivism among adulterers and other criminals or for treasonous conspiracy [193, 123]) or exile (again, for religious intolerance [223]).

Much more pervasive than any of these sentences is the exercise of an artificial "shame culture."[64] Throughout the text of *Utopia*, reputation and recognition act as the first line of correction for behavior. Privatizing tendencies and withdrawal from the community are "not thought proper" (141); it is "contemptible" to insult fools and "ugly" to mock the disfigured (193). Even those crimes with set punishments also rely upon public disgrace. Premarital intercourse brings "public disgrace" on the entire family (189), the atheist is "entrusted with no offices . . . and universally regarded as low and torpid" (225), and travel without permission earns "contempt" (145).[65] The overall impression is of a society that does not have many fixed penalties because it does not need them (cf. 193) and would just as soon use honor to encourage virtue as shame to punish its absence (195).

Consonant with their hedonistic moral psychology, the theoretical background behind the Utopians' punishments is based on a sort of cost-benefit analysis considering both deterrent power and productivity. "Generally, the gravest crimes are punished with slavery, for they think this deters offenders" as much as capital punishment would, "and convict labor is more beneficial to the commonwealth" (193). There is also the hint of a rehabilitative element to Utopian punishing. "When subdued by long hardships, if they show by their behavior that they regret the crime more than the punishment, their slavery is lightened or remitted altogether" (193).

More evidence of a reformative aspect to More's theory of punishment can be found in the treatment of heterodox beliefs. Anyone who denies the idea of reward and punishment in the next life, either because of outright atheism or some other sort of materialism, is, as mentioned above, shamed but not punished (*nullo adficiunt supplicio*) (224). In a passage that borrows very freely from the *Laws* (907d–909d),[66] Hythloday says that rather than being forced to dissemble, unbelievers are encouraged to express their views "in the presence of priests and other important persons. . . . For [the Utopians] are confident that in the end his madness (*vesania*) will yield to reason (*ratio*)" (224). Here, More imports both the Platonic metaphor, crime as sickness, and the Platonic cure—dialectic with experts.

If all we had of *Utopia* was book 2, we would still be able to conclude that education and punishment are closely related in More. But the theoretical framework behind this relationship, which seems to contain a mixture of Ciceronian/utilitarian and Platonic/reformist future-directed tendencies, has not yet achieved the clarity of the original

Platonic arguments, which grounded penal institutions in first philosophy. What does More really want from punishment, and does he have a convincing method by which to achieve his ends? Is More guilty of philosophical "institution begging"? Importantly for the answers to these questions, *Utopia* contains not one account of punishment but two. In addition to the parsimonious penal code of the "best commonwealth," More revisited the question of punishment in the work, though his second discussion appears first, in the set piece of the dialogue of counsel at Cardinal Morton's house in book 1.[67]

The conversation in front of Cardinal Morton is used by Hythloday to illustrate a point about the role of the philosopher in politics. This was a contentious question for Renaissance intellectuals, particularly for those who identified with the Platonic tradition.[68] Instead of an abstract treatment of the problem, More chose to grapple with the challenge of "counsel" through an examination of a few issues in which the views of philosophers differ from the instincts of most rulers and their advisory class. One of these issues is punishment.[69]

In a pattern that would be repeated again and again over the next two hundred years, early sixteenth-century English authorities attempted to respond to rising petty crime by taking a freer hand in capital punishment.[70] Hythloday, as he reports it to Morus, took issue with this approach. He told Morton and his guests that capital punishment "goes beyond the call of justice (*supra justum*), and does not in any case contribute to the public good (*usu publico*)" (56).[71] The question of what "just" punishment means is answered by Hythloday's choice of metaphor. "In this matter . . . [England and much of the world] seem to imitate bad schoolmasters, who would rather whip their pupils than teach them" (57). More thus affirms that punishment is analogous to education and should operate according to a similar logic. This is the very same comparison that first emerged in full in Plato's *Protagoras*. Thus, More suggests, Platonic arguments can govern punishment not only in Utopia but out of it too, in the decidedly non-ideal conditions of Tudor England.

In the later discourse on Utopia, Hythloday gives a picture of the psychic causes of crime, including pride and false pleasure, but here his focus is on the social causes of crime—largely poverty, encouraged by an indolent nobility and insufficient attention to legal equity.[72] Under such conditions, Hythloday argues, harsh punishment fails the classic Cicero-nian test for moral action—it is neither just nor expedient. When people are badly socialized (*educari*), the community itself is in effect "first making them thieves and then punishing them for it" (67). Even in an imperfect society, Hythloday insists, punishment is merely an outgrowth of education. It can safely be said that the same combination between "utilitarian" considerations (such as what punishment will most deter others and how to prevent major crimes from being more attractive than minor ones), and reformative/educative concerns identified in book 2 exist in book 1 as well. In this extended discussion, however, More gives his character the opportunity to provide a rationale for the *technique* of punishment itself—penal servitude.

Servitude as it existed in the late Renaissance world would not have been a very educational punishment. This is why Hythloday introduces his acquaintances to the Polylerites, a nation that practices slavery in a very different way from what was familiar to Europeans (it is worth noting that it is at this very point, in presenting an argument for penal slavery, that More first introduces the reader to the exotic world of Utopia and its neighbors). Their course of punishment consists of resti-tution to the victim, followed by hard labor on projects in the public good. Prisoners live in cells (*cubiculi*) at night, and their upkeep is paid for by taxes or charity. Private individuals can hire their service at a spe-cial rate. More calls this hard labor and explicitly denies that it is a workhouse (*ergastulum*) because the work is done in public. Despite this denial, Hythloday reports on measures like uniforms, distinctive hair-cuts, and special badges (all of which will find a place in later literatures of incarceration) (73). In this regime, "the aim of the punishment is to destroy vices and save men" (75).[73] The rehabilitative nature of this system is vouchsafed by its low recidivism and the constant promise of pardon.[74]

His discussion of the Polylerites allows More to be both more ex-plicit about the continuity between education and punishment and to use punishment as a point of entry into the broader imaginative project of the world as it might be in book 2. The Polylerites do not inhabit an undiscovered country; they are vassals of Persia (though they live in splendid isolation, much as Plato imagined the city of the *Laws* could exist on Crete). Unlike Utopia, where perfect education makes punishment almost otiose, the Polylerite penal system is closer to what could exist in England or Europe. It is a form of education after the fact, a second-best solution. The lawyer who is arguing with Hythloday in front of the Cardinal scoffs that "such a system could never be established in England without putting the commonwealth in serious peril" (75). The lawyer's scoffing self-confidence is an invitation to the reader to ask what sort of system of government would be more fully compatible with "just punishment." The answer to that question is Hythloday's discourse on Utopia.

To return to the technique of punishment itself, penal servitude does what no other form of punishment can—it corrects behavior both justly and usefully. The usefulness of servitude is obvious—the labor power of the criminal is placed at the disposal of the state. What is "just" about this punishment seems to be its refusal to discard citizens based on their misdeeds (and based on their insufficient education). It makes "men necessarily become good" (75) first, by giving them the opportunity to unlearn their bad habits—to "regret the crime more than the punishment," that is, to demonstrate that their prudential calculation based on pleasure has changed. More envisions this institution as a civilized alternative to corporal and capital punishment as it existed in his own time. Some impoverished members of less fortunate societies, Hythloday reports, even prefer slavery in Utopia to freedom elsewhere (the principle of lesser eligibility is culturally relative) (187).

Until this point, we have been at pains to emphasize the continuities between Plato's theory of punishment and More's "educational" account of penal servitude. Also important, however, are the significant differences. Plato developed a complex and extensive explanation for how corporal punishments could reorder the psychopathologies of some criminals while imprisonment worked for others. More is not as clear about the reason that penal servitude works as a form of correction.[75] He also seems almost indifferent to the scope of rehabilitation. It may take "the rest of their lives" for criminals to improve (75), or they may earn their release, and More seems to have little preference between the two options. Does this mean that *Utopia* is guilty of "institution begging" and proposing an institution for whose desired effects it lacks proper philosophical cause? To fully understand the technique of punishment in Utopia and the reasoning behind it, it is necessary to turn to one of the other differences between More and Plato—the Englishman's theory of labor.[76]

Labor is the essence of More's penal technique—"apart from constant labor, [convicts'] lives are not uncomfortable" (73), but it is also essential to the entire project of Utopia. The benefits of hard work are visible at the founding moment of the state, when Utopus, the founder, puts both the defeated aboriginal inhabitants and his own soldiers to work digging a channel to separate Utopia from the continent "so that the vanquished would not think the labor a disgrace" (42).[77] And the emphasis on the value of work is ever present in the established Utopian constitution as well. "The chief and almost the only business of the syphogrants [the lowest level of magistrate] is to . . . see to it that no one sits around in idleness, and to make sure that everyone works hard at his trade" (127). The social structure of Utopia prevents idleness in two senses. Large swaths of the social order in England who, at least in More's view, are not productive members of society (including women, the wealthy, and the indigent) are either eliminated from or are made to work in Utopia. This increased labor pool is complemented by fewer goods produced (only those things consonant with the necessities of life and the "natural pleasures"). The result is a significant decrease in the number of hours required to produce the means of subsistence for all (129–31).

The second reason that Utopia is free of idleness has to do not with the inputs or outputs of the economy but with productivity itself. "Because [the Utopians] live in the full view of all, they are bound to be either working at their usual trades or enjoying their leisure in a respectable way" (127). The value of surveillance for correct behavior, which is so crucial to the Utopian religion, is revealed to have an economic function as well, and this laboring society in turn ensures social stability. The regime of production is meant to serve "the chief aim of [the Utopians'] constitution" that, "as far as public needs permit, all citizens should be free to withdraw as much time as possible from the service of the body and devote themselves to the freedom and culture of the mind" (135). This idea, that extensive political intervention is necessary to preserve the sphere of private freedom, is perhaps the most recognizable of all of More's innovations. It is an extreme version of a trade-off that exists at the heart of many liberal states.

These nascent modernizing aspects aside, Utopia's institutions of correction are still broadly consonant with their models in Plato's *Laws*. In both texts, punishment is just one element of a broad scheme of social education (*paideia, educatio*) that includes formal schooling, informal customs of shaming and honoring, and, in extremis, legal sanction, whether corporal or carceral.[78] In the Platonic institution of correction, it is not enough to have disciplinary techniques that claim to educate. There must be some moral logic that explains why a given punishment— whether whipping, jailing, or killing–fulfills the aims of making the criminal better, or at the very least deters others. If the Platonic parallel is to hold, More's affinity for penal servitude and the salutary effects of labor cannot merely be a response to the economic crises and vagrancy that plagued early modern Europe. The usefulness of labor must address both the social and the individual causes of crime. More suggests as much. Penal servitude can make men "necessarily become good," preparing them to "make up for the damage they have done" and all but banishing the danger of recidivism (75). But labor as a technique of behavioral reform is one aspect of Utopia that cannot be traced back to Plato.

THE SOURCES OF REHABILITATIVE PENAL SERVITUDE IN MORE

None of More's Greek or Roman models was particularly enthusiastic about the psychological effects of hard work. Plato famously equates working with one's hands (*cheirotechnia*) with "baseness" (*banausia*) (*Rep.* 590c); and according to the moral psychology of the *Laws*, "illiberal" labor is a sort of baseness that prevents the formation of a liberal character (*ēthos eleutheron*) (*Laws* 741e). Aristotle's disdain for the effects of hard work on the soul are equally notorious: those people whose function (*ergon*) is the use of the body are "naturally" slaves (*Politics*, 1254b15ff).

There were some ancient thinkers who had a more measured attitude toward hard work. The Cynic tradition, from Antisthenes and Diogenes through Dio Chrysostom, shows an appreciation for toil (*ponos*) as a training ground for virtue, and the Stoic school, especially as expressed in Epictetus, viewed work as just another of the morally indifferent phenomena (*adiaphora*).[79] On the whole, however, Roman political thought followed its Greek predecessors. Cicero's distinction between the gentlemanly professions (*liberales*: medicine, architecture, teaching, trade on a grand scale, and especially and mostly agriculture) and the base or vulgar ones (*sordidi*: everything else) is often taken to be paradigmatic of elite Roman attitudes toward work (*Off.* 1.150–2).[80] For the Romans, it is precisely the "liberal arts" whose "care is virtue" and which "make a man good."[81] Labor is for the lowly.[82]

Thomas More's vision of reformative carceral slavery did not, then, emerge from the classical philosophers. It can, however, be traced at least in part to antiquity. By the first or second century of the imperial era, the ambiguous role of labor in customary Roman law began to coalesce into a series of related custodial punishments for low-status offenders.[83] More, who trained as a lawyer, would have been familiar with the Roman codes and their various forms of punishment and must certainly have read or known secondhand about several forms of penal servitude used more or less widely in the later centuries of the empire.[84] These included sentencing *ad metallum* (to the mine) and *ad opus publicum,* or to public works.[85] It is the later of these that More seems to have adapted for his *Utopia.*

Penal servitude on the island consists of constant work (*in opera . . . perpetuo*) while chained (184);[86] and the more polished account of punishment among the Polylerites in book 1 even makes use of the full phrase *opus publicum* (73). Perhaps to distinguish this penalty from its sources, More is careful to emphasize a set of penological aims utterly foreign to the Roman lawyers. His goals are purely Platonic. Incarcerated labor both deters offenders and benefits the republic. (More emphasizes this penological utility, repeating it chiastically.) It also modifies the behavior of criminals, aiming to make them docile (*domiti*) and leading them toward penitence (*ad paenitentiam*). If, after prison (*carcer*) and chains (*catena,* standing in for *vincula* for the purposes of alliteration), the criminals remain "like wild beasts" (*indomitae beluae*), they are executed (192).[87] On the whole, however, in both penological passages the final stress is on the "hope" and "patience" for a return to society—a very different possibility than that which awaited Roman criminal slaves (193, 75).[88]

More's penology is a mix of Roman technique and Platonic rationale, but the Romans did not think their punishment could reform, and

Plato would not have dreamed of educating through labor. We have still not explained how labor became a method of rehabilitation. Perhaps it is best to begin with the broader question of labor. The revaluation of labor from the disdainful attitude of the ancients to the assiduous toil of early modern Protestants has occasioned a great deal of scholarly interest. Some have traced the shift to a change in the attitude toward the menial professions that began to occur at the beginning of the high medieval period.[89] Others have identified the rise of laboring, self-sustaining monastic communities in western Europe as a pivotal moment, particularly given the ideological importance of the work-friendly Rule of Benedict for constituting later monastic practice.[90]

The most outstanding philosophical exemplar of this shift, and one very dear to More's heart, was St. Augustine.[91] The Bishop of Hippo, who was familiar with the works of Cicero and Seneca in praise of leisure (*otium*), took up the cause of labor within the Latin church. In his influential work *De opera monachorum,* he addressed the question of physical labor in the community of saints. Castigating those ascetics who claimed that their holy life excused them from providing for themselves, Augustine insisted that work can improve men, teaching virtues like pride and humility,[92] and is a human obligation emphasized in both the Old and New Testaments.

Whatever the particular origins of the work ethic of Western Christianity, by More's lifetime the lion's share of the transition from ancient attitudes to modern ones had taken place.[93] This was especially true in monastic communities, which, as Max Weber himself recognized, had begun to rationalize the practice of labor, if only for otherworldly ends.[94] More was very probably influenced by Augustine's intellectual arguments, and he was almost certainly influenced by the monastic practices of his own day.

In the years after his lectures on Augustine but before his eventual marriage, More spent as many as four years living in close communion with the Charterhouse of London.[95] The Carthusians were known for organizing their habitation in individual cells around the central cloister, an architectural novelty that has its origins in the idea of the monastery as a preparation for the even more ascetic life of the hermitage. The Carthusians were notable not only for their architecture, intended to promote the individual's communion with God, but for their considerable devotion to a discipline that forbade all private property, even books.[96] The rigor of the Charterhouse made a lifelong impression on More, who even compared his room in the Tower to a monk's cell, noting to his daughter, "If it had not been for my wife and you that be my children . . . I would not have failed long ere this to have closed myself in as strait a room, and straiter too."[97] More's idea of penal incarceration, though fundamentally Roman, seems to borrow something from this monastic heritage. The penal slaves are locked away each night individually, "in their *cubiculi*" (72).[98] Another possible influence on More is the practice of ecclesiastical and monastic imprisonment, then in common use. The Rule of Benedict, for instance, calls for penal isolation to induce penitence (*paenitentia*), and there are other early examples of the cenobitic prison (*carcer*) as a place to address sins of pride and laxity.[99]

More's depiction of a reformed system of punishment thus combines three disparate elements—the institution of penal servitude as it survived in the compendiums of the Roman lawyers,[100] the idea of deterrence and reform as the chief aims of incarceration as argued by Plato in the *Laws* (among other places), and finally, the conviction that hard work and isolation were not only not detrimental; they were essential to the sort of discipline that belongs to the care of the soul, a sentiment found very clearly in the monastic communities to which More was drawn.

This chimerical combination of labor and discipline fits well with what More identified as the chief causes of social disturbance—indolence on the level of society and overweening pride in the soul of the individual.[101] The form of incarceration used by the Polylerites and the Utopians puts to work those most likely to tend toward indolence and forces them to toil toward the public good, both making idle hands active (*publicae rei servient*) and causing proud souls to become tame (*domiti*). In doing so, More could plausibly claim to have fulfilled the fundamental aim of the New Learning, to combine the best philosophical arguments of the Greeks with the best spiritual practices of the church.[102] From the vantage point of our "genealogy" of penal incarceration, we can see that More and his Renaissance counterparts reversed the process initiated by Philo and the early church. The spiritual practices and ecclesiastical institutions of Christianity, especially monasticism, again became a resource for thinking about political institutions, whether on the island of Utopia or in the urban centers of northern Europe.

CONCLUSION

The theoretical origins of punishment in More are an admixture of Platonic reasoning and Roman jurisprudence, both firmly rooted in the ancient world. But More picked up his Plato after two thousand years of political, religious, and cultural change. It is worth asking what effect this distance had on More's adaptation of Platonic punishment and incarceration.

The first place to look for disparities between Plato and More is in the role of "shame" and "shame culture." More, writing in Christian Europe at the height of the Renaissance, should be well on his way to the sort of guilt-based thinking about punishment and retribution that characterizes the modern ethics of autonomy. And yet, as we saw, Utopia is still very much a reputational society, similar in size and demeanor to Plato's ideal cities (and the honor-based moral economy of the classical world). More's use of shame and social sanctions assumes the sort of iterative, unmediated interactions that characterize small communities. Indeed, the cities of Utopia are kept at an ideal size of no less than sixty and no more than about a hundred thousand people, divided into quarters, and ensuring that social and political life is conducted among acquaintances, if not intimates (54).[103]

More wrote not only out of an admiration for the scale of the ancient polis/civitas but in the context of an England that had not yet begun its climb out of the demographic abscess of the late Middle Ages. More's own London was a town of some sixty thousand. Its economic and social relations were largely governed by personal reputation, and the problems of an anonymized urban underclass were not yet fully in view, although they were clearly on More's mind.[104] Both the scale of social interaction and demands of social order in More's day were arguably closer to the ancient world than to the postindustrial one.

Even the most obvious cultural difference between More's world and Plato's, Christian hegemony, is pointedly excluded from *Utopia*. The Utopians are not Christian, but they are amenable to it, perhaps because Christianity expresses the same ethical monism that their own indigenous philosophy recommends. For all that More's Utopia contains "proto-liberal" elements like the preservation of a (very limited) private sphere, and the assertion of some version of the "harm principle," or even the suggestion of religious toleration, the society of the Utopians remains fundamentally oriented toward an idea of virtue as the pursuit of *true* pleasure.[105] The tolerance of dissent (including from atheists) is presented as a sort of forbearance toward those who are foolish rather than a sign of approbation (and that patience only extends so far). It would probably be churlish to recall More's polemical works against the Reformation in this connection, but Utopia is located somewhere between the Hellenistic schools and the Augustinian church in its ideas about moral virtue and religious belief, and it is certainly not pluralistic in the modern sense.

That said, there is at least one clear way in which More's political thought reflects a theory of society distant from that of Plato (or most other Greek writers). Athenian writers agreed that the most serious problem facing the social order of a city is the challenge posed by elites, whether they are oligarchical plotters (as per Demosthenes) or atheistic intellectuals (in Plato's *Laws*). More, for his part, is far more concerned with the material causes of crime, the indolence of the rich and the desperation of the poor. In fact, in his prosecution of the "pride" associated with the aristocracy and his appreciation of the laboring classes (who, he acknowledges, are honest but exploited), More seems to anticipate the reordered priorities of a nascent bourgeois revolution. Whether it is due to the influence of Christianity, monasticism, or some other less tangible source, More's egalitarian impulses are far stronger than the ancient ideal states that were his models. He wants to understand social order from the perspective of work or labor, that is to say, from the bottom up.

With hindsight, More and his *Utopia* can be understood as a transitional moment for the political theory of incarceration and punishment. Little of the philosophical, legal, and institutional aspects of More's theory of punishment would have been foreign to a reader living in the Roman Empire, and More adheres to classically Platonic ideas about both the ends of punishment and the relationship between punishment and education. But his technique of penal imprisonment and improvement with hard labor is absolutely new, as is the fully utility-based psychology that supports it. (As we saw, utility played an ancillary role for Plato, in the service of constructing a system of laws that would lead the citizen toward virtue.) More has accepted that social order can be maintained in a society that values pleasure for pleasure's sake (though the nature of pleasure is not yet fully localized in the mind of the solitary Cartesian subject). This means that the psychological mechanism used to influence criminal behavior can be much simpler than it was in Plato. Hard labor is both useful for the society and painful enough to change a convict's mind. More's Augustinian ideas about labor open an entire horizon of possible prisons, ones that even those Roman politicians who so prized the idea of the "useful" (*utile*) could not have imagined.

More's social theory, his suspicion of the "pride" of the few (to be tempered by communism) and the "indolence" of the many (to be corrected by compulsory labor), helped him to adapt the Platonic vision of reformative incarceration into a formula that perfectly fit the emerging bourgeois societies of early modern northern Europe. Whether by coincidence or by fate, More's proposals were published just before these societies began to take their own first steps toward experimenting with incarceration as an actual penal practice. The prison was about to leave Utopia for the real world.

4

"ALL RESTRAINT OF MOTION"— INCARCERATION IN HOBBES

WITHIN TWENTY YEARS of Thomas More's death, the Utopian proposal for penal confinement with hard labor had begun to take root across northern Europe. Nurtured by a humanistic habitus similar to More's, the burghers of London (1555), Amsterdam (1596), Hamburg (1618), and dozens of other cities from Oxfordshire to East Prussia began to construct special buildings for the punishment and reform of minor criminals.[1] Judges began to treat prisons as a form of incarceration through "public works" like that described in *Utopia*,[2] and penal incarceration based on reformative labor found a central place in the urbanizing landscape of northern Europe. So began what was perhaps the first intentional experimentation with penal incarceration in European penal practice since the abortive attempts in democratic Athens almost two thousand years earlier.

As Europe started to explore the possibilities of the prison, it fell to another Englishman to point out a possible problem with the increasingly widespread form of punishment.[3] According to Thomas Hobbes, the bodily punishment of citizens (for Hobbes, subjects) by the sovereign to whose authority they accede entails a contradiction. Penal incarceration threatens to break the social contract between sovereign and subject that lies at the foundation of the state (or commonwealth); but Hobbes acknowledges, and indeed insists, that to administer such punishment is still an inalienable right and responsibility of the sovereign. By placing penal confinement in tension with the consent of subjects to be governed, Hobbes stated a distinct form of the paradox of popular authorization of imprisonment posited by Demosthenes: certain forms of punishment can be at the same time both advisable and illegitimate given the structure of the relationship between subject and regime. Although the precise nature of this paradox in Hobbes is very different from the ideological conflicts among Athenian democrats, the similar logical structure of this contradiction is nonetheless noteworthy.

This chapter elucidates Hobbes's discovery of a contradiction between popular power and penal practice. It begins by examining Hobbes's general theory of punishment and the paradox within it. Next, it turns to the specific role of imprisonment within Hobbes's philosophy. Hobbes takes incarceration, which in seventeenth-century England was almost exclusively a short-term form of discipline for sundry misdemeanors, and treats it as equivalent to capital punishment. We can trace this somewhat apparently outsized role for the prison to the central importance of physical restraint in Hobbes's theory of liberty and, ultimately, to his theory of the social contract.

In addition to Hobbes's theory of punishment and contracting, we will also examine how Hobbes thought punishment *worked*. Like Plato, Hobbes views law and punishment as twin facets of the relationship between government and subject. Although he does not make the sort of explicit and extensive arguments about soul craft and punishment that characterize the Platonic tradition, Hobbes nevertheless insists that punishments must either reform criminals or deter them. And Hobbes's theory of moral psychology implies that, despite its drawbacks, imprisonment is well suited to effect this reform. Viewed from within Hobbes's system, the prison's advantage is that although it severs the obligations of the subject to the sovereign, incarceration also produces similar conditions to those under which it is rational to exit a state of nature and rejoin the social contract. That is, the prison has the potential to fix the problem of punishment in a popular regime. After establishing the outlines of Hobbes's theory of imprisonment, we venture a more complete account of the social theory behind the Hobbesian prison (including who should be imprisoned and why). Finally, the chapter concludes by restating the version of the paradox of popular incarceration that emerges in Hobbes.

PUNISHMENT AND INCARCERATION

To understand why Hobbes found it necessary to grapple with incarceration, which, despite shifting public opinion around punishment, remained an apparently minor phenomenon in seventeenth-century England, it will be helpful to situate the prison within his broader theory of punishment, a theory that has been an object of perplexity for readers since the seventeenth century.[4] The problem that has bothered critics, ranging from Hobbes's Royalist contemporaries to the rational choice critics of the twentieth century, is an apparent contradiction between Hobbes's theory of authorization—that parties to the social contract authorize every action of the sovereign as if it were their own—and his theory of reserved rights: that there are some things, including the right to self-defense in the face of bodily harm, that a person cannot give up.

Hobbes's views on the rights of subjects seem to have changed somewhat over the course of his career,[5] but in the version of the theory in *Leviathan,* Hobbes wrote that there are "some rights which no man can be understood . . . to have abandoned or transferred." Among these is the "right of resisting" (1) deadly or violent assaults and (2) "wounds, and chains, and imprisonment." (*L* IVX.8, 82).[6] Yet Hobbes also seems to include punishment as a part of how subjects authorize sovereigns to act in their name, stating, "If he that attempteth to depose his sovereign be killed, or punished by him for such attempt, he is author of his own punishment" (*L* XVIII.3, 111). On the one hand, the right to resist physical punishment is absolutely and conceptually inalienable. On the other hand, Hobbes provides at least one example where physical punishment is authorized by the person punished.

Hobbes addressed this apparent discrepancy directly in his most extensive discussion of punishment, the twenty-eighth chapter of the

Leviathan. After defining punishment as "an evil inflicted by public authority" (a definition to which we will return), Hobbes takes up a "question . . . of much importance" concerning "by what door the right or authority of punishing . . . came in." He resolutely reaffirms the right to resist punishment, stating that "no man is supposed bound by covenant not to resist violence" and confirming that "the right which the commonwealth . . . hath to punish is not grounded on any concession or gift of the subjects" (*L* XXVIII.2, 203–4). Instead, Hobbes suggests, the sovereign's right to punish comes from the fact that the sovereign never gave up its rights from before the social contract. In the precontractual state of nature, "every man had a right to everything," including "subduing, hurting, or killing any man" for his own self-preservation. Hobbes calls this "the foundation of that right of punishing which is exercised in every commonwealth." Subjects, as parties to the social contract, have laid down almost all of their rights, while the sovereign has not laid down any of its rights. Therefore the sovereign rightly uses forms of violence (including punishments) that were not (and could never be) included in a contract between parties.

This solution to the contradiction between his general theory of authorization and the case of the right to resist punishment is not entirely satisfactory. For one, it is not clear what exactly Hobbes is saying. If punishment is a sort of prepolitical violence, is the criminal in a state of nature with respect to the sovereign?[7] If so, is this because the crime she committed itself ruptured the social contract, or is it because the sovereign has ejected her from the state by the act of punishing her? And if, under threat of punishment, subjects can decide to leave the state, can the sovereign still be said to be the sole judge and authority within the commonwealth?[8] For some critics, Hobbes's admission of a right of resistance to punishment undermines the very structure of the state; for others, it is proof of the fundamentally liberal character of Hobbes's thought—and that whether he intended it or not, Hobbes had laid the groundwork for a regime whose power could be constrained by individual rights.[9]

To understand how Hobbes's justification for punishment and his rationalization of resistance can exist side by side, we have to understand punishment as a legal process that, like all legal processes in Hobbes, both emerges from the sovereign and guides the sovereign's behavior. As

Arthur Yates points out, Hobbes talks about the sovereign's situation as a natural person in the state of nature as the "foundation of that right of punishing" (*L* XVIII.2, 204). While the violence of punishment is reminiscent of the state of nature, punishment itself is constrained by legal categories, such as due process, and by legal principles, such as *nulla poene sine lege* (there can be no crime unless a law has been broken).[10] This means that punishment cannot simply take place in a lawless state—rather, the sovereign is *authorized* by the law to use the violent means that it (alone) retained from the state of nature.[11]

Signy Gutnick Allen pursues a similar observation from a different direction. She notes that Hobbes repeatedly and consistently makes a distinction between "rebels" who exist in a state of "hostility" to the sovereign and "criminals" who are punished according to the laws of the commonwealth.[12] Traitors explicitly breach the social contract and are treated by the sovereign accordingly (as an enemy in a state of war). Criminals, however, are dealt with within a system of civil law that has very little in common with the state of nature. It is true, that, once the sovereign threatens them with a violent punishment, criminals can be justly expected to resist—but from the perspective of the sovereign, they are still subjects, with the accordant rights and privileges. The sovereign's power to punish is thus bound up in the sovereign's discretion over the boundaries of citizenship. Hobbes's theory of punishment is "trying to maneuver . . . between two conflicting points of view"—the view of the sovereign, for whom violent punishment is a social necessity, and the view of the criminal/subject, for whom it is rational to break the contract once the sovereign has threatened her body or life.[13]

These explanations of Hobbes's theory still leave a final question. Given the strain it places on the social contract, why should Hobbes countenance violent punishments in the first place? After all, although we have been using the word "punishment" rather freely, it is only a certain set of extreme penalties that trigger a right to resistance. Other punishments discussed by Hobbes, including pecuniary punishments or the sorts of shame punishments familiar to us from Plato and More (which Hobbes calls "ignominy"), would not provide any pretext for resistance and would thus avoid the conceptual contradictions of which Hobbes stands accused. To understand why Hobbes nevertheless insists on violent forms of punishment, including incarceration, we must better understand the aim and function of punishment in the *Leviathan.*

From the very first pages of the book, Hobbes gives the institution of punishment pride of place, calling it the "nerve" by which every member "is moved to perform his duty" (*L* introduction 3; elsewhere he calls reward and punishment "nerves and tendons" XXVIII.26, 209). The priority given to punishment in Hobbes's system can be explained by the simple fact that no contract, including the original contract between subject and sovereign, can exist without "some coercive power to compel men equally to the performance of their covenants, by the terror of some punishment greater than the benefit they expect by the breach of their covenant" (*L* XV.3, 89). Accordingly, Hobbes lists punishment as one of the explicit responsibilities of the sovereign, who should aim at the "correction, either of the offender or of others by his example" (*L* XXX.23, 230; cf. XVIII.14, 115). In fact, it is precisely this corrective aspect, "disposing the delinquent (or, by his example, other men) to obey the laws" that separates punishment from hostility (and the criminal from the rebel, *L* XXVII.7, 204).

The first condition of punishment then is that it reforms a criminal. This, in and of itself, would not necessitate harsh penalties. But Hobbes also worries that "if the harm inflicted" by a punishment "be less than the benefit or contentment that naturally followeth the crime committed," it will merely be thought of as the "price" of committing the crime (*L* XVIII.9, 205). That is, the aim of punishment is to stop crimes entirely, so if a criminal weighs his options and decides that, all told, the punishment is worth bearing, he will commit the crime, and the system of punishment will have failed.[14] As Hobbes states more clearly in *De Cive,* this fact about cost-benefit analysis and the "pricing" of crimes solicits harsher penalties (cf. *L* XVII.8, 192).[15]

The importance of punishment for social stability, and the necessity of making sure that the costs of crime outweigh the benefits, means that the specifics of how to punish are of utmost importance to the success of the state. And indeed, Hobbes takes an exceptional interest in the practicalities of punishment. In chapter 28 of the *Leviathan,* he lists five main techniques of punishment: corporal, pecuniary, shame based ("ignominy"), exile, and incarceration (or some mixture of these). Hobbes is not only interested in categorization, however; he is concerned to show that his system, as one scholar puts it, can "plausibly achieve its aims."[16]

To figure out which punishments will reform criminals and discourage would-be offenders to the correct degree requires Hobbes to analyze particular punishments at the level of practical politics.[17] Upon closer examination, for instance, pecuniary punishment "is not properly a punishment, but the price of privilege and exemption from the law" (*L* XVIII.18, 206), which only ends up forbidding the offense to those who cannot afford to pay the fine. Given that Hobbes is particularly concerned, for reasons we soon discuss, that the "rich and mighty . . . may have no greater hope of immunity when they do violence" (*L* XXX.15, 226), fines, which are the easiest for the rich to avoid, are singularly unattractive.

The place of shame-based punishment is less clear-cut. Hobbes thinks "that it is necessary there be laws of honor and a public rate" for deserving subjects (*L* XVIII.15, 115), and consequently it is possible to "degrade" subjects, to deny or remove them from office (*L* XXVIII.19, 207). But the sort of social honor that interested the Greeks and their Renaissance pupils is studiously absent from *Leviathan* (things "honourable by nature" cannot, Hobbes avers, be legislated by the state). The usual markings of shame punishment—"words of disgrace" and "contempt"—are merely "phantastical" injuries. Hobbes even historicizes his own dismissal of shame, noting that "this corner of the world" was "made sensible" to the unimportance of slights of honor "by a custom not many years since begun" (*L* XXVII.20, 196). In any event, punishment must only be concerned with the honors bestowed by the state, and subjects are expected not to act rashly out of concern for their honor.[18]

Exile is another punishment Hobbes catalogs, only to implicitly reject. Hobbes, himself an exile, would have seen the beginnings of penal transportation to the colonies of the New World, but he dismisses the idea of banishing criminals, concluding that exile "seemeth not in its own nature . . . to be a punishment" because "the mere change of air" does not tend "to the forming of men's wills to the observation of the law" (*L* XXVIII.21, 207). When Hobbes later talks (approvingly) about colonization, it is as a form of poor relief (cf. *L* XXX.19, 228), not a form of punishment.

This leaves only two plausible techniques of Hobbesian punishment:[19] corporal punishments, including death ("either simply, or with torment"), "stripes, wounds, chains, and any other corporal pain," (*L* XXVIII.17, 206) on the one hand; and imprisonment on the other. These are also the two forms of punishment that immediately trigger a criminal's right to resist (cf. *L* XIV.8, 82; XXI.11–12, 141–42). And it is perhaps no mistake that the same activities both enforce the contract and rupture it. Although writers on Hobbes's theory of punishment have usually focused on the role of capital punishment, Hobbes makes no distinction between corporal punishment and imprisonment—both are harsh enough to deter criminal behavior (cf. *L* XI.4, 58), and both, it must be inferred, have a reformative potential.

Nevertheless, it is not difficult to think of reasons why Hobbes *could* have rejected some forms of corporal punishment. As one game theorist argues, it would have been more logical to minimize "the maximal penalties to the level below that of people in the state of nature," in order to encourage people to join the commonwealth.[20] And in Hobbes's own time, Hugo Grotius explicitly rejected capital punishment as insufficiently compatible with reform. Surely Hobbes, who had read this passage in the *De jure belli ac pacis* (but to which, unlike other points of Grotius's, he does not respond), would have seen the difficulty that capital punishment poses to any rehabilitative theory.[21] Another reason that capital punishment seems superfluous is the psychological continuity between death and other forms of physical danger (as noted above, forms of corporal punishment and imprisonment accomplish the same things, *L* XI.4, 58; cf. IVX.8, 82; IVX.29, 87)—if the same ends can be accomplished without the death penalty, why does Hobbes insist on capital punishment?[22]

To see how Hobbes can both insist on the primacy of reform and entertain the use of execution "with torment," it may help to examine the immediate penological context within which Hobbes wrote. We have already mentioned Grotius's humanistic defense of rehabilitative punishment,[23] but it was not only scholarly readers of Plato who were proposing changes to the penal codes of sixteenth-century Europe. The English Civil War saw a lively debate among anti-Royalists over how to reform the legal system, including the techniques of punishment. The more radical elements among the Parliamentarians, including the

Levellers and the Diggers, made the case that capital punishment should be greatly curtailed (or even abolished), and even more conservative figures like Matthew Hale were involved in attempting to soften the force of capital punishment.[24]

Hobbes was not the only Royalist to stand up for the sovereign right to capital punishment, but, given his theory of sovereign power and his distaste for parliamentarian critics of sovereign authority, his strong need to reaffirm the harshest aspects of corporal punishment begins to make more sense. This is especially true given the widespread prevalence of capital punishment in early modern England. To question capital punishment was to question a tool of government that, even if not the most effective from a philosophical perspective, was among the most identifiable markers of the sovereign authority that it was Hobbes's chief intention to defend.[25]

This leaves us with the final technique of punishment discussed in the *Leviathan* and our central subject, imprisonment. If Hobbes's seventeenth-century context helps to make sense of his commitment to capital punishment, it does precisely the opposite in the case of imprisonment. The more we examine the penal practices of Hobbes's own time, the stranger his inclusion of incarceration as one of the main pillars of social order seems. Hobbes defines imprisonment as "when a man is by public authority deprived of liberty," and he distinguishes between custodial incarceration and "the inflicting of pain on a man condemned." Only the latter form is a punishment, and this penal incarceration can be in a "house" (prison), an island, or a place of enslavement (the penal quarries of the ancient world; now, slave galleys) or simply to be put in chains "or any other such impediment" (*L* XXVIII.20, 207).[26]

The "houses" to which Hobbes refers are most likely the "houses of reformation" and "houses of correction" that, beginning with the London Bridewell, had begun to appear in English cities and across the continent.[27] This situates Hobbes squarely within the seventeenth-century prison-building moment with which we began this chapter. But prisons, bridewells, and houses of correction were almost entirely places of brief or temporary confinement, for very minor crimes.[28] The nascent practice of incarceration was addressed to the margins of social life—the blasphemers, the itinerants, the peddlers, and the prostitutes—and certainly not intended to punish felons. Hobbes is thus making the curious claim that an institution heretofore mostly used to police the minor delinquencies of urban order gives anyone condemned to it an excuse for out-and-out rebellion. He is, at the same time, elevating imprisonment to the level of capital punishment in the power of its reformative and deterrent effects (Grotius, perhaps the most influential reformative penal theorist of Hobbes's time, does not even mention the prison).[29] While Hobbes seems to give incarceration an outsized role in punishment and reform, the salutary effect of labor, which was at the basis of both More's theory and contemporary seventeenth-century civic encomiums to the prison, is largely absent from Hobbes's discussion.[30] Hobbes's use of the prison seems both uncanny and untimely. We can resolve some of these riddles by examining the philosophical underpinnings of incarceration in the *Leviathan*.

THE PHILOSOPHY OF THE PRISON IN HOBBES

The prison is not ever taken as an independent object of analysis by Hobbes, but, nevertheless, the philosophical significance of incarceration clearly crossed his mind, as evidenced by a shift in terminology between *De cive* (1642) and the *Leviathan* (1651). The basics of Hobbes's theory of the right of resistance, as we noted above, were already in place by *De cive*. Hobbes noted that bodily suffering (and especially the threat of death) absolves the subject of any responsibility to obey, even in the case of legally executed punishment. But while in *De cive* we read that it is "death, wounds, or other bodily harm" (*DCiv* II.14, 39) that trigger this exception, in *Leviathan* it is more explicitly death, "wounds, chains, and imprisonment" (*L* IVX.8, 29, 82, 87). Similarly, in *De cive,* we find prisoners being led to "punishment, whether capital or not" (*DCiv* II.14, 39), as evidence of the implicit right to resist. In the *Leviathan*, Hobbes describes the practice of prisoners being led "to execution or prison" under armed guard. If the prison (and even the somewhat synonymous *vincula,* or "chains") is absent from the accounts of punishment and resistance in *De cive*, it is squarely in the center of the parallel passages in *Leviathan*.

This is not to say that the prison is entirely absent from *De cive*, and in fact, the philosophical uses of the prison as a metaphor or an image of unfreedom provide an important clue as to why Hobbes may have decided to give incarceration a more central role in the later work. The first appearance of imprisonment in *De cive* is in the example of the formation of an association (*societas*) by conquest. The victor places the vanquished in chains (*vincula*) and compels him to agree to obey (*DCiv* I.14, 30). Hobbes later qualifies this, noting that a person can only be said to be obedient or obliged when he is not in chains or imprisoned (*vinctus . . . vel incarceratus, DCiv* VIII.3, 102); and in fact, "a slave who is thrown into chains, or is deprived of his liberty in any way, is released" from obligation (*DCiv* VIII.9, 105).

What is true of slaves is also true of free citizens because the liberty of slaves and of citizens is, Hobbes argues, conceptually identical.

> LIBERTY (to definite it) is simply the *absence of obstacle to motion. . . .*
> Every man has more or less *liberty as he has more or less space in which to*
> *move*; so that a man kept in a large jail (*carcer*) has more *liberty* than
> a man kept in a small jail. . . . Obstacles of this kind are external
> and absolute; in this sense all *slaves* and *subjects* are *free* who are not
> in bonds or in prison. (*DCiv* IX.9, 111)

Hobbes's famous definition of "negative liberty" as freedom from direct physical constraint is in effect built around the image of the prison. If we put these passages together, we can see that in *De Cive,* Hobbes had all the conceptual elements of incarceration as a punishment that would sever the social contract by releasing the criminal from her obligation to obey, but he did not yet make this argument explicit.

In the *Leviathan,* not only does Hobbes make the role of penal incarceration clearer; he also expands upon the philosophical importance of physical restraint as the prime example of unfreedom. Hobbes avers, as he did in *De cive,* that a covenant cannot exist without trust and that, as in the example of the vanquished captive, incarceration is a (perhaps *the*) sign of distrust (*L* XX.10, 130). He also returns to his definition of liberty as "the absence . . . of external impediments of motion," which means "in the proper sense . . . corporal liberty (that is to say, freedom from chains and prison)" (*L* XXI.1, 6, 136, 138).

Hobbes is also interested in demonstrating the difference between the real restraint of liberty (for instance, in a prison) and the "artificial chains, called *civil laws,*" through which subjects are ruled by a sovereign (*L* XXI.5, 138). This juxtaposition of the "weak bonds" of law, which do not violate liberty (in the proper Hobbesian sense of corporal liberty), and the actual chains of a prison emphasizes that "laws are of no power to protect . . . without a sword in the hands of a man, or men, to cause those laws to be put in to execution" (*L* XXI.6, 138). The "artificial chains" of law, which do not constrain liberty, are dependent on the real threat of punishment (which, in *Leviathan*, now explicitly includes chains and prisons). It is the specter of unfreedom, in Hobbes's strict sense, that makes the "liberties of the subject" (that is, life in a law-governed commonwealth) possible.

In the *Leviathan*, the prison as a form of physical constraint now joins corporal (and capital) punishment as one of the boundary situations of the relationship between subject and sovereign. Earlier, we examined this from the perspective of the condemned criminal, whose right of resistance is triggered by her violent punishment or prison. Now we can examine this boundary from the other direction—why would the sovereign choose to make use of the definitional case of unfreedom, the prison, in the normal practice of punishment? And what did Hobbes intend by giving incarceration such a prominent place in his discussions of contract, punishment, and law?

To help illuminate the connection between confinement as it relates to the social contract and incarceration as a punishment, it may help to turn to the work of one of his contemporaries—Gerrard Winstanley, a leader of the proto-communist Diggers and a writer whose political thought is about as diametrically opposed to Hobbes's as can be imagined. It is unclear whether Winstanley read Hobbes (although by the time his tract *The Law of Freedom* was published in 1652, Hobbes's arguments, if not Hobbes's texts, were in wide circulation),[31] but, in any case, Winstanley had a keen eye for important aspects of the arguments for sovereign authority, including the relationship of punishment to law. "For what are prisons, whips and gallows," Winstanley asked, "but the laws and power of the sword, forcing and compelling obedience and so enslaving, as if the sword raged in the open field?"[32] Winstanley recognizes and abhors the Hobbesian premise that law-governed society and punishment are two sides of the same coin. He pinpoints the nature of this relationship even more precisely in a related passage: "For what are prisons, and putting others to death, but the power of the sword to enforce people to that government which was got by conquest and sword and cannot stand of itself, but by the same murdering power?"[33]

Punishment is not only law—it is specifically part of the law of conquest: "What are [laws] but the cords, bonds, manacles and yokes that the enslaved English, like Newgate prisoners, wears upon their hands and legs as they walk the streets? by which those Norman oppressors and these their successors from age to age have enslaved the poor people."[34] It is worth unpacking Winstanley's choice of metaphor here. The image of the "Norman Conquest" appears again and again in the radical literature of the Diggers. They trace the authority of the state and its legal and administrative power back to an original act of illegitimate violence by the "Bastard William" (the Conqueror) and his victory at the Battle of Hastings. If laws are the chains that the invaders used to "enslave" the English people, punishment is their tool to secure the social order by repeatedly reproducing the moment of conquest anew.

Hobbes basically agreed with Winstanley about the relation between sovereignty and war. The difference for Hobbes is that what he calls "dominion acquired by conquest" is anything but illegitimate. Hobbes takes up the old Roman law tradition around the origins of slavery in the right of the victor over the vanquished and uses it to develop a new theory of conquest and covenant.[35] At the moment of victory, the defeated party is, in all likelihood, "kept in prison or bonds." The right of dominion is established (the vanquished party's "service is due") at the moment "when the victor hath trusted him with his corporal liberty" (L XX.12, 131). "It is not, therefore, the victory that giveth the right of dominion over the vanquished, but his own covenant" (L XX.11, 131). For Hobbes, the fact that the vanquished is eventually released from his state of unfreedom (physical confinement) means that the victor now trusts the vanquished and that the vanquished, in turn, is under some obligation to the victor (according to whatever conditions he was released). The release from incarceration becomes, in Hobbes, evidence of a trustworthy contract.

As we saw, Winstanley extended this moment of conquest to the apparently "legal" institution of punishment, and it is fair to ask whether punishment might also function in a similar way for Hobbes. The central tension in Hobbes's discussion of punishment, once again, is the mismatch between the punished person, who is free (or even rationally obliged) to resist her punishment and act as if she is once again in a state of nature, freed from all obligation, and the sovereign, who has discretion as to whether to treat the criminal as a subject (and therefore entitled to legal protection) or to declare the criminal a "rebel" and treat her according to the state of war.

Punishment in Hobbes can be seen as a sort of liminal condition between full citizenship and the state of war.[36] In his account of conquest, Hobbes gives imprisonment an eerily similar role. The vanquished prisoner is in a state of war with the sovereign, but prevented by her lack of liberty from doing anything about it. When (and if) she is freed, it is because her jailer is certain that she is docile and prepared to join (or rejoin) the social contract. In a similar way, penal incarceration is the only technique of punishment that allows the sovereign to temporarily exclude a subject from political society under, as it were, controlled conditions. A convict can be kept in prison until such a time as she can be trusted to behave according to the law. And indeed, for Hobbes, the release of a prisoner from chains is an unambiguous sign of trust in future behavior. Given that Hobbes is explicitly committed to rehabilitative punishment, it is clear that the preference of the sovereign should be to return the citizen from the state of war to the political covenant. Imprisonment, with the presence of reform embedded in the very concept of release, seems to align perfectly with Hobbes's first stated aim in punishing: to dispose the delinquent to obey the laws.

It is one thing to have a well-grounded theory of punishment and its ends; it is quite another to have an explanation of how a technique of punishment—in this instance, incarceration—can accomplish those aims, in this instance, the formation of criminals' wills. While scholars have often argued over the punitive aspects of Hobbes's thought, they have only very rarely recognized that a more fully worked out theory of how punishment works is present as well. In this section, we try to reconstruct the moral psychology of punishment in Hobbes from its various constituent parts and show how incarceration was a plausible means to accomplish the psychological process demanded by Hobbesian reformative punishment.[37]

Hobbes's main priority in punishment is to banish the widespread but destructive understanding of punishment as revenge (*ultio sive poenae*) and to reorient the practice of punishment entirely toward the future.[38] Although deterrence is an important part of this future-directed strategy, at every point that Hobbes discusses punishment, he places reform first, suggesting that the first aim of punishment is to change the reasoning of the person being punished. In Hobbes's own words, the end of punishment is "not to force a man's will but to form it (*formare*), and to make it what he who fixed the penalty desires it to be" (*DCiv* XIII.16, 152). Hobbes further insists that "it is only permitted to inflict a penalty in order to correct (*corrigavi*) the wrongdoer or so that others may be reformed (*esse meliores*)" (*DCiv* III.11, 49).[39] This reformative priority is preserved in the account of the Laws of Nature in *Leviathan* and in Hobbes's expectation that punishment must be inflicted with the "intention or possibility of disposing the delinquent (or, by his example, other men) to obey the laws" (*L* XXVIII.7, 204).[40]

Even if Hobbes is truly concerned with reforming the "disposition" or "will" of the criminal, these passages do not explain just how punishment can change the criminal's mind, other than by inducing "terror" (which Hobbes connects with forming the will).[41] Hobbes does not provide an explicit answer to this in the way that, say, Plato or Bentham does. Nevertheless, the elements of such a theory are present in his work, from a theory of the psychic causes of crime to an explanation of practical reasoning, decision-making, and psychic change.

To understand how reformative punishment might work, we must first understand the causes of crime. Like Plato in the *Laws,* Hobbes has a tripartite theory of criminal psychology: "The source of every crime is some defect of the understanding, or some error in reasoning, or some sudden force of the passions" (*L* XXVII.4, 191). The first cause of crime is "ignorance," of the law, the sovereign, or the penalty. Ignorance can be addressed by proper promulgation of the laws and need not concern us here. The second cause of crime is "error" or "defect in reasoning." Hobbes gives three examples: that of an immoralist who does not believe in keeping his contractual promises, that of a natural law theorist who thinks nature's (or God's) laws trump those of the state, and those who make hasty inferences "from true principles" (*L* XXVII.10–12, 193–94). Although, as we will see, these are important cases for Hobbes, they are not what we usually associate with the majority of criminal activity. That falls to the last cause of crime, the force of passions like anger, hate, lust, ambition, and covetousness.[42]

Aside from being implicated in the causes of crime, reason and passion more generally define how people think, make decisions, and act in the world. Reason, for Hobbes, is simply the deductive science of adding and subtracting the consequences of the correct definitions of things (L V.2, 22). Rational thought (or "science") is thus a method and a process of thinking, one that, on the whole, is "motivationally inert."[43] Although it has the strongest potential to tell a person which means or ends will have positive consequences, scientific reasoning relies on acquiring true knowledge of correct definitions and is therefore rarely in evidence in everyday life, where most people "are so far from [science] that they know not what it is" (L V.18, 26). This reinforces the sense that crimes of reason are exceptional (though perhaps all the more significant for that).

The second sort of cognition, the passions, are much closer to the "will" or "disposition" that inspires most human activity. The passions, as Hobbes says, "are the beginnings of all [man's] voluntary motions" (EL V.14, 23) and are themselves "small beginnings of motion within the body of man" (L VI.1, 28). To a large extent, the "will" that leads to action can simply be reduced to these passions. Will "is the last appetite in deliberating" (L VI.53, 33), and deliberation is nothing other than "the whole sum of desires, aversions, hopes and fears, continued till the thing be either done or thought impossible" (L VI.49, 33). Changing (re-forming) the criminal "will" therefore means changing the process of deliberation, or, at the very least, its final outcome.

The simplest way to change the outcome of deliberation is to boost the presence of some of the passions. Hobbes writes, "Of all passions that which inclineth men least to break the laws is fear. Nay . . . it is the only thing . . . that makes men keep them" (L XXVII.19, 196). If fear is the lawful passion, it is specifically "bodily fear" that has the most powerful effect on human activity (L XXVII.20, 196). Bodily fear overwhelms the deliberative process. This explains both the reformative and deterrent powers of corporal punishments (capital punishment, of course, can only ever be deterrent).

It is tempting to stop there and to posit fear ("terror") as the only tool of psychic change in Hobbes. There are reasons, however, to look for an additional psychic cause of reform. One such reason is the fact that incarceration is not classified by Hobbes as a corporal punishment.[44] Therefore, it is not clear that bodily fear fully explains how prisons work. Another reason is that Hobbes actually provides an additional pathway for affecting deliberation, and he explicitly connects this pathway both to rational cognition and to criminal behavior. This second pathway is prudential reasoning, for example, when "he that foresees what will become of a criminal re-cons [remembers] what he has seen follow on the like crime before, having this order of thoughts: the crime, the officer, the prison, the judge, and the gallows" (*L* III.7, 13; cf. *EL* IV.7, 15). Prudence, for Hobbes, is the process of induction from experience. As a rational faculty, prudence is less reliable than deductive reason or "science," but prudence nevertheless clearly plays an important role in voluntary deliberation and is, predictably, in much wider use than scientific reason, as all human beings have access to experience (cf. *L* VI.57, 34; V.22, 27).

Fear acts by weighing in the balance of deliberation (recall Hobbes's metaphor of "scales" for the process of how a prospective criminal decides to act, *De Cive* XIII.16, 151). Prudence acts in a slightly different manner. Some of the most serious sorts of criminals err because they "have a great and false opinion of their own wisdom" (*L* XXVII.16, 194). Such criminals are a special case of the sort of citizen who does not understand why sovereign authority is necessary and thus have not reasoned correctly about obeying the law. Hobbes explains similar errors by noting "all men are by nature provided of notable multiplying glasses (that is their passions and self-love) . . . but are destitute of those prospective glasses (namely moral and civil science), to see afar off the miseries that hang over them" (*L* XVIII.20, 118). Criminals (and not only criminals) therefore often reject the *real good* of law-governed obedience for the "apparent good" of their own interest. This sort of conclusion is the product of faulty deliberation, and inducing more fear would not necessarily fix the underlying problem.[45] Ideally, perhaps, criminals would be taught to act according to the "certain" knowledge of "civil science" (one of the two true sciences according to Hobbes, along with geometry). But given that scientific reason is the hard-won product of a long process of education, criminal law must look for an easier solution. Fortunately, both prudence and reason act on the deliberative process in a similar way "so that he who hath by experience or reason the greatest and surest prospect of consequences deliberates best himself" (*L* VI.57, 34; cf. IX.1, 57).[46]

From this point, it is simple enough to see how time in prison might contribute to the experience, and thus the prudential deliberation, of a convicted criminal (here the *durational* aspect of incarceration makes it especially important for affecting experience). But there is one other pathway by which prison can have a special effect on the wills or "voluntary acts" of criminals. We have already cited Hobbes's statement in the *Elements of Law* that the passions "are the beginnings of all [man's] voluntary motions" (*EL* V.14, 23). The significance of motion, while not always explicit, is ever present in Hobbes's moral psychology, and he affirms that "the best signs of passions present are in the countenance, motions of the body, actions, and ends or aims which we otherwise know the man to have" (*L* VI.56, 34). Given the psychic importance of movement, Hobbes's definition of imprisonment as "all restraint of motion caused by external obstacle" (*L* XXVIII.20, 207) should be seen in a new light. The prison, precisely in the way that it acts against the expression of passions as a form of motion, not only presents the prisoner with a controlled experience of being unfree and excluded from the benefits of law-governed society; it further constrains the moral psychology of the prisoner. With her voluntary motion and activity prevented by unfreedom, the prisoner is "freed" to reexamine her own prudential interests. The real good of the sovereign, obedience, and the real good of the prisoner, release, become one and the same.

HOBBES'S SOCIAL THEORY OF CRIME AND INCARCERATION

We have seen how Hobbes made use of the prison and suggested why Hobbes made use of the prison—all that remains is to ask, for whom did Hobbes make use of the prison? One of the most important shifts in the larger history of ideas about incarceration is the transition from ancient writers' focus on incarcerating elites to the modern theoretical concern with delinquent masses. Thomas More was already sensitive to the way social and economic changes could determine the patterns of crime through enclosure and immiseration of the poor, but rather than picking up where More left off, Hobbes's criminological priorities seem to owe more to the classical affectations of Tacitean (or Thucydidean) humanism than they do to the rapidly ramifying urban centers of the early modern period. Like the classical authors we have examined, Hobbes is mostly interested in imprisoning elites.

Hobbes is unambiguous about the fact that "all crimes are not . . . of the same allay" (*L* XXVII.21, 197). Some of the extenuating and aggravating circumstances of crimes are obvious. Abnormal mental states or the threat of force majeure, for instance, make a criminal less culpable. More unexpected is Hobbes's assertion that destitution and famine excuse crime and that the presumption of "strength, riches, or friends" aggravates it. Contrary to More's observations about the dangers posed to English society by enclosure, Hobbes is ready to forgive the desperate actions of the poor, while he sharply condemns the crimes of the rich (cf. *L* XXVII.27, 198; XXVII.30. 199). This makes sense given Hobbes's theory of rationality—the closer a poor person is to the conditions of death or bodily injury, the less the law can be said to obligate her.[47] The powerful, on the other hand, "have least need to commit" crimes (*L* XXX.16, 227). Perhaps for this reason, when a grand or wealthy person does commit a crime, Hobbes views it as the symptom of a much more serious problem.

In two related passages, Hobbes makes a case for the dangerous elite few as the greatest threat to political order. The first comes during his discussion of the two major causes of crime, faulty reason and uncontrolled passions. The first crime of reason, we read, is the result of "potent men" who have learned the wrong lessons from history and take it as an established truth that might makes right (*L* XXVII.10, 193).[48] The next type of crime is the false teaching of natural law, and the last is the crimes of "they that have both a great opinion of their own understanding, and believe that things of this nature require not time and study, but only common experience and a good natural wit" (*L* XXVII.12, 193), or in other words, the sorts of people who pretend to know what they do not really know.[49]

But it is not only the crimes that rely on knowledge or elite learning where the rich and powerful predominate. In discussing crimes of passion, Hobbes's first attention is to "vain glory, as if difference of worth were an effect of their wit, or riches, or blood, or some other natural quality, not depending on the will of those that have the sovereign authority." Vainglorious people explicitly expect to be treated differently than "poor, obscure, and simple men . . . the *vulgar*" (*L* XXVII.13, 194). Wealth and power magnify the ill effects of already dangerous passions.

The good and great—whether it is from their wealth, connections, or "false opinion of their own wisdom"—often think that the law does not apply to them or that they will be able to escape punishment by "corrupting public justice" when the time comes (*L* XXVII.14–16, 194). But most seriously, it is especially those who think they know what they do not who "are the first movers in the disturbance of commonwealth" (*L* XXVII.16, 195). Even if Hobbes looked around him and saw that most crimes are committed by the many, he also saw that the crimes that really matter, the crimes that pose the deepest threat to peace and public order, tend to be committed by those with some financial, social, or intellectual power.

The second passage that discusses the sociology of crime is even more direct. Because the end of punishment is "correction[,] . . . the severest punishments are to be inflicted for those crimes which are of most danger to the public," particularly when "they are committed by sons, servants, or favourites of men in authority." But in "crimes of infirmity," on the other hand, "there is place many times for lenity" (*L* XXX.23, 230). Even in the case of public disorder, "the punishment of the leaders and teachers[,] . . . not the poor seduced people," is to be preferred. All in all, one of the main tasks of criminal law for Hobbes, the way that it acts to "fasten subjects to the seat of sovereignty," is by vanquishing the proud. It is no coincidence that Hobbes places his explanation of the name of *Leviathan,* and its biblical moniker "King of the Proud," at the end of the chapter on punishment.

Hobbes's concern with elite crime, and particularly his obsession with grandees and others who have "a fake presumption of their own wisdom," is reminiscent of Plato's discussion of the *doxosophia* of the misbelievers in the *Laws* and places Hobbes within classicizing, or even Machiavellian, currents in seventeenth-century thought,[50] as opposed to More and those of Hobbes's contemporaries who were concerned with pressing social problems like full employment.[51] Despite his place at the beginning of "social contract theory" and his interest in the scientific method, Hobbes's theory of society should be understood as a fundamentally Renaissance-aristocratic one.[52] Hobbes, a young man during the Essex Rebellion and a middle-aged one during the crises that led to the civil war, was simply not concerned with pacifying the restive masses through penal labor, let alone in putting them to use for social gain. Rather, Hobbes always viewed the threat to social order as largely coming from above. In this respect, *Leviathan* is not a prophetic blueprint of bourgeois society, and, despite his unusual attention to incarceration, Hobbes is not really predicting penal modernity.

Modern or not, Hobbes did break with earlier currents in political thought by making punishment entirely a question of the expression of the sovereign and thus detaching the theory and the practice of punishment from the sort of informal "shame culture" that might operate outside the law. This was a major departure from theories of punishment in the ancient world and even from that of More's ideal state, where the boundary between social pressure and civil law as mediators of behavior was still blurry or nonexistent.[53]

Hobbes was highly attuned to the effects of society and culture on political life at the time in which he wrote, and his ideas about political behavior (and emotions like vainglory, sudden glory, and the like) reflect this.[54] But when it came to punishment he insisted that "the commonwealth wills that public words, i.e., laws, count for more with citizens than the words of a private citizen."[55] Rather than using "disgrace" or shame to shape behavior, Hobbes excluded these forms of social control from public law, much as he tried to exclude other forms of superstition. Similarly, informal types of social commitment like oaths, which were so important for earlier cultural-penal theories, have little or no force in Hobbes's thought.[56] When Hobbes's principle that punishment only exists within the law (and, therefore, as part of the direct relationship between subject and sovereign) is combined with his dictum that "where the sovereign has prescribed no rule, there the subject hath the liberty to do or forbear, according to his own discretion" (*L* XX.18, 143), punishment in Hobbes's state appears to be potentially more circumscribed than in many earlier thinkers and even than some later ones.

CONCLUSION

Despite Hobbes's considerable attention to incarceration, long an insignificant or ambiguous form of punishment, and despite the interaction between penal confinement and Hobbes's philosophical interest in physical freedom (and unfreedom), Hobbes is unique among the thinkers treated in this book in never explicitly drawing attention to incarceration. At no point does Hobbes favor incarceration over corporal (and capital) punishment, and he does not make explicit any of the arguments about the moral psychology of reform and the restraint of motion that we have shown were available to him. Of course, the fact that Hobbes was also unconcerned with the place of capital punishment in his work has not stopped scholars from puzzling over the similar contradictions between the social contract and the death penalty. But in the context of the story we are trying to unravel about theoretical tendencies in philosophy's engagement with incarceration, we may be able to go a bit further than simply saying that Hobbes's intentions do not matter. Even if incarceration as a punishment was not particularly important to his project (it was indisputably important as an image and analogy), Hobbes's positioning of incarceration within the justificatory structure of the commonwealth is nevertheless both novel and significant for understanding the place of the prison in the modern, liberal state.

For the first time since the discussion of the prison in Athens, it is the political principles of the regime, in this case Hobbes's theories of authorization and contracting, that define and delimit the practice of imprisonment. Hobbes's use of the prison depends on the importance of physical freedom (and physical unfreedom) to the boundary conditions of political membership. And, as in democratic Athens, incarceration, while attractive in some respects (it produces the requisite amount of terror, it affects prudential reasoning, it does not favor the wealthy and powerful), also poses a serious conceptual problem to this political structure. We can identify, in Hobbes, a different version of what we identified in the case of Athens as a paradox of popularly authorized imprisonment. Just as we opened this chapter with the paradox of the authority to punish and the right to resist, we conclude with this second paradox in Hobbes's penology.

In the first paradox, recognized by centuries of readers, a punishment that negates the incentives one would have for joining the social contract (such as preserving one's life, body, or physical freedom) automatically releases the punished person from her obligations to that contract. But contracts by themselves are insufficient to maintain public order, so punishments that violate the contract are necessary to maintain the force of the contract, and the subject is said to authorize acts of the sovereign, including those needed to maintain the contract. Incarceration is a punishment that both triggers this paradox and simultaneously offers a way out of it: Prison is violent enough to release an inmate from her obligations, but at the same time, it does not let her actually leave or resist the sovereign. Both the inmate and her jailer know that the only condition under which she will be released is if she is once again trusted by the sovereign (by analogy with the case of a vanquished prisoner of war who is released from her chains). The prison therefore has the unique ability to reproduce the moment of contracting, a hypothetical moment that becomes analogous to the actual moment of release. The final aim of punishment for Hobbes is "disposing the delinquent to obey the laws" (XVIII.7, 204), and the prison offers a paradoxical mechanism for reconciling the criminal with the sovereign's will: by exclusion from and then reinclusion into the political community.

It may not seem obvious that the contradictions within Hobbesian imprisonment should be thought of as a form of the paradox of popular incarceration; after all, the Hobbesian sovereign is not (necessarily) a democratic government, and Hobbes is not concerned with the way incarceration might impinge on equality or political freedom or any of the other "democratic" values that interested Demosthenes and his Athenian contemporaries. But incarceration nevertheless bears on precisely the aspect of Hobbes's thought that is most closely bound up with popular authority—the moment of contracting. The authority of Hobbes's sovereign is ratified one of two ways: by "institution," when a body of people come together to constitute a sovereign by shared assent, and by "acquisition," when vanquished parties agree to obey their victor in return for their physical freedom. Without wading into the debate over whether these initial moments of agreement are themselves essentially democratic,[57] we can see that imprisonment, which cancels the prisoner's assent to the sovereign's rule and takes away her physical freedom, threatens the very conditions that Hobbes thinks are necessary for both types of contract.

Whether the contractual relationship between citizen (subject) and sovereign emerges from a form of democratic procedure (as seems to be the case in the account of contracting in *Elements of Law* and *De Cive*) or from the individual authorizations of the citizens (in *Leviathan*), that is, whether this is a "thick moment" of popular consent or a very "thin" one,[58] it is precisely this consent that incarceration vitiates, immediately and continually. This contradiction seems not to have bothered Hobbes, for whom the conditions of peace within a state would justify any number of broken contracts, but it does show that, by making a form of freedom the precondition for popular consent (whether individually or as a body), Hobbes placed the "unfreedom" of the prison in direct conflict with the popular foundations of the state. It is not wrong to see in this the seeds of later contractarian objections to penal conditions (for instance, Tommie Shelby's analysis of the right to resist the carceral state).[59] And, given that these later theories often have much more capacious understandings of the sort of freedom that is "reserved" by citizens than Hobbes did, their objections to modern forms of incarceration along Hobbesian lines can be made with considerably more force.[60]

If Hobbes's statement of the contradiction between freedom and confinement seems both philosophically prescient and very germane to liberal-democratic concerns about freedom and incarceration, his social theory of punishing the wealthy and forgiving the poor is much more distant from most later approaches (if, as we suggested in the introduction, also preferable to them). Hobbes provided what is probably the first account of the prison within a theory of a "modern" state, but his views on the sociology of crime still bear the mark of a different social world. To understand how the theory of the prison was integrated with a theory of society more like that of contemporary liberal states, we must jump forward another hundred years, to the penal theory of Jeremy Bentham.

$$5$$

BENTHAM'S PANOPTICON—
BETWEEN PLATO AND THE
CARCERAL STATE

IN JULY 1776, a month that would go down in American history for different reasons, a twenty-eight-year-old lawyer named Jeremy Bentham wrote a biting letter to the London *Gazetter and New Daily Advertiser* about the worsening crisis in the thirteen colonies. Bentham was incensed by the letter of one pseudonymous "Ignoramus," who had attacked the arguments of Bentham's friend John Lind as "Utopian." Utopia, Bentham reminded readers, was "a country imagined by Sir Thomas More . . . where, without any adequate cause assigned, every thing went well." But "utopian" has become an adjective "of undiscriminating reprobation." In fact, Bentham claimed, "where I have seen it used, I have as often observed it to indicate a want of virtue in the censurer, as of merit in the plan he censures." Too often, "men in power" use the word to dismiss any plan that threatens to "reform abuses by which they profit" or "disturb the indolence in which they wish to slumber." Bentham, it seems, was squarely on the side of Utopia.[1] Today, Bentham is best known as the father of utilitarian moral philosophy and as the designer of the Panopticon prison, but, from the very beginning of his career, he was not afraid to associate himself with the Utopian tradition in political thought. In fact, he would fondly refer to the Panopticon as "my own utopia."

This chapter reexamines one of the most well-studied aspects of Bentham's thought—his writings on punishment and incarceration.[2] By positioning himself as a successor to More, Bentham was making a claim about the comprehensive nature of his theoretical ambitions that links him not only to the author of *Utopia* but, indirectly, to More's Platonic models and thus to a long history of thinking about penal institutions.

Bentham's prison theory is interested in the classical idea of discipline as a learning process. But Bentham is not only Platonic in his devotion to soul craft. As in *Utopia* and Plato's *Laws* before it, Bentham's approach to the prison is fully integrated into a broader theory of society and the social world. The foundation of Bentham's idea of social order is, as it was for More, human labor. Labor is the source of property, which, for Bentham, grounds people's expectation of their own happiness and place in society. Consequently, the sort of people who acquire property through their work (earnings) are the foundation of a secure and happy society. The aim of punishment, for Bentham, is not to return criminals to a civic community; it is to nudge them, as far as is possible, into behaving like the productive workers of the middle class.

Bentham is known for his late conversion to radical democracy. Nevertheless, this chapter situates his Panopticon prison squarely in the Platonic reformative tradition of incarceration.[3] In spite of his interest in democratic government, Bentham's penology is strictly technocratic and, in his own words, "despotic" (B iv.63).[4] This makes Bentham one of the last prison theorists to stay wholly within one tradition of prison theory, before, as we have argued in the introduction, modern penology entangled popular authorization with reform. Bentham's contribution to the Platonic reformative tradition is sui generis. Bentham thinks about criminality, on the order of the population, demographically. He writes with an industrial society of middle-class property owners and lower-class laborers in mind. He openly conceives of prisons as a place to punish the poor, reforming them into productive laborers. And this penal vision is in service of an almost Utopian notion of a rationally ordered society. Bentham's prison theory holds a mirror up to the contemporary world both in the way in which he envisioned the punishment of an entire demographic class (in his case, the poor) and in the way his Platonic commitment to the perfect penal technique contrasts so starkly with the contemporary loss of faith in the rehabilitative ideal.

The chapter begins by situating Bentham's theory of punishment alongside his participation in the Utopian tradition. The second section takes up Bentham's central innovation in prison theory—the Panopticon. Bentham's prison is a paradigmatic example of the "total institution" in contemporary social theory. It is also, however, a planned, rationalized institution of correction of the sort that was theorized by Plato and More. We examine the Panopticon as both a site of behavioral intervention and as a reimagination of the relationship between education and correction that characterized other Platonic theories of incarceration. Finally, the chapter grapples with the links between behavioral intervention, punishment, and social class in the context of Bentham's liberal political thought—a tangled set of relationships that has continued to haunt the history and theory of incarceration down to the present day.

BENTHAM ON PUNISHMENT

Best known as the founder of utilitarianism, Jeremy Bentham is rarely connected to the Platonic tradition in the history of political thought, a tradition more associated with idealism, rationalism, and authoritarianism than the empirical materialism that underlies Bentham's philosophy. Although Bentham is often thought of as a harbinger of the leading ideas of the nineteenth century, utility and democracy, he grew up under the rationalistic auspices of the French Enlightenment, and with a particular weakness for the political utopianism of Fenelon's *Telemachus*.[5] The connection between utopian literature and political progress was obvious and important for the philosophes among whom the young Bentham hoped to place himself. Fenelon's text, especially the idealized city of Salente, stood for legal reform and limited government.[6] Cesare Beccaria, another important influence on both the French Enlightenment and Bentham more directly, traced his own theories back to Montesquieu's Orientalizing utopian work, the *Persian Letters*.[7] And, in a letter to Bentham, the Chevalier de Chastellux points out that Beccaria, whose influence on Bentham's early penal writings was clear, owes "the germ of [his] principles" to More's *Utopia*.[8]

Considering this intense cross-pollination between utopian romances, materialist philosophy, and the intellectual habitus of the young Bentham, it is less of a shock to see the father of utilitarianism repeatedly refer to his own institutional plans, and especially his Panopticon designs, as "Utopias."[9] Utopia was not an abstract designation for Bentham. As he made clear more than once, his projects should be compared with those of the sixteenth-century chancellor of England, and the comparison would, Bentham thought, be favorable to himself:[10] "In the Utopia of the sixteenth century, effects present themselves without any appropriate causes; in this of the nineteenth century, appropriate causes are presented waiting for their effects."[11]

Bentham was certain that the decisive difference between the old utopias and his new one lay in his discovery of the real standards for connecting human morality and matters of fact—pleasure and pain.[12] Punishment, whatever More or Plato might have thought of it, is nothing other than a word for a certain relation to the creation of pain in human bodies and minds. According to the principle of utility (or, in Bentham's later formulation, the "greatest happiness" principle), any production of pain "is mischief," and therefore "all punishment in itself is evil" (Introduction to the Principles of Morals and Legislation, 158).[13]

By grounding punishment entirely in pleasure and pain, Bentham has left it subject to a sort of paradox (IPML, 74, 158).[14] Insofar as law and government exist to promote the common good, they will, Bentham insists, need to conform to the principle of utility, aiming "to prevent the happening of mischief, pain, evil, or unhappiness" (IPML, 12). But punishment is at the same time the production of an evil by political authority or law. Governments use pain to prevent pain.

As opposed to Hobbes, who was prepared to tolerate a great deal of harshness to ensure political stability, Bentham's theory requires that the state minimize punishment as far as is possible. "If [punishment] ought at all to be admitted, it ought only to be admitted in as far as it promises to exclude some greater evil" (IPML, 158). Inherent to the very nature of punishment is a trade-off, a calculation of the smallest measure of pain needed to prevent an equal or greater quantity of pain. Given this, it is perhaps unsurprising that Bentham begins his account of punishment by elucidating cases where, despite the commission of some crime, punishment should not be administered at all.[15] Punishment is always a last resort.

The costliness of punishment is central to Bentham's discussion. His language is shot through with the metaphors of expense and profitability. Because punishment, as a form of pain, is fully commensurable with the pain it is trying to prevent, the metaphors of bookkeeping are especially fitting. If the credit gained by punishment does not outweigh the debit of the mischief, if "it's *unprofitable*, or too *expensive*," or if mischief can be prevented "at a cheaper rate," punishment must be eschewed (IPML, 159; Bentham's emphasis).

This feature of Bentham's theory of punishment confounds the stereotype of the philosopher as a disciplinarian. Instead of absolute control, Bentham is after a sort of maximization—the most result for the lowest cost given the constraints.[16] This principle applies not only to the question of whether to punish, but also to the mode of punishment itself. Punishment can manage costs in several ways (keeping in mind that the currency under discussion is pain). It can deter future crimes, it can encourage fewer offenses and offenses of a less harmful sort (e.g., assault versus assault with a deadly weapon), but whatever it does, it should do "at as *cheap* a rate as is possible" (IPML, 165; Bentham's emphasis). For the most part, Bentham suggests, these aims can be accomplished by adequate attention to proportionality. The rule of proportion in Bentham is not a universal scale; it is a measure of what Bentham terms in a related context "frugality." The limits of frugality are not measured by the smallest crime and the largest but rather by the "maximum" deterrence produced and "minimum" pain delivered in each situation.[17]

The general principle behind Bentham's theory of punishment is the proportion of pain administered against pain prevented as constrained by frugality. This is a far cry from the explicitly virtue-oriented approaches in Plato and the Platonic tradition discussed in earlier chapters. (Plato used pleasure and pain, of course, but only ever in the service of the rule of reason in the soul.) But although Bentham differs from earlier authors in his "frugal" approach to punishment, he is close to the spirit of More and Plato in his dedication to finding the right "how" to accomplish the aim of frugal punishment.

To this end, Bentham lists three main elements to be aimed at in punishing—example (deterrence), reform (the improvement of the criminal), and incapacitation (IPML, 158n, 180)[18]—and even notes that particular techniques will be most efficient given particular ends, but at first it seems that no punishment can be philosophically perfect. Punishments must be mixed and matched ad hoc (IPML, 185). The neutral calculation of pain is indifferent to means.[19] If the only source for Bentham's philosophy of punishment were the *Introduction to the Principles of Morals and Legislation,* that might be an appropriate conclusion. Bentham, however, mentions in a footnote that the aims of punishment are to be treated in a separate work, *The Theory of Punishment.* It is to that work, or a simulacrum of it, that we must turn if we hope to understand the connection between the theory and practice of punishment (IPML, 185n).[20]

Punishment as Intervention

In *The Theory of Punishment* and the manuscripts related to it, Bentham provides a clearer picture of punishment. He notes an essential confusion in English between (1) the form of punishment (incarceration is a punishment) and (2) the social category it occupies (a thief undergoes punishment). Bentham signals that he will analyze both elements of the word.[21] There is also a fuller account of what punishment is aiming at—taking away the physical power to offend (incapacitation), by changing the criminal's will or desire (reform), and by inducing fear (B i.396; see UC 96.260). In order to provide a plausible connection between the two meanings of punishment, however, Bentham needed to answer the question that proved so important (and difficult) for Plato—*how* a given form of punishment can accomplish its aim. Despite the simplicity and elegance of the "proportionality" of mischief, Bentham's discussion nevertheless depends, like Plato's and More's before him, on the technical plausibility of his moral psychology.

To ask after Bentham's moral psychology may seem unnecessary, given his reputation as English philosophy's preeminent hedonist. The psychology of the principle of utility begins with a statement about human nature. "By the natural constitution of the human frame . . . men in general embrace [the principle of utility] . . . if not for the ordering of their own actions, yet for the trying of their own actions, as well as those of other men" (IPML, 13). The idea that an act is right or wrong ultimately depends, in the eyes of observers, on its ability to "promote or oppose" happiness (IPML, 12), but Bentham does not claim that this principle alone explains or motivates human action.

Bentham, not far removed from the main sources of Scottish sentimentalism, also allows for the influence of emotion ("passions") on decision-making. The form that practical reasoning takes, however, is the same with or without emotion—it is the study and calculation of foreseeable consequences (see IPML, 174).[22] Such calculations vary with the state and identity of the agent, both in terms of what Bentham calls "circumstances influencing sensibility" and the temper of the individual at the time of the decision (IPML, 52). This is what Bentham means by calling punishment an "artificial consequence"—it is a tool to alter the practical reasoning both of the criminal undergoing it and of the public that witnesses it. Punishment does not require the exact computation of a unit by some "felicific calculus"; it is enough that, given a knowledge of the general circumstances that have an impact on practical reasoning, the "*quantity actually inflicted on each individual offender may correspond to the quantity intended for similar offenders in general*" (IPML, 169; Bentham's emphasis). Punishment, viewed under the aspect of psychology, is not merely about the evil of pain; it is about pain in its guise as an "efficient cause" of human practical reasoning. Punishment must be designed based on a knowledge of what people have a tendency to do and thus what they may be "*made* to do" (IPML, 34).[23] It is a matter, in Bentham's later language, of changing interests.[24]

As with pleasures, interests are naturally varied. Punishment must be measured according to the psychological state of the criminal, or, more precisely, to the *tendency* of a certain type of criminal. "There are some appetites which are circumspect and reflective, such are the appetites for riches, for power and for honour. There are others which are precipitate and blind—such are the physical appetites" (UC 27.63). This account of psychology suggests certain not entirely comfortable penal consequences, as Bentham admits both obliquely and directly. One such result is that the crimes of the poor must be punished more severely, because the interest of the poor criminal is, in a sense, stronger in trying to achieve his aim (UC 27.63). Bentham even projects the psychology of interest on to the aims of punishment. Incapacitation attacks the physical power that accomplishes interest, deterrence raises "up an artificial interest" to outweigh the original interest, and reform "weakens" the original interest, changing how the agent calculates consequences.[25]

Understood psychologically, punishment's simple connection to pain becomes ever more mediated. Pain is only one means to the end of creating "artificial consequences" and thus "artificial interest." The best means of influencing interest is therefore still something of an open question.[26] In elucidating the broader structure of means at the disposal of the legislator, of which punishment is but one option, Bentham has recourse to a distinction he did not use in the *Introduction*—that between "direct" and "indirect" legislation (B i.367; see UC 87.42). Of all the ways of effecting "inclination, knowledge, power," the "three expedients" of "influencing conduct," punishment works most successfully on the first and the third (UC 87.3; cf. UC 17.208). There is an obvious drawback, however, to punishment as mode of law. "The mischief must, in some degree, have already taken place before the remedy can be applied" (UC 87.42). Indirect legislation is thus "whatever else can be done in the way of law" to prevent mischief and delinquency (UC 87.3). In writing a law, the lawgiver should always have in mind how best to shape the knowledge and inclinations of the unsuspecting agent. Indirect legislation stretches across every possible area of legal design, from how the tax code is structured to how poor relief is given out. If at the root of punishment was a sort of efficiency function, it will always be more parsimonious to nudge than to punish.[27]

Bentham recommends what is now called "choice architecture" as a supplement to the penal code in modifying interests, and as a result, the line between punishing and not punishing grows less clear (UC 87.11).[28] A tax on a dangerous substance, for instance, may cause the very same amount of pain that a fine on the same substance would have exacted, but it minimizes disutility by discouraging antisocial behavior before it happens and avoiding punishment after it has occurred. When describing the points at which intervention will be inefficient (the contexts where the "spontaneous action" [*sponte acta*] of agents tends toward higher universal utility), Bentham writes of the "comparative inefficiency of such means . . . [of transfer] by taxes—that is by punishments" (UC 17.217).[29] Bentham's reasoning seems to be that a tax is a direct form of intervention that causes pain, making it for all intents and purposes indistinguishable from punishment.[30]

The troubling ramifications of this unbroken spectrum of intervention from the framing of legislation to the carrying out of penalties are not difficult to discern. One example Bentham gives of "indirect legislation" is the institution of national identification procedures, up to and including mandatory personal tattoos. On balance, he claims this "would become favorable to personal liberty" by making criminal investigations and proceedings more "relaxed" (B i.557). Better the "invisible chain" fashioned by indirect legislation than the heavy chains of the prison.[31]

In searching for a theory of punishment to anchor the theoretical understanding of incarceration in Bentham, we find instead that Bentham has less a theory of punishment than a general theory of legislative intervention, of which punishment is an important but secondary part. The connection between proportion and utility that Bentham inherited from Beccaria and others points toward the heart of Bentham's thought, the minimization of pain. When pain can be minimized by other forms of intervention or by nonintervention, punishment is needless, and some forms of intervention, like taxes, might as well be punishment, even if they do not fit the strict definition of "a post-facto pain caused by some sanction." What is important is not the word "punishment"; it is rather

> legislation as a state of warfare: political mischief the enemy: the legislator is the commander: the moral and religious sanctions his allies: punishments and rewards (raised some of them out of his own *demesnes peculiaire*, others borrowed from those allies) . . . direct legislation, a formal attack made with the main body of his forces in the open field: indirect legislation, a secret plan of connected and long-concerted operations, to be executed in the way of stratagem or *petite guerre*.

Most important of all is frugality: "the oeconomy with which [this war] may be carried on and the ingenuity which it is thought to require."[32]

Punishment, then, is one locus among many where the legislator can balance the behavioral scales against public mischief. Like Plato and

More, Bentham has integrated his theory of punishment into a much more ambitious theory of how law should interact with human nature. In fact, what Bentham calls "indirect legislation" is closely analogous to the broad sense of education (*paideia, educatio*) that accompanied the penal theories of Plato and More. It is in light of this broader project that we turn to Bentham's writings on incarceration. It turns out that imprisonment is a preferred penal technique, not because of its inherent advantages in fulfilling the aims of punishment but, as in Plato and More, for its inherent advantages in shaping human behavior.

INTERVENTION, INCARCERATION, AND THE PANOPTICON

Bentham's Panopticon, besides being the "total institution" familiar to readers of Goffman and Foucault, is an institution of correction not unlike Plato's prison or More's use of penal servitude. Like its predecessors in the reformative tradition, the Panopticon aims to modify human behavior according to a particular theory of moral psychology, and, like them, the panoptic system is integrated into a large vision of society and law. To demonstrate this institutional affinity requires canvassing evidence from each of the four uses of panoptic architecture in Bentham's corpus, as, unlike the sometimes scant evidence of prison thinking in Plato, More, or Hobbes, Bentham's writings on incarceration span decades of his life and take up many hundreds of pages.

Incarceration before the Panopticon

The Rationale of Punishment initially displays a marked skepticism about two aspects of imprisonment—its lack of frugality and the inequality of its effects. (The loss of income for a poor man is much worse than that for a rich man; meager rations are much worse for the rich man than the poor.) Skepticism aside, Bentham concluded that "if any punishment can in itself be popular, this, I think, promises to be so" and wrote that incarceration, correctly applied, could combine the religious, moral, and political sanctions in one institutional framework (B i.426).[33] Bentham even tentatively proposed a three-tiered system of prisons to address the full gamut of menial and capital crimes (B i.430).[34] Tellingly, the discussion of "laborious punishment" falls under a separate heading, suggesting that, initially, incarceration and labor occupied entirely separate categories in Bentham's scheme. Labor possesses the chief properties of punishment "in greater perfection, upon the whole, than any other single punishment" and has much greater claim to being both frugal and equal than imprisonment does (B i.437–41, quote from 439).[35]

When the American Revolution (1776) made the popular solution of penal transportation less feasible, England suddenly found itself on the verge of a full-blown crisis in punishment. Around this time, a series of penal reformers including Bentham's hero John Howard and his fellow nonconformist author Jonas Hanway published two immediately popular books on a novel penal solution that came to be termed the "penitentiary." The history of this reform movement has been ably told elsewhere, but the combination of labor and incarceration in one site was an idea that had a tremendous impact on Bentham's thought.[36]

Howard's and Hanway's suggestions were almost immediately taken up by the political elite. Within two years of the publication of Howard's *State of the Prisons,* a law funding the construction of a high-capacity penitentiary made its way through Parliament. Bentham saw this act as a chance to finally make a show of his "genius for legislation." In his response to the proposed Penitentiary Act (16 Geo. III, c. 43, 1778), Bentham brought to bear his entire theory of punishment, excoriating the "unequal, unexemplary, unfrugal" methods of punishment then in use.[37]

Several of Bentham's particular suggestions in his *A View of the Hard Labour Bill* are of interest for the way they foreshadow elements of his later plans, including the role of vocational and religious instruction, the collection of criminological data, considerations of inspection, and the division of criminals into various classes (B iv.17–18, 29, 27). But what marks this work as a real advance and the beginnings of Bentham's mature penal thought is his admonition to the "Utopian speculator" who "unwarrantably presumes, that a man's conduct . . . *will* quadrate with his duty, or vainly regrets that it will *not* so" (B iv.12). Here, Bentham is establishing a standard regarding the principles of institutional design, a standard explicitly set against the example of More. He will not make claims about human conduct that do not have a clear warrant in human interests. "Economy" and "morality" depend on the mastery of interest and incentive by philosophers as well as administrators.

Bentham's Total Institutions

Bentham's most important and substantial work on incarceration related to his several ill-fated attempts to build a Panopticon prison of his own design. Many readers will be familiar with the Panopticon, at least in outline, and this chapter does not dwell on the particulars of how "inspection" of the inmates was to work, the circular layout of the cells, the single warden spying on inmates with his lamp and one-way screens, or any of the other details that stick so vividly in the mind. The aim of this section is to elucidate elements of the Panopticon that have been less recognized or not recognized at all but that bear directly on important tendencies in Bentham's penal thought.

Bentham's Panopticon was a paradigmatic example of what Erving Goffman termed a "total institution."[38] Goffman's total institutions share a certain "family resemblance" in their organizational characteristics but fill distinct social roles.[39] Indeed, from his earliest proposals, Bentham proposed the Panopticon not only as a prison but as a hospital, an asylum, a school, and, more generally, a tool for experiments in social engineering.[40] While many readers have treated the later passages suggesting panoptic schools and seraglios as a sort of jeu d'esprit, Bentham devoted considerable time and energy to panoptic projects beyond the prison, and even his late *Constitutional Code* carries the telltale marks of the principle of inspection.[41]

The first and most familiar use of the Panopticon design was as a penitentiary. This was proposed by Bentham as early as 1787 and the subject of a decades-long practical effort to secure funding and support for its realization.[42] The main feature of the Panopticon prison was to have been what Bentham termed the "inspection principle"—the idea that as there would be no way to know whether an inspector was observing at any given time, prisoners would have to behave at all times as if the inspector was watching them. The internalized feeling of being watched makes inspection omnipresent (B iv.44–45).

The usefulness of a prison building that promises such levels of control over the inmate seems obvious, and Bentham savors the completeness with which the Panopticon can accomplish the aims of punishment. Constant labor in a building whose form offers itself as the perfect "manufactory" will create "inward reformation" through the ordering of behavior in those who enter it and provide exemplary images for public consumption (B iv.168, 49fn). And the potential for extracting the labor power of inmates suggests the salutary ways that labor can serve as a variable, commensurable, and frugal punishment (see B iv.142–44).

The next form of total institution designed by Bentham was presented as a solution to the problem of pauperism. Bentham referred to this application of his plan as the "Industry House" or "pauper Panopticon." Although less well-known than the prison design, the two institutions could be seen as a sort of family, "the Panopticon in both its branches—the prisoner branch and the pauper branch" (B xi.103).[43] The aim of incarcerating in the case of punishment is familiar from earlier penal thought, including Bentham's own work. Bentham's use of incarceration in the case of "indigence" is less familiar.

In Bentham's social thought, "poverty . . . is the natural, the primitive, the general, and the unchangeable lot of man,"[44] while the condition of leisure ("opulence") is an "exception." The necessary conjunction between labor and the creation of wealth might as well be described by the biblical adage: "By the sweat of your brow you shall eat." Living at subsistence levels (poverty) is a natural condition, but being unable to support oneself to subsistence level ("indigence") is a threat to the lives of the impoverished and therefore a significant source of pain. To starve the indigent when things might be otherwise is therefore, in effect, to punish them for being poor.[45] Bentham returns more than once to the relation between poor relief and punishment. A key reason (perhaps, it will turn out to be *the* key reason) to provide poor relief is to ensure "the security of the affluent"[46] by removing the motive for crimes against property. Poor relief is thus a form of indirect legislation.[47]

The vision of incarceration presented in the plan for a "system of Industry Houses" is like that of the prison Panopticon. At the heart of the design is a location where the connection between the labor of the indigent and their subsistence can be monitored and "secured."[48] Only people who work deserve to eat, but no man deserves to starve— therefore, it makes sense to ensure that people work to ensure that they do not starve. This logic is behind the "work before eat" principle. Paupers are to be fed after they have worked off the equivalent value of their food.[49]

"The limits to power," Bentham writes, "are the limits to responsibility."[50] With the Industry House, society takes responsibility for the sustenance of the lowest of its members, but it also demands the power to ensure the results it desires. The Panopticon, as a specialized device for the manufacturing of power over bodies and minds, is the perfect tool for such a task. Rather than the "short-sighted eye of false humanity" that recommends lenience for the delinquent and handouts for the poor, the Panopticon is a philanthropic method of making both crime and poverty rarer, or at the very least less eligible.[51]

The Industry Houses function as a "net-work,"[52] introducing a banking system, a coordinated labor market, a site for unified medical records, a national identification system, a centralized postal service, and much more.[53] Bentham, who had read the great debates about centralization stimulated by Jacques Neckar, Jakob Friedrich von Bielfeld, and others, began to see the Panopticon not merely as a building but as a site of police power, in both eighteenth-century senses of the word—a site beneficial for both the maintenance of security and for the optimal use of the state's forces.[54]

The pauper Panopticon has elements of both direct and indirect intervention in behavior. To a large extent, what would be mandated for a pauper by Bentham's Poor Law is very similar to what a delinquent would have to undergo in Bentham's version of a penitentiary bill. Bentham insists, however, that it is not a form of punishment. It is an indirect intervention to prevent crime and "mischief" in the future. He does not deny that the very same technique may be used on both a felon and a pauper, but he denies that the same technique has the same social meaning.[55] Given Bentham's fondness for nonpenal forms of incarceration, this slipperiness in Bentham's definition of punishment has important consequences for understanding his theory of the prison. In the Industry House, direct and indirect legislative interventions and punitive techniques for nonpunitive ends seem to cohabit under the same roof.

Bentham's third total institution is his planned school, the "Chrestomathia" (a neologism meaning "useful knowledge"). From Bentham's earliest plans for penal incarceration, he foresaw both vocational and religious education as elements in the reformatory project (B iv.18). The pauper Panopticon, as discussed below, had a full educational complement for training the destitute children who would work there. Long after any hope for the political future of either Panopticon had passed, Bentham conceived of yet another educational use for his inspection house. In the "chrestomathic" school, the "monitorial" Lancaster-Bell system could be combined with the architecture of the "inspection principle" and a specially designed curriculum to ensure useful education at low cost to a growing middle class.[56]

Although not as explicitly carceral as his other projects (Bentham does not specify barred doors or indicate a protocol in case of escapees), the school must be included in the account of Bentham's total institutions, if only for his insistence that by building a panoptic school "security is *maximized*, and rendered entire," eliminating the distance between the teacher's eye and the student's behavior.[57] Education is also worthy of its own location on the spectrum of interventions. The usefulness of carceral architecture for instruction relates to two of Bentham's examples of indirect legislation, "the power of instruction" and "the power of education" (B i.567–70). The school is a site of legislative intervention, but it is on the other end of that spectrum from punishment. The lawmaker may—indeed, should—make use of the school curriculum to both promulgate the laws and to shape the students' knowledge of the world in such a way that they are inclined to follow them (B i.567–70; cf. B i.157–63). Education, as an ideal, is intervention without pain.

THE TECHNIQUE OF PANOPTIC INCARCERATION

One of the most famous aspects of the panopticon is what Bentham called the principle of inspection and Michel Foucault immortalized more generally as "panopticism"—the idea that the knowledge that one is always potentially under surveillance leads one to internalize the expectations of the watcher. Bentham was proud of the way in which the Panopticon exercises absolute power over the bodies of inmates. Through inspection, the master of the building controls "authority so much exceeding anything that has been hitherto signified by *despotic*" (B iv.63).[58] The power of observation is the power to stifle "dispositions unfavorable to security," including those of "vigour and courage" (B iv. 142). The common goal of this discipline across every application of the inspection idea is to cause the inmate "to be industrious."[59] But this characteristic, what Foucault termed the production of "docile bodies" through the application of a "new mode of power," is only one of the many "advantages" that Bentham identified in his prison design, and for Bentham, it was not even the most important advantage.

For Bentham, the most important process that took place in a panoptic prison was not corporal; it was intellectual. The Panopticon inculcated a form of self-government in its inhabitants, teaching them the art of managing themselves by teaching them to recognize both their own interests and the most efficient way to pursue them and by realigning their interests to better fit the demands of social life. The Panopticon is therefore as much a model of social reform as it is a site of penal discipline.

In the *Panopticon Letters*, Bentham identifies three "joint purposes of *punishment*": securing the body of the inmate (control), reforming the conduct of the inmate (ultimately through labor),[60] and "pecuniary economy" (see, e.g., B iv.9, 17; B i.424–31). When Bentham weighs these three principal purposes against one another, he finds that "the very existence of the system" of incarceration depends largely on economy. This is not only a question of mere pounds and pence—economy is closely related to the concept of penal frugality traced out above. For the prison to be run *economically* means to administer no harm that is not necessary and to provide no pleasure that does not produce an adequate profit. Once again, frugality slips between the sense of cost saving and the sense of conceptual efficiency, and the Panopticon excels in both senses (B iv.47; cf. B i.424).

It is not the arrangement of brick walls and iron bars that produces economy, and it is not even the method of central inspection, per se. The engine of frugality in the Panopticon is the organizational structure of contract management.[61] Contract management appears alongside the inspection principle in the earliest Panopticon texts, and it remained a crucial element of the plan until Bentham's death.[62] The basic premise was that a contractor would bid on the right to run the Panopticon and would be entitled to a portion of the profits.[63] The profit motive would lead the administrator of the prison to look for efficiency gains in every place he could, and carefully designed checks, such as high fines for the death of inmates, would make sure he did not cut corners too far.[64] The "punishment" of financial loss combines with the "reward" of profit to direct the conduct of the official.

In essence, the economy of the Panopticon derived from what Bentham saw as a perfect balance between the tremendous control over costs allowed for by the Panopticon's delivery of power over the laborer and the checks on avarice provided by adequate publicity. The architecture of the building would allow transparency, both in the views of the cells and in the openness of the central inspection shaft to the outside world. This meant that the contractor could design a business plan based around a monopoly on labor at or just below the cost of subsistence wages, but his treatment of the prisoners, the behavior of his staff, and the content of his bookkeeping would all be open to salutary scrutiny (B iv.47–48, 127–28).[65] Bentham was confident that with the correct incentive structure, the private interests of the parties and their duties as public officers could always be made to align.[66]

Bentham wrote at the end of a century that had seen the abuses of private contracts finally lose ground to nascent structures of bureaucratic oversight.[67] Consequently, he knew his support of private contract management was a minority position even among the most devoted theorists of the new political economy. Bentham explicitly took aim at the very thinker who had first opened his eyes to the possibilities of market efficiency and accused Adam Smith of making contract management into a "hobgoblin."[68] Although sometimes described as a theorist of mistrust, Bentham fundamentally believed "it is only by accident that private and public interest are at variance."[69] Contract management and the architectural design of the Panopticon itself combine "to join interest with duty," where the profit motive of the administrator serves the "aim of the act," that is to say, frugal management (B iv.125).

This "interest-duty principle" does not only apply to the manager; it applies equally to the managed. The "end" of the inmate is "the extraction of labour, to as great a value as may be" consistent with health and custom. (Bentham greatly resented mandatory rest on Sundays.)[70] This, as far as the total institution is concerned, is the "duty" of the inmate. The warden will use the inducement of pleasure and the threat of pain to make the inmate's interest align with this duty. This process is a form of socialization and interest formation. While the contractor gains a profit from the labor of the workman, "the moral habits of the workman himself will in the same proportion be receiving improvement from the same cause."[71] The Panopticon serves the interests of the manager even as it corrects the interests of the managed.

The role of the Panopticon in reeducating interest might seem surprising. An underlying element of Bentham's moral theory is often thought to be that people are the best judges of their own interests.[72] As was noted above, however, interest itself is mutable for Bentham. It is closely tied to the ability of an agent to correctly discern and calculate consequences.[73] Bentham accepts the reality of situated, motivated reasoning and knows that different agents will calculate their interests differently based on external factors such as age and wealth.[74] This has important implications for how Bentham understands the behavior of his inmates. "To be engrossed by the present moment is among the characteristics of that lowest class of individuals" who are likely to populate the Panopticon (B iv.140). The lowest classes reason about consequences in a limited way; that is what led them onto the "path of delinquency" in the first place. The Panopticon can train them, using the tools of punishment and reward, into understanding how to both calculate consequences more directly and how to work toward delayed gratification via "projects of productive industry and innocent enjoyment" (B iv.140).

The pauper Panopticon offers more evidence of these aims. Its additional functions, or "collateral uses," include a "poor man's loan office," which would offer microfinance services in place of pawnbrokers, banking facilities amenable to impoverished clientele, and remittance services so that both inmates and other laborers of the pauper class might be enabled to save and send their wages rather than keep and spend them.[75] The wage structure in the pauper Panopticon even carried with it forced savings mechanisms to create sufficient capital for the pauper inmates to become self-sufficient.[76]

The project of the Panopticon is thus a project of reforming interest. Labor does not only offset costs in the service of economy. "The habit of industry is a source of plenty and happiness," and insofar as the Panopticon creates industriousness, it creates welfare.[77] The Panopticon allows its managers to create a constant conjunction between certain concepts in the minds of inmates. Relief, liberty, and all other long-term goals are connected to labor. Personal identity and personal worth are connected to productivity. In Bentham's vision of the Panopticon "low wages would thus be, and be seen to be, the punishment—the natural punishment—of bad character." Bentham calls this the Panopticon's "advantage in point of morality," that it makes value visually manifest in a way certain to operate on the minds of the prisoners and the public.[78]

A related advantage of the Panopticon as a form of behavioral intervention is the sterile environment it provides for the fabrication of certainty. Inside the building's walls, particular causes (work) always lead to certain effects (reward). Bentham more than once refers to the Panopticon as the ideal experimental chamber for any number of fanciful ends, but this mastery of cause and effect is directed to one goal above all other.[79] Whether one refers to the managerial aim of the Panopticon as an education in acquisitiveness or refers more bluntly to an "antechamber of the market economy," the form of practical reason taught in the Panopticon is that of a rational actor in a competitive market.[80]

Bentham's Panopticons can thus be said to be frugal in two senses. They use the least resources while maximizing production, but they are also devoted to producing frugal behavior in their inmates.[81] The aim of the Panopticon is the production of *self-government,* actors who police their own behavior in a manner befitting their self-interest. The art of "self-government," Bentham writes, is the fundamental content of ethics, while legislation is the art of the whole community's government.[82] The correct interpretation of means, ends, consequences, and interests (government, correctly construed) is thus the ultimate aim of all legislative intervention, direct or indirect. Nudges and prison cells arrive at the same outcome.

Viewed from the aspect of the broader history of prison theory, Bentham appears at the other end of a process begun by More's penological appropriation of slave labor. Bentham does not privilege "reform" in his theory of the aims of punishment, but he does view a certain type of behavior, or a certain model of practical reasoning, as best from the perspective of aggregate public utility and the public good. Incarceration, whether as punishment or as poor relief, is a site of the inculcation of this practical reasoning. The final achievement of Bentham's prisons is the creation of a connection between labor and reward in the minds of the prisoners, paupers, and the public.

In earlier models of the education/incarceration spectrum, incarceration was a corrective to be supplemented by the power of social custom.

From Protagoras, through Plato, and in More, citizens were to be formally educated by parents and teachers; informally educated through mechanisms of shame, praise, and blame; and, in the case of misdeeds, corrected through punishment. Bentham's institutional model provides for the first and the third cases of intervention, but Bentham does not envision an informal aspect to social control. All interventions in behavior take place through the medium of the law. This aspect of Bentham's theory is fundamentally Hobbesian—sovereign power "upon the principle of utility, can never be other than fiduciary."[83] And while the sovereign's power *within* the medium of law is theoretically limitless, where "the thunders of the law prove impotent, the whispers of simple morality can have but little influence."[84]

In Plato and More, the law was to be minimal, and social coercion, maximal. Incarceration was the rare moment when intervention was required. In Bentham, social coercion can be neither relied upon nor trusted, and intervention must take place not only at the moment of correction but continuously, through the indirect modes of legislation. Neither Plato nor More intended incarceration to stand on its own. The idea of the prison always existed in tandem with a larger vision of law and society. But for Bentham, the use of "private ethics" is not directly available to the liberal legislator, so the interface between the rationality of the prison and the rationality of everyday life must be accomplished some other way. The final section of this chapter examines how the total institutions described by Bentham fit into his broader social theory.

BENTHAM'S THEORY OF CLASS AND LIBERAL INCARCERATION

The first two sections of this chapter have presented a general account of Bentham's theory of incarceration, from its relation to his utilitarian theory of punishment to the technique of behavioral correction. The last section attempts to draw some lessons about what Bentham called the "advantage point in morality" created by penal labor and contrasts Bentham's version of carceral political philosophy with the earlier versions treated in this book. For Bentham, labor is not only the sign of a stable society, as it was in More—it is the marker for a particular attitude toward rationality, cause and effect: that effort begets reward and that those who have "earned" property can expect to enjoy it. Prison labor is implicated in a whole set of relations between utility, property, and class—relations that ultimately stand behind Bentham's entire logic of intervention.

BETWEEN REHABILITATION AND SOCIAL ENGINEERING

For most of the thinkers studied in this book, the simplest and most direct connection between institutions of correction and the broader society was the ideal of reform—the rehabilitation and reintegration of inmates and their return to society. Bentham often praises the reformative aspect of the Panopticon. Inspection, "the only effective instrument of reformative management," aims to cure delinquents of their ailment (chiefly, idleness) rather than to cast them out of society as transportation does (B iv.175; cf. 186n). There is "no trade that could be carried on in this state of thraldom, but could be carried on with at least equal advantage in a state of liberty" (B iv.55). In the plans for the pauper Panopticon, Bentham affirms that in the case of those consigned to the system as suspected paupers, "the primary object will [be], because it ought to be, to restore them to society."[85] The inmate is released on probation, and his name published in the "Employment Gazette" for prospective employers to peruse.

In this vein, Bentham's deeper ambivalence about the released penal inmate is worthy of some attention. At the end of his term, "after a long seclusion, the convict is once more turned adrift into society." His "former connexions are . . . dissolved"; his prospects of employment, dismal (B. iv.21–22). Bentham offers two solutions to the problem of reintegration—one is to institute a system of "good behavior" certificates to mollify prospective employers, and the other is impressment into the army or navy. Despite the repeated mention of reform as one of the essential elements of punishment, and despite the protocols for probation and release, it is not certain that Bentham envisions a return to society as the standard outcome of incarceration. In the passage above about trades carried on in liberty, Bentham goes on to say that "both parties would probably find their account in continuing their manufacturing connexion" (B iv.55). That is to say, a new position for the recently released convict would be found back in the Panopticon. From the very beginning of his carceral project, Bentham is not sure that it will be realistic to expect the return of the convict to an unmonitored civic life—such a scenario may require effects that do not have adequate causes. It is a hope that verges on the utopian.

This feature, that the inmate may choose or be forced to choose to stay in the Panopticon after his sentence is over, returns repeatedly throughout the texts on incarceration. Bentham sets a series of varying (but invariably stringent) conditions for release. In the case of the Panopticon prison, this means impressment into the army or navy or finding a householder to post a fifty-pound bond. Bentham recognizes that many (even most) inmates will be unable to obtain such a sum and suggests that they be made to enter a "subsidiary establishment," also a Panopticon (B iv.166).[86] In unpublished drafts of the Panopticon Bill, Bentham named this building the "Metasylum" and called for its terms to last no less than a year, to be renewed annually (UC 119.154).[87] The prisoner thus becomes a "Metasylum man," entering a new system of labor exploitation (UC 119.222).[88] Bentham requires a similar bond from a "responsible Housekeeper" in the case of paupers released from an Industry House, though the probationary period is only a year.[89]

The more one looks, the more all-encompassing Bentham's conception of the panoptic system becomes. Bentham divides the inhabitants of the pauper Panopticon into "two correspondent classes": the "*indigenous*," those who are "born into the House"; and "the Secessionists," born without.[90] This is connected to Bentham's unpublished plans for a baby Panopticon, or "Paedotrophion," and subsequent Panopticons that would see a child grow from infant to adult, working all the way (UC 107.54ff).[91] Bentham is not insensitive to the way in which his conception ruptures the relations between parents and children and "bursts asunder" the "closest ties" of family.[92] The objection to the Panopticon as a cause of "natal alienation" is uncannily close to Orlando Patterson's definition of slavery as social death. Bentham's response is that pauperism and the cure for pauperism are both matters of choice (the same could be said of crime) and that given the plurality of goods, "there must be a subordination had amongst ends."[93]

From the picture that emerges from the various discussions of life after the Panopticon, it seems clear that rehabilitation is not the point of incarceration. Bentham might, in principle, agree with More's determination that penal labor can "destroy vices and save men,"[94] but he has a very different view of the "usefulness" of incarceration from More. If the law must directly intervene in human affairs, as in the case of the creation of "artificial consequences" through punishment, it is best to do this in such a way that as much is gained by the intervention as is possible. One gain in efficiency is the yoking of interests to duties through the profit motive. Another such gain is the inculcation of motives, the training of minds to see profit and perceive the conjunction of cause and effect, in a new way. In addition to these cognitive achievements, there is an additional gain to utility from the Panopticon hiding in plain sight—the efficient use of excess capacity in the labor supply and the creation of laborers where there were none before.

Bentham himself refers to the population of Panopticon inmates as the "stock of hands" or "species of Cattle," whose "capacity" would yield profit to be "reaped."[95] This aspect of the Panopticon is the turning of "idle hands" into active hands.[96] "Idle hands" is a category with wide catchment, from the temporarily unemployed pauper, to the mistrusted former sex worker, to the convicted delinquent, who is, after all, only another species of unexploited labor.[97] Most important, at least in the case of the pauper Panopticon, is the species known as "unripe hands," indigent minors, who have not yet been trained and can legally be treated as "apprentices" without any right to a wage. It is from this class that much of the profit of nonpenal Panopticons will be derived.[98]

The question of underexploited labor capacity is an empirical one, and Bentham was well aware that if too many of the poor were disabled, or too many convicts were unproductively insane, incarceration by Panopticon would cease to be economical. For this reason, his project was deeply invested in the collection of statistical knowledge of populations. Bentham attempted to analyze flawed data from the nascent demographic experiments of the Royal Society and ultimately tried to create his own data set through the distribution of a "Pauper Population Table" to be filled out and returned, parish by parish.[99] His interest in the labor market as an empirical phenomenon positions Bentham as a pioneering figure in a shift from the general debate about the organization of the *forces* of the state to the understanding of those forces as answerable to the statistical sciences, chief among them political economy. The Panopticon is thus not only an attempt to produce self-governing citizens; it is also an experiment in what Foucault called "governmentality," the measurement and arrangement of society according to the analysis of population-level data and the postulation of an empirical mean.

Aside from a commitment to a certain empirical method, Bentham's carceral scheme carries with it a series of additional social-theoretical assumptions. Bentham subscribes to a broadly Lockean view of the creation of value through labor. "In every country, the whole stock of existing wealth . . . is the *product* of the labour of individuals, deriving their subsistence from their own labor."[100] This "class of persons maintained by their own labour" is the lynchpin of social and political life. Neither the wealthy, who are exceptional in not having to work, nor the poor, who are "hangers on," provide any model for behavior. Bentham thinks it self-evident that people will not work if they do not have to. Therefore, making industrious behavior "more eligible" is necessary to avert "the destruction of society."[101] In the context of a Poor Law, the key is to create a system of relief that prevents paupers from choosing to be indigent.

The role of labor, who works doing what and how, forms a focal point of Bentham's social thought. A person's place in the labor force is a more important identifier than almost anything else, including her legal status. "The legal distinction between felons and non-felons is . . . little more than nominal" while the difference between being employed (especially employed in an "avowed" profession) and unemployed suggests "a habit interwoven with the very texture of a man's life."[102] The importance of identity to labor is such that a "universal Register of employment" is as essential a statistical tool as national identification papers. In lieu of such publicly available information, Bentham suggests that a person should be considered unemployed and subject to consignment into the Panopticon system unless they can prove otherwise.[103] Given his dismissal of both the idle rich and the hungry poor, Bentham seems to want to bring the whole of the population into the middle category, those who work for their sustenance. This can also be understood in psychological terms—the middle classes, those who support themselves through labor, exhibit most clearly the connection between labor and reward that Bentham sees as the essence of prosocial behavior. Both Bentham's picture of interest and duty and his understanding of the structure of society are rooted in the middle class.

The idea that class and utility may go hand in hand was not unique to Bentham. In the famous words of the Declaration of the Rights of Man, "Social distinctions may be founded only upon the general good [*l'utilité commune*]." With the example of class in mind, we might can say that one way in which the Panopticons produce utility for society is by reproducing society itself—its distinctions, its divisions, and its classes. If, for whatever reason, upper-class prisoners ("decayed gentility hands") make their way into the pauper Panopticon, they are to have separate treatment, meals, and maintenance.[104] This is largely because of the role of what Bentham called "expectation" in the construction of social life "Expectation! . . . Expectation is the basis of every proprietary right: it is this affords whatever reason there can be for giving a thing to one man rather than another. Keep the current of expectation inviolate, in these words are contained the quintessence of everything which utility can dictate on this extensive ground."[105] Expectations play a fundamental role in Bentham's utilitarian theory.[106] Because a person's expectations are drawn from the constitutive elements of her identity, violated expectations cause a great deal of pain and should be considered a significant threat to human security and thus to utility. Property and wealth are an important foundation of expectation, and the utilitarian legislator will need to treat those with property and wealth according to their expectation of how they should be treated (B i.308–309). Because presumably few wealthy people will end up incarcerated, it is "economical" to treat them as a class apart.

Such treatment would not be economical for the lower classes, who are expected to fill the Panopticons—these inmates will be delinquents, paupers, and especially children (B iv.140). It is no coincidence that all these categories of person share the general characteristic of an inability to reason completely. Bentham explicitly likens delinquents to children or the mentally ill (B iv.175). The expectations of a child, of course, do not need to be respected. The expectations of a child should be managed.

One way to manage expectations is through education, "the art of conducting man" toward well-being. Education is also "government in miniature: legislation and administration in miniature," and here, the question of management again breaks down along class lines.[107] In a remarkable excursus in his account of the pauper Panopticon, *Pauper*

Management Improved, Bentham gives what he describes as a sort of educational treatise, taking up the heretofore neglected question of education for the poor. Thinking of Rousseau, Bentham writes that rich are to be educated in and for distinction and competition. It is not, however, the task of the Panopticon to produce an Emile.[108]

Rich students learn through play, but the poor should have no play "but that of the best sort, which is work at the same time."[109] Bentham systematically dismisses everything from badminton to marbles. "There may be great hardship in disappointing and frustrating an appetite already created, there can be none in ordering matters so as to prevent the creation of it."[110] This is Bentham's crucial strategy for the education of the poor and for life in the panoptic institutions in general. The management of expectations is the optimal strategy for the production of utility. Managed correctly, the impoverished youth are "a vast mine of national wealth," and the "parentage of Plutus (Wealth) is no secret. He is the child of Earth by Labour . . . and Adam Smith for his head Genealogist."[111]

The logic of class maintenance is as important as that of subject formation for understanding the texts on the Panopticon. Simply put, the preexisting class system is favorable for utility, as Bentham understands it. "In the world at large, the inconveniences dependent on the unavoidable dominion of the rich over the poor are tempered at least, if not outweighed, by the advantages that are attendant on them."[112] Whether he is dividing paupers in "two classes with a firm and steady hand" or admitting the "superior importance" of education in the superior classes, Bentham uses incarceration as a sorting device, making distinct forms of behavioral intervention based on class identity.[113]

To attempt a structural comparison, class plays a similar role for Bentham to that played by shame in the classical and early modern theories of incarceration of Plato and More. It is an extant fact of social organization that Bentham incorporates into his institutions of correction. He does not need to legislate class ex nihilo but can make use of it as both a paradigm for social order and a parallel in the outside world for the practices within the Panopticon. Like shame, class turns out to play an important role in how practical reason situates individuals within the social structure, and Bentham recognizes the importance of class for the type of reasoning in which both direct and indirect legislation aim to intervene.

The concept of "expectation" is just as important here as it was to Plato's conception of shame in the *Laws*. There, shame was used to lead people to "expect" the social consequences of bad behavior. Here, inmates are led to expect and accept both a moral relation between labor and survival and to internalize that relationship. As important as docile bodies may be for the construction of class in the industrial age, from a strictly utilitarian perspective, industrious minds are even more important.

A conceivable objection to the account of Bentham's theory laid out above is that it has not done justice to the distinction between incarceration as punishment (the activity of the prison Panopticon) and other uses of incarceration (provision of relief, education). To adequately answer this objection, it is necessary to return to the question of the conceptual distinctness of punishment introduced above. Bentham's discussion of punishment varies between the ordinary sense of the term and his usage of the word to mean a particular form of legislative intervention. At one point, Bentham seems to acknowledge that what he might call an "instrument of discipline" would be generally called a "punishment," but methods of effectively compelling behavior are scarcer than the modes of inflicting pain (which are near infinite); therefore, modes of discipline/compulsion must be distinguished from punishments, *stricto sensu*.[114]

Bentham himself foresaw the sort of interpretation that confused his institutions of compulsion for institutions of punishment. Confinement in the pauper Panopticon "is no punishment—no injustice—but a measure partly of humanity, partly of security." Bentham's reason for this is that the pauper Panopticon "does not administer [pain] with any of those views with which punishment is administered."[115] It does not aim to deter, either the inmate or others. "This may be the result—and happy it is . . . when it is really the effect, but it is not the object in view."[116] In effect, Bentham is saying that the effect may be to punish, but if that is not the intention, it cannot be called punishment.

Bentham sensed the implausibility of this argument but could not quite get himself free of it. "What is it then, if not a punishment? . . . It is a measure of simple precaution and security, operating indirectly to the benefit of him who is the subject of it . . . instituted and observed *for* the benefit of community at large."[117] This sentence could just as well apply to the prison Panopticon, with the replacement of "operating directly" for "indirectly." Here, it is the poor who are "froward children" "in a state of wardship," the same comparisons Bentham used to justify coercive force applied to delinquents through punishment.[118] Lastly, the difference between incarceration as punishment and as poor relief is that the latter "has no limit." The very instant a pauper obtains "a means of lively-hood," he is released. Given Bentham's enthusiasm for "metasylums" and other paracarceral institutions meant to keep inmates within the panoptic system, the "lack of limit" to incarceration envisioned by Bentham gains a darker double meaning.

Bentham himself asked, "as to the means of producing economy, where then is the difference, between a House of Correction [and] an industry house?"[119] In the end, the difference is only a procedural one—the former is housed with those who have committed a transgression in the past, and the latter with those who, though under compulsion, have not yet transgressed. Given that in both cases Bentham entertains the idea of incarcerating people who have not yet undergone a trial, even this question of time, a "before" and "after," begins to break down.[120] The pain produced by these two interventions, whatever the intention, seems to be of the same nature. Bentham fulminates that such objections emerge from a demagogic obsession with "liberty" and an unfounded fear of "inquisition."[121] But the unintended collapse of the prison/jail/welfare distinction in Bentham's conceptual scheme seems almost prophetic considering a similar collapse visible in contemporary societies. As critics of the prison note, there is often little real difference between pretrial detention and punishment in its conditions or social effects, and the connection between welfare systems and prison systems is equally stark.[122] This is not to say that we should read Bentham in light of subsequent developments in incarceration but rather to stress to what extent the later difficulties of the modern prison form are visible already at its inception.

Bentham's theory of punishment is really part of a broader theory of frugal intervention in behavior. In punishment, as in law more generally, Bentham aspires to the least amount of meddling needed to get the desired change in interests. The form and character of this meddling, however, is almost entirely governed by class. The lowest classes will undergo incarceration, whether "penal" or "charitable," while the middle and upper classes will be trained both through schooling and through the "invisible chain" of the laws themselves.

CONCLUSION: BENTHAM, CLASS, AND THE PLATONIC TRADITION IN INCARCERATION

The emergence of class from the background to the foreground of Bentham's Panopticon plans necessitates a final reappraisal of the "system of rationality" operating at the nexus of labor, incarceration, behavior, and frugality.[123] This chapter has focused on frugality as a crucial conceptual theme in Bentham's prison theory, but frugality is only a formal quality—it requires content (frugality of what?). Above, this content was described by the shorthand "pain" as the thing that was to be minimized to maximize happiness or "utility."

Upon closer examination, Bentham's idea of utility has "four subordinate objects—Subsistence. Abundance. Equality. Security."[124] Bentham has no doubt that "the most important object is security. . . . When security and equality are in opposition, there should be no hesitation: equality should give way" (B i.302, 311). Security, and security of expectation, depends on "the fixed and durable possession" of property (B i.307). Property itself is "an established expectation," and the preservation of property through law is "the most splendid triumph of humanity over itself" (B i.309).

Bentham knew that under conditions of scarcity, where "subsistence" is threatened, the poor will be tempted to take from the rich; "and in proportion as endeavours to this purpose are employed, or believed to be intended to be employed . . . security . . . is diminished."[125] It is this impulse that lies behind his Poor Law proposals. The "economy" of the Panopticon is ultimately in the service of property as security.[126] At every step of Bentham's reasoning, the institution of incarceration was tested and honed for frugality of cost, frugality of pain, and optimization of outputs. In the end, this logic of frugality results in a massive intervention in the service of a particular notion of security. It is one class, the property-owning middle class, who both produce the most utility through the entrepreneurial use of their holdings and have the most to lose (in terms of violated expectations) by giving them up. The entire carceral apparatus of the penal and pauper Panopticons is justified by the need to keep this property safe.

Behind the spectrum of legislative interventions, from punishment to legislative architecture, lies a consistent justification of greater political intervention in the lives of one class in the name of lesser intervention in those of another class. This is the suggestive paradox in Bentham's vision of the prison—the best way to ensure the frugal nonintervention is to intervene appropriately via institutions that impress the modes and methods of efficiency and productivity on the minds and the bodies of the delinquent, the poor, and the young.[127]

This population-directed aspect of the Panopticon, epitomized by Bentham's desire to house an entire class of people in his "Houses" from birth until death, shows an essential continuity between Bentham's theory and contemporary penal institutions. Bentham theorized how the same legal justification (i.e., the pursuit of negative liberty or "security") could look different, applied across different strata of the population via different forms of direct and indirect intervention. This facet of liberal law is visible in a "carceral state" that continually imprisons the same sort of ("unproductive") person, while addressing other forms of intervention to "productive" class and status groups.

Foucault suggested, rather impishly, that the soul or subjectivity of the modern individual was invented to control the bodies of restive workers. Our analysis of early theories of rehabilitation and reform in Plato, Philo, and More shows that, even when they were concerned with the moral psychology of crime and the motivation for behavior, these thinkers did not treat the "soul" as something distinct from the totality of the social world. The "shame culture" that is described by Plato's *Laws*, the ideal ascetic communities of late antique Judaism and Christianity, and even the imaginary island nation of *Utopia*—these contexts imagined punishment as an intersubjective process, mediating between the soul and the community, without ever taking the perspective of an individual's "subjectivity." From this perspective, Bentham and the modern prison really do represent a turning point in the history of reformative reason. To understand utility as a matter of an individual's interest privileges the perspective of the subject as entirely distinct from the community—and presages a new form of penal subjectivity.

But the real aim of Bentham's project was the rationality of society, understood and analyzed *via* the rationality of individuals and using the heuristic of classes.[128] Punishment changes the rational interest of criminals: incapacitation attacks the physical power that accomplishes interest, deterrence raises "up an artificial interest" to outweigh the original interest, and reform "weakens" the original interest, changing how the agent calculates consequences. Bentham refers to this process of interest formation as the development of "moral habits."[129] In the Panopticon, "low wages would thus be, and be seen to be, the punishment—the natural punishment—of bad character."[130] The panoptic system reinforces a moral and social hierarchy based on Bentham's understanding of means-ends rationality.

Plato's ideal state in the *Laws* determined whom and how to incarcerate by reference to elite intellectual threats to the rule of reason. Thomas More's *Utopia* widened the scope of reformative confinement to the indigent and poor. Bentham's "own Utopia" contains elements of each approach. Penal incarceration in the Panopticon is largely directed at the poor, as a "class." But this is done in the name of reason. Bentham's final justification for his carceral intervention is that a certain understanding of rationality is conducive to the greatest happiness for the greatest number of people. This is, in the final analysis, still a justification in the name of a higher understanding of reason.

As we noted at the beginning of this chapter, one might have expected to find, in the writings of as systematic a thinker as Jeremy Bentham, some political justification for the panoptic project. But as we have now shown, Bentham's enthusiasm for the prison form had, like his predecessors in the Platonic reformative tradition, everything to do with the art of changing minds and very little to do with the correct form of regime. Bentham was farsighted in his conviction that interventions, what are now called laws and policies, would ultimately have to operate on the level of the population and demographic tendencies within it. He was more forthright than later architects of intervention in directing his carceral policy largely at a single class, the poor. The administration of punishment according to class has little to do, and is in fact at odds, with the formal equality of democratic citizens.

Bentham's work is a fitting close to the story of early theories of incarceration. He was premodern, even Platonic, in his ambition to design a comprehensive system of law, with a rational and ultimately a moral justification for every clause. But he also imagined a system of incarceration that both directly inspired two hundred years of penal policy to come and anticipated the "despotic" potential of incarceration to confine and "intervene" on entire social classes. Bentham demonstrates, as much as anyone can, the extent to which the prison before the Panopticon is still with us.

CONCLUSION

BENTHAM'S PANOPTICON PRISON defines the boundaries of three distinct penal eras. The first of these, the era of the prison before the Panopticon, has been the central subject of this book. The next era is the era of the Panopticon itself, and of the countless penitentiaries and reformatories around the world that modeled themselves after it. The final era is our own time, the time of the prison after the Panopticon. This third penal era is one of transnational penal populism, of the widespread abandonment of reformative punishment in favor of incapacitation or "warehousing," and of American mass incarceration.[1] To some observers, ours seems like the final era of the prison, conceptually if not politically. The liveliest debate among philosophers of incarceration today considers not what incarceration should look like but whether incarceration should exist at all.[2]

An insurmountable distance seems to separate the present moment from the early theories of incarceration explored in this book. Arguments akin to those of the Platonic reformative tradition have fallen out of fashion since the radical turn against paternalism and the general penal skepticism of the late twentieth century.[3] Democratic theories of incarceration today are more likely to recommend the abolition of the prison than to consider its justification.[4] It would be reasonable to conclude that the story of the prison before the Panopticon has very little to offer the prison after the panoptic era. But in these final pages, we will revisit the early philosophy of incarceration with the present condition of prisons and punishment firmly in mind. While the early history of prison theory holds no final answers to our present carceral dysfunction, it nevertheless ought to inform our efforts to punish better.

****

The Platonic reformative tradition, set as it is against the exotic backdrop of Plato's Magnesia or Thomas More's Utopia, seems far from the present and its penal problems. But at the heart of the Platonic approach to incarceration lies a simple conceptual standard, one that appealed to Plato, More, and Bentham alike: penal means, including incarceration, must fit penal ends. When imprisonment fails to do what it is meant to do, it is guilty of what M. M. McCabe called "institution begging."[5]

Plato and his followers thus sought to ascertain the best method for what they viewed as the correct ends of punishment: reformation and rehabilitation. Apart from the rare "incurable" criminal, the aims of Platonic imprisonment were first to change criminals' minds and second to deter them and others. Of course, none of the actual penal techniques proposed by Platonic theorists—whether dialectical education, penal labor, or panoptic interest management—is a plausible idea for contemporary punishment. But the philosophical standard to which these proposals held themselves is still both sound and valid. The Platonic tradition reminds us that the justificatory standard for imprisonment should remain high, especially considering the serious consequences of unjustified incarceration.[6] This standard poses a challenge to contemporary proponents of penal reform precisely because so many attempts at theorizing reformative imprisonment fail to clear the Platonic bar for penal justification.

The Platonic tradition of incarceration can be broadly summarized as investigating the "how" of incarceration—the technique, the aim, and even the architectural and procedural details of punitive confinement. The other major early tradition of prison thinking, that of popularly authorized imprisonment, is much more concerned with the "who" of punishment—who is imprisoned and who does the imprisoning. From Demosthenes onward, this approach distinguishes between two different types of punishment. The first, horizontal type is administered by democratic citizen equals who, according to Demosthenes, should strive to treat one another leniently, as befits fellow rulers. But Athenian democracy also grappled with the vertical axis of punishment—how to deal with the elite members of society who participate in democratic politics but may still pose a threat to popular rule. For Demosthenes incarceration is a harsh penalty. To violate the dignity of free citizens by placing them behind bars may be appropriate in the case of "vertical threats" from elites, but it is otherwise inappropriate for a community of free and equal citizens.

Contemporary political theorists find attractive the idea that punishment in a democratic society should focus on the generosity that citizen equals owe one another.[7] In this liberal-democratic context, as in Athens, incarceration is once again considered a harsh punishment.[8] But philosophers have been slower to adopt the second, vertical axis of Athenian penal ideology. Even advocates of a reformed prison system do not see incarceration as part of the arsenal of democratic rule, to be mobilized against restive and dangerous elites. This silence about vertical punishment is especially perplexing because incarceration today often functions vertically in the opposite sense—punishing the poor, minorities, and other marginalized populations.[9]

Thomas Hobbes further elucidates the ambiguities of popularly authorized incarceration. Hobbes's focus on physical liberty as the basis of the social contract between sovereigns and citizens explains why the deprivation of physical liberty is both a harsh and a reasonable punishment in a state founded on popular authorization. Hobbes took incarceration seriously, making it equivalent to capital punishment in terms of its consequences. His theory of physical liberty and freedom of choice point to prison as a possible tool to regulate the relationship between subjects who have broken the law and the sovereign who wants to reform them and make them obedient. This is Hobbes's proto-liberal ideal theory of incarceration as "all restraint of motion." Hobbes, like the Athenian democrats, identifies elite political crime, which threatens the equilibrium of the commonwealth, as the proper political context for such a harsh punishment.

Hobbes, however, moves beyond the Athenian approach to incarceration in his adaptation of horizontal and vertical forms of punishment to the sorts of massive, differentiated states that characterize modern societies. For Hobbes, all punishment is fundamentally vertical because punishment concerns the relationship of the sovereign and the subject, not the relationship of subject citizens to one another. The sovereign in a popularly authorized state nevertheless has good reason to tend toward leniency, all else being equal, because harsh punishments like incarceration rupture the social contract that grounds authorization. Further, Hobbes—like the Athenians—believes that the major threats to political order come largely from jealous and entitled elites, not from the impoverished citizens whose crimes are often those of circumstance and necessity. Ultimately Hobbes, like the Athenians, considers the question of equality before the law to be part of reason of state. According to this tradition, to treat poor and weak citizens and rich and powerful citizens alike is not justice; it is shortsightedness.

The Athenian model of horizonal and vertical forms of punishment, or the Hobbesian model of vertical punishment allotted differentially between elite crimes and crimes of the poor will be more or less attractive depending on how one conceives of the relationship between citizens and the state in a liberal democracy. But both challenge the present regime of liberal criminal law. This is not to say that it is impossible to imagine a liberal state that differentially incarcerated the infractions of the wealthy few instead of the impoverished many, while still maintaining rule of law.[10] Such a regime is clearly possible. After all, the contemporary penal system differentially punishes the poor, as well as racial and other subgroups within the population. The United States has witnessed a shift in these penal strategies over a period of decades, as have other democratic countries. The priorities of punishment are always contingent.

The tradition of popularly authorized imprisonment is univocal in insisting that our priorities be oriented around who is punished, as much as how. And the who in question should be the wealthy and powerful. The popularly authorized approach demands a war on tax evasion rather than a war on drugs. After all, the case for Athenian imprisonment with which we began this book was about wealthy deputies of the state who refused to pay their fair share of profits to the public coffers. In Athens, the misdeeds of the powerful were the proper grounds for the harsh punishment of incarceration.

Disfigured by the tendency to punish the poor and fragment the citizen body, incarceration as it exists in the United States and other liberal-democratic states stands in sharp contrast to this democratic tradition. As in the case of the Platonic reformative tradition, incarceration as widely practiced today falls short of the standards of these early attempts at prison thinking. But despite its necessary opposition to incarceration today, the popular authorization approach to incarceration is not inherently abolitionist. For Demosthenes and Hobbes, the idea of entirely eliminating a punishment like the prison was not a reasonable or desirable goal. Punishments, including incarceration, are tools that allow popularly authorized regimes to self-regulate. Unlike some abolitionists, then, the popular authorization tradition accepts the idea of a harsh punishment like incarceration in principle. Harsh punishment might be applied to both serious violent crime (premeditated murder, sexual assault) and to the crimes of the most powerful (tax evasion, election denial, fraud, corruption).

The aim of democratic incarceration, from this perspective, is not first and foremost the protection of private property, as Bentham and other voices have insisted. It is the preservation of political principles like equal voice, equal respect, and people power.[11] Today, in the United States, the use of incarceration is antithetical to all these values. The philosophy of the prison from before the Panopticon therefore pushes us to imagine a future of thinking about incarceration that rises to the moral challenges set by the past.

NOTES

ACKNOWLEDGMENTS

INDEX

.

NOTES

INTRODUCTION

1. By "prison" and "penal incarceration" this book will generally mean *only* punitive incarceration, that is, the use of imprisonment as a judicial sentence, as opposed to the custodial or coercive forms of incarceration that have existed at many times and places. This distinction dates to Roman law, and in modern scholarship, at least to Gotthold Bohne, *Die Freiheitsstrafe in den italienischen Stadtrechten des 12.–16. Jahrhunderts* (Leipzig: Leipziger Juristen-Fak., 1922). For the reasoning behind this usage, see below. For the history of the prison in perspective, see the introduction by the editors in Norval Morris and David J. Rothman, eds., *The Oxford History of the Prison: The Practice of Punishment in Western Society* (New York: Oxford University Press, 1997).

2. For the effects of mass incarceration on political equality, see Amy E. Lerman and Vesla M. Weaver, *Arresting Citizenship: The Democratic Consequences of American Crime Control,* Chicago Studies in American Politics (Chicago: University of Chicago Press, 2014); Andrew Dilts, *Punishment and Inclusion: Race, Membership, and the Limits of American Liberalism* (New York: Fordham University Press, 2014); and Peter Ramsay, "A Democratic

Theory of Imprisonment," in *Democratic Theory and Mass Incarceration,* ed. Albert Dzur, Ian Loader, and Richard Sparks (Oxford: Oxford University Press, 2016), 84–107.

3. The question of "how to punish justly" can have two meanings. Usually, it is taken to refer to the moral principles that justify the infliction of pain by an authority. In this book, we will be concerned with a more practical or material sense of "how," namely, "by what means?" Within the history of political philosophy, the evidence concerning incarceration is often wrapped up in discussions of the aims of punishment and other arguments more usually associated with the philosophy of punishment. The ambitions of the present study, however, are limited to the theoretical origins of a particular institutional form. We will frequently need to discuss philosophies of punishment, particularly the well-known contributions made to the genre by Plato and Bentham, but the analytical thrust of the argument will be at incarceration as a particular technique and political institution, not about the many problems, solutions, and controversies around the correct aims of punishment (reform, retribution, deterrence, etc.).

4. Edward M. Peters, "Prison before the Prison," in *The Oxford History of the Prison,* ed. Norval Morris and David J. Rothman (Oxford: Oxford University Press, 1997), 3–47. Recent work by Matthew Larsen, Julia Hillner, Guy Geltner, and others, to which we will refer throughout, has complicated this story without entirely refuting it. We should note that a growing chorus of scholars continues to challenge the standard eighteenth-century origin story for penal incarceration. Pieter Spierenburg traces the prison back to the workhouses of the sixteenth century. Petrus Cornelis Spierenburg, "Four Centuries of Prison History: Punishment, Suffering, the Body, and Power," in *Institutions of Confinement,* Publications of the German Historical Institute (Cambridge: Cambridge University Press, 1996), 17–35. And others have begun to push the story of penal incarceration back into the Middle Ages. See Guy Geltner, *The Medieval Prison: A Social History* (Princeton: Princeton University Press, 2008), which makes a strong case for incarceration as a "coherent experience" (p. 27) in late-medieval Italian city-states. The prisons he discusses there look very much like the Athenian prison discussed in Chapter 1. Despite the intriguing relation between such city-states and nascent early modern Republican theories of government, Geltner does not identify a guiding theory behind historical incarceration (see, e.g., p. 16). In Julia Hillner, *Prison, Punishment and Penance in Late Antiquity* (Cambridge: Cambridge University Press, 2015), the author finds traces of incarceration in late-imperial Roman law but admits that this is not the "autonomous, government run" institution (p. 351) with which the current book is

concerned. To this can be added Matthew Larsen's forthcoming work on early Christians and incarceration *Early Christians and Incarceration: A Cultural History* (New York: Oxford University Press, forthcoming), which, while not concerned with penal incarceration in the strict sense, helps to fill in an important piece of the story of how ideas about incarceration were transmitted from antiquity forward. For a broader perspective on the prison beyond Europe, see Mary Gibson, "Global Perspectives on the Birth of the Prison," *American Historical Review* 116, no. 4 (2011): 1040–63.

5. For the earliest recorded evidence of incarceration in the nonpunitive, broad sense, see J. Nicholas Reid, *Prisons in Ancient Mesopotamia: Confinement and Control until the First Fall of Babylon* (Oxford: Oxford University Press, 2022, ebook). See Reid's acknowledgment that in writing about Mesopotamian prisons, he is not discussing "the prison in the strict sense" (p. 45).

6. One crucial moment in the creation of this distinction was the work of John Howard, whose report *The Principal Prisons of England and Wales* (1777) helped to inspire Britain's Penitentiary Act of 1779 and served as inspiration for the young Jeremy Bentham.

7. The ambivalent status of harsh pretrial conditions seems to be a feature of even the most "advanced" correctional systems. See Peter Scharff Smith, "A Critical Look at Scandinavian Exceptionalism: Welfare State Theories, Penal Populism and Prison Conditions in Denmark and Scandinavia," in *Penal Exceptionalism? Nordic Prison Policy and Practice,* ed. Thomas Ugelvik and Jane Dullum (London: Routledge, 2012), 38–57. For detailed studies of prisons as sites of mortality, morbidity, and other forms of pretrial injustice, see Prison Policy Initiative, "Jails and Bail," accessed December 5, 2022, https://www.prisonpolicy.org/jails.html. For statistics about the significant role that nonpunitive jails play in mass incarceration, see Peter Wagner and Wendy Sawyer, "Mass Incarceration: The Whole Pie 2023," Prison Policy Initiative, accessed August 1, 2023, https://www.prisonpolicy.org/reports/pie2023.html. For these reasons, contemporary critics of incarceration pointedly reject the prison/jail distinction. See, for instance, Angela Y. Davis, Gina Dent, Erica R. Meiners, and Beth E. Richie, *Abolition. Feminism. Now.,* Abolitionist Papers Series (Chicago: Haymarket Books, 2022, ebook), 132–37.

8. I borrow this language from Demetra Kasimis, *The Perpetual Immigrant and the Limits of Athenian Democracy,* Classics after Antiquity (Cambridge: Cambridge University Press, 2019), 9.

9. Perhaps the earliest literary consideration of the meaning of incarceration, the Hymn to Nungal (discussed in Reid, *Prisons in Ancient Mesopotamia*) clearly denotes the prison (*ennuĝ*) as a sort of discursive site (see

especially pp. 134–38). So too the many Christian martyrologies set against the backdrop of a Roman *carcer* helped to fix the importance of chains and confinement in late-antique Christian theology. Such moments, and other literary considerations of prisons, are certainly discursive sites, but their political-theoretical content can be retrieved only tentatively and with great difficulty. For this reason (as well as a lack of expertise and a paucity of space), I have not included them in this book, which limits itself to texts that are either explicitly political, explicitly philosophical, or explicitly both.

10. For the philosophical proponents of prison abolition, see, inter alia, Angela Y. Davis, *Are Prisons Obsolete?* (New York: Seven Stories, 2003); Steve Martinot, "Toward the Abolition of the Prison System," *Socialism and Democracy* 28, no. 3 (September 2, 2014): 189–98; Allegra M. McLeod, "Envisioning Abolition Democracy," *Harvard Law Review* 132, no. 6 (April 2019): 1613–49; and Dorothy E. Roberts, "Abolition Constitutionalism," *Harvard Law Review* 133, no. 1 (November 2019): 1–122. For a systematic nonabolitionist response, see Tommie Shelby, *The Idea of Prison Abolition* (Princeton, NJ: Princeton University Press, 2022).

11. For the particular and recurrent nature of physical liberty as a problem in the history of political philosophy, see Efraim Podoksik, "One Concept of Liberty: Towards Writing the History of a Political Concept," *Journal of the History of Ideas* 71, no. 2 (2010): 219–40.

12. For the autonomous authority of Athenian juries, see Danielle Allen, *The World of Prometheus* (Princeton, NJ: Princeton University Press, 2000).

13. See *Leviathan* XXI.7, 139. Page references will be to Thomas Hobbes, *Leviathan: With Selected Variants from the Latin Edition of 1668,* ed. Edwin Curley (Indianapolis: Hackett, 1994).

14. *L.* XIV.8, 82.

15. See *De Cive* XIII.16, 152. Page numbers and translation from Thomas Hobbes, *Hobbes: On the Citizen,* ed. Richard Tuck, trans. Michael Silverthorne (Cambridge: Cambridge University Press, 1998).

16. For a forceful exploration of this tension, see George Kateb, "Punishment and the Spirit of Democracy," *Social Research* 74, no. 2 (2007): 269–306. See also the discussion of Hobbes in Keally D. McBride, *Punishment and Political Order* (Ann Arbor: University of Michigan Press, 2007).

17. For the emergence of Platonizing ecclesiastical prisons in late antiquity, see Hillner, *Prison, Punishment, and Penance.* This process is briefly treated at the beginning of Chapter 3.

18. On this aspect of Bentham, see Spencer J. Weinreich, "Panopticon, Inc.: Jeremy Bentham, Contract Management, and (Neo)Liberal Penality," *Punishment and Society* 23, no. 4 (October 1, 2021): 497–514.

19. As recognized by Michael Ignatieff, "State, Civil Society, and Total Institutions: A Critique of Recent Social Histories of Punishment," *Crime and Justice* 3 (1981): 153–92. See also David Garland, *Punishment and Modern Society: A Study in Social Theory* (Oxford: Clarendon, 1990).

20. For the tradition of "Whig histories" of the prison, see Michael Ignatieff, *A Just Measure of Pain* (London: Macmillan Education UK, 1978), ch. 1; and Gibson, "Global Perspectives," 1043.

21. For the theoretical significance of Tocqueville's prison investigations, see Bernard E. Harcourt, "The Invisibility of the Prison in Democratic Theory: A Problem of 'Virtual Democracy,'" *Good Society* 23, no. 1 (July 10, 2014): 6–16.

22. Benjamin Rush, *Essays, Literary, Moral and Philosophical* (Philadelphia: Thomas and William Bradford, 1806), 137.

23. Z. R. Brockway, *Fifty Years of Prison Service: An Autobiography* (New York: Charities Publication Committee, 1912), 389 (italics in original).

24. Brockway, *Fifty Years,* 393–94.

25. For an overview of the "rehabilitative ideal," see Francis A. Allen, *The Decline of the Rehabilitative Ideal: Penal Policy and Social Purpose* (New Haven, CT: Yale University Press, 1981). Rush predicted the democratic response to released convicts would be "This our brother was lost, and is found— was dead and is alive." Rush, *Essays,* 157.

26. Michel Foucault, *Discipline and Punish: The Birth of the Prison* (New York: Pantheon Books, 1977), 23.

27. "The soul is the prison of the body." Foucault, *Discipline and Punish,* 29–30.

28. Ignatieff, *Just Measure of Pain,* 210. See also the discussion of Tocqueville, p. 212.

29. Ignatieff: "Social stability had to be founded on popular consent, maintained by guilt at the thought of wrongdoing" (p. 211). Modern prison theories not only made a claim to an effective method of rehabilitation but also suggested that a social structure with formal legal equality but lacking real social equality could be justified due to the psychic imbalance of the disadvantaged classes (an imbalance that would be repaired by imprisonment).

30. Around 1971 the number of prisoners in the United States began an exponential climb that would last for more than thirty years, resulting, at its peak, in over seven million people either behind bars or in some other form of penal custody and an incarceration rate that rose from 61 per 100,000 in 1972 to 767 per 100,000 in 2007. See National Research Council, "The Growth of Incarceration in the United States: Exploring Causes and Consequences" (Washington, DC: National Academies, 2014), 33. A hugely disproportionate percentage of these new prisoners came from Black and minority communities. As early discussions of the

term explain, mass incarceration is defined not only by the number of people incarcerated but by the demographic patterns behind those numbers. Mass incarceration is characterized by the incarceration of *entire demographic categories.* See David Garland, "Introduction: The Meaning of Mass Imprisonment," *Punishment and Society* 3, no. 1 (January 1, 2001): 5–7; and Bruce Western, *Punishment and Inequality in America* (New York: Russell Sage, 2006).

31. An observation inaugurated by Malcolm M. Feeley and Jonathan Simon, "The New Penology: Notes on the Emerging Strategy of Corrections and Its Implications," *Criminology* 30, no. 4 (1992): 449–74, and taken up by, among others, David Garland, *The Culture of Control: Crime and Social Order in Contemporary Society* (Oxford: Oxford University Press, 2002). For a recent examination of the current "state of the question" on prisons and mass incarceration, see David Garland, "Theoretical Advances and Problems in the Sociology of Punishment," *Punishment and Society* 20, no. 1 (January 1, 2018): 8–33; Garland, *Culture of Control,* ch. 1.

32. See, for instance, American Friends Service Committee, *Struggle for Justice: A Report on Crime and Punishment in America, Prepared for the American Friends Service Committee,* 1st ed. (New York: Hill and Wang, 1971).

33. Important early statements of this position can be found in Herbert Morris, "Persons and Punishment," *Monist* 52, no. 4 (1968): 475–501; and Jeffrie G. Murphy, "Marxism and Retribution," *Philosophy and Public Affairs* 2, no. 3 (1973): 217–43. See also James Q. Whitman, *Harsh Justice: Criminal Punishment and the Widening Divide between America and Europe* (New York: Oxford University Press, 2005), 194: "The shift of the mid-1970s also brought the return of a style of retributivism that, in American practice, is closely associated both with populist justice and with deep-seated Christian sentiment—much though the academic philosophers who advocated retributivism at the same time may have hoped to encourage a kind of gentler Kantianism."

34. See Allen, *The Decline of the Rehabilitative Ideal.*

35. An influential text in the decline of rehabilitation and the rise of proportionality is Andrew Von Hirsch, *Doing Justice: The Choice of Punishments: Report of the Committee for the Study of Incarceration,* 1st ed. (New York: Hill and Wang, 1976). See also the contributions to Hyman Gross and Andrew Von Hirsch, eds., *Sentencing* (New York: Oxford University Press, 1981).

36. For this dynamic, see Albert W. Dzur, Ian Loader, and Richard Sparks, "Punishment and Democratic Theory: Resources for a Better Penal Politics," in *Democratic Theory and Mass Incarceration,* ed. Albert W. Dzur, Ian Loader, and Richard Sparks (New York: Oxford University Press, 2016), 1–17. Rebecca U. Thorpe, "Democratic Politics in an Age of Mass Incarceration,"

in *Democratic Theory and Mass Incarceration*, ed. Albert Dzur, Ian Loader, and Richard Sparks (Oxford University Press, 2016), 18–28.

37. Dzur, Loader, and Sparks, "Punishment and Democratic Theory."

38. For one account of this history, see Elizabeth Hinton, *From the War on Poverty to the War on Crime: The Making of Mass Incarceration in America* (Cambridge, MA: Harvard University Press, 2017).

39. Davis et al., *Abolition. Feminism. Now.*

40. For shifts within the legitimation structure (and institutional structure) of the prison and of reform in the nineteenth century, see David J. Rothman, *The Discovery of the Asylum: Social Order and Disorder in the New Republic* (Boston: Little, Brown, 1990); David J. Rothman, *Conscience and Convenience: The Asylum and Its Alternatives in Progressive America* (Glenview, IL: Scott, Foresman, 1980). I have pursued one possible reason for this ideational transformation elsewhere. See Jacob Abolafia, "Rehabilitative Faith," *Point* 17 (Spring 2018): 85–91.

41. For the former, see the introduction in Perry Zurn and Andrew Dilts, *Active Intolerance: Michel Foucault, the Prisons Information Group, and the Future of Abolition* (New York: Palgrave Macmillan, 2016); and for the latter, American Friends Service Committee, *Struggle for Justice*.

42. See again Von Hirsch, *Doing Justice*. For a recent restatement of "nothing works," see James Q. Wilson and Joan Petersilia, *Crime and Public Policy* (New York: Oxford University Press, 2011).

43. Ignatieff points out that from the penitentiary's earliest days, no method of reform had ever been shown to work. Ignatieff, *Just Measure of Pain,* 209. But it was only in the late twentieth century that liberal societies stopped trying. See also Abolafia, "Rehabilitative Faith."

44. The most famous version of this racial story is Michelle Alexander, *The New Jim Crow: Mass Incarceration in the Age of Colorblindness,* rev. ed., with a new foreword by Cornel West (New York: New Press, 2011). But one need not accept the grand historical comparison between the oppressive social forms of slavery, Jim Crow apartheid, and mass incarceration to accept that the racial politics (and political economy) of midcentury America are an important piece of this story. For the latter, see Nicola Lacey and David Soskice, "Crime, Punishment and Segregation in the United States: The Paradox of Local Democracy," *Punishment and Society* 17, no. 4 (October 1, 2015): 454–81; Nicola Lacey and David Soskice, "American Exceptionalism in Inequality and Poverty: A (Tentative) Historical Explanation," in *LSE International Inequalities Institute Working Paper* (British Academy, 2021), 41–67.

45. See Marie Gottschalk, *The Prison and the Gallows: The Politics of Mass Incarceration in America* (Cambridge: Cambridge University Press, 2006); Marie Gottschalk, *Caught: The Prison State and the Lockdown of American Politics* (Princeton, NJ: Princeton University Press, 2014); Naomi Murakawa, *The*

First Civil Right: Race and the Rise of the Carceral State, Studies in Postwar American Political Development, (Oxford: Oxford University Press, 2014).

46. Lerman and Weaver, *Arresting Citizenship*; Amy E. Lerman, *The Modern Prison Paradox: Politics, Punishment, and Social Community* (Cambridge: Cambridge University Press, 2014).

47. Davis, *Are Prisons Obsolete?* The language of abolition had been applied to the prison by the first generation of critical incarceration scholars in the 1970s, notably in Thomas Mathiesen's *The Politics of Abolition* (1974). For context, see Thomas Mathiesen, *The Politics of Abolition Revisited* (London: Routledge, 2016).

48. Davis, *Are Prisons Obsolete?*; Angela Y. Davis, *Abolition Democracy: Beyond Empire, Prisons, and Torture,* 1st ed., Open Media Book (New York: Seven Stories, 2005). Davis et al., *Abolition. Feminism. Now.*

49. For a version of liberal theory that tries to establish the principles of justified incarceration see Shelby, *Idea of Prison Abolition.*

50. For the disappointed fortunes of various prison management systems, see, inter alia, Rothman, *Discovery of the Asylum*; Rothman, *Conscience and Convenience*; Michael Meranze, *Laboratories of Virtue: Punishment, Revolution, and Authority in Philadelphia, 1760–1835* (Chapel Hill: University of North Carolina Press, 1996); Adam Jay Hirsch, *The Rise of the Penitentiary: Prisons and Punishment in Early America,* Yale Historical Publications (New Haven, CT: Yale University Press, 1992); Rebecca M. McLennan, *The Crisis of Imprisonment: Protest, Politics, and the Making of the American Penal State, 1776–1941,* Cambridge Historical Studies in American Law and Society (Cambridge: Cambridge University Press, 2008).

51. For the failure of reform in American, see the previous note. Some scholars have made the argument that the world is witnessing a form of "penal convergence," wherein the post-reformative American approach is increasingly visible in other jurisdictions, including western Europe. See John Pratt, *Penal Populism: Key Ideas in Criminology,* Key Ideas in Criminology (London: Routledge, Taylor & Francis, 2007); and John Pratt, *Populism, Punishment and the Threat to Democratic Order: The Return of the Strong Men,* 1st ed. (London: Routledge, 2023); for another comparative approach, see Michael Cavadino and James Dignan, *Penal Systems: A Comparative Approach* (Los Angeles: Sage, 2006).

52. For the classic version of this claim, see John Pratt, "Scandinavian Exceptionalism in an Era of Penal Excess: Part I: The Nature and Roots of Scandinavian Exceptionalism," *British Journal of Criminology* 48, no. 2 (March 1, 2008): 119–37.

53. For the drawbacks of this comparative approach and the dangers of "commodifying" the Nordic model, see Thomas Ugelvik and Jane Dullum, eds., *Penal Exceptionalism? Nordic Prison Policy and Practice* (London: Routledge, 2012).

54. Jeremy Bentham, *Official Aptitude Maximized, Expense Minimized*, ed. Philip Schofield (Oxford: Clarendon Press, 1993), 37.

55. See John Pratt, "Scandinavian Exceptionalism in an Era of Penal Excess: Part II: Does Scandinavian Exceptionalism Have a Future?," *British Journal of Criminology* 48, no. 3 (May 1, 2008): 275–92; the editors' introduction in Ugelvik and Dullum, *Penal Exceptionalism?*; Smith, "Critical Look"; Thomas Mathiesen, "Scandinavian Exceptionalism in Penal Matters: Reality or Wishful Thinking?," in *Penal Exceptionalism?*, 13–37.

56. This parallel has been drawn by Angela Davis in, e.g., Angela Y. Davis, "From the Prison of Slavery to the Slavery of Prison: Frederick Douglass and the Convict Lease System," in *The Angela Y. Davis Reader*, ed. Joy James (Malden, MA: Blackwell, 1998), 74–95; as well as by Alexander, *New Jim Crow*. The analogy is questioned on philosophical and historical grounds by critics including Shelby, *Idea of Prison Abolition*, 44–86; and James Forman Jr., "Racial Critiques of Mass Incarceration: Beyond the New Jim Crow," *New York University Law Review* 87, no. 1 (2012): 101–46. The causal or historical links that scholars have drawn between mass incarceration of Black Americans and chattel slavery are less important here than the undemocratic image that is created when one (demographically discrete) part of the political community is imprisoned while others are not.

57. Lerman and Weaver, *Arresting Citizenship*; Lerman, *Modern Prison Paradox*.

58. For the former reason, see Ramsay, "Democratic Theory of Imprisonment," 106. For felon disenfranchisement and democracy, Dilts, *Punishment and Inclusion*, 1–21.

59. Kateb, "Punishment and the Spirit."

60. Vanessa Barker, *The Politics of Imprisonment: How the Democratic Process Shapes the Way America Punishes Offenders* (Oxford: Oxford University Press, 2009); Thorpe, "Democratic Politics."

61. See below for a case where citizens were hesitant to carry out a retributive punishment, an "unwelcome mission" in Thucydides's words (III.49.4).

62. See Chapter 4.

63. Kateb, "Punishment and the Spirit," 271.

64. See Chapter 1; and Ramsay, "Democratic Theory of Imprisonment," 89–92.

65. See Chapter 4. In "crimes of infirmity there is place many times for lenity" (*L.* XXX.23, 230).

66. See Kateb, "Punishment and the Spirit"; Ramsay, "Democratic Theory of Imprisonment."

67. Demosthenes 22.68, *paradeigma poiēsai tois allois,* a predecessor of Voltaire's *pour encourager les autres.* I use the Greek text from Demosthenes. *Orations, Volume III: Orations 21–26: Against Meidias. Against Androtion. Against Aristocrates. Against Timocrates. Against Aristogeiton 1 and 2.* Translated by J. H. Vince. Loeb Classical Library 299 (Cambridge, MA: Harvard University

Press, 1935). Translations from the Greek are my own unless otherwise noted.

68. *L.* XXVII.16, 195.

69. For neoliberal social policy and its correlation with penal policy see, inter alia, Jonathan Simon, *Governing through Crime : How the War on Crime Transformed American Democracy and Created a Culture of Fear* (New York: Oxford University Press, 2007); Ruth Wilson Gilmore, *Golden Gulag: Prisons, Surplus, Crisis, and Opposition in Globalizing California*, (Berkeley, CA: University of California Press, 2007); Pratt, *Penal Populism*; Loïc J. D. Wacquant, *Punishing the Poor: The Neoliberal Government of Social Insecurity*, English language ed., Politics, History, and Culture (Durham, NC: Duke University Press, 2009); and for a forceful summation, Ramsay, "Democratic Theory of Imprisonment."

70. For Demosthenes's equivocations about whether incarceration is a high-status punishment, see Chapter 1. For Whitman's argument that the European history of imprisoning high-status political prisoners influenced their differentially less harsh practices, see Whitman, *Harsh Justice,* 197.

71. *euthunai, Protagoras,* 326d. The Greek edition of Plato used is *Platonis Opera,* ed. J. Burnet (Oxford, Oxford University Press, 1903). All translations are mine unless otherwise noted.

I. THE PARADOX OF INCARCERATION IN DEMOCRATIC ATHENS

1. Demosthenes 24.11.

2. See, for instance, Edward M. Peters, "Prison before the Prison," in *The Oxford History of the Prison,* ed. Norval Morris and David J. Rothman (Oxford: Oxford University Press, 1997), 3–47. Both the general accounts of Athenian law and the specialist literature on prisons remain split. Danielle Allen, "Imprisonment in Classical Athens," *Classical Quarterly,* n.s., 47, no. 1 (January 1, 1997): 121–35, follows Irving Barkan, "Imprisonment as a Penalty in Ancient Athens," *Classical Philology* 31, no. 4 (October 1, 1936): 338–41, in finding the evidence on the whole supportive of the development of imprisonment as a normal punishment. Virginia Hunter, "The Prison of Athens: A Comparative Perspective," *Phoenix* 51, no. 3/4 (October 1, 1997): 296–326, in the tradition of Kurt Latte, "Beiträge Zum Griechischen Strafrecht. II. Die Strafen," *Hermes* 66, no. 3 (1931): 129–58, is much more skeptical, as is Stephen Todd, *The Shape of Athenian Law* (Oxford: Clarendon, 1993), who describes the evidence as "tendentious" and "odd" (p. 143). For more extensive discussion of the literature, see Allen, "Imprisonment in Classical Athens," 121; Hunter, "Prison of Athens," 296; and the bibliographic material collected in

Marcus Folch, "Political Prisoners in Democratic Athens, 490–318 BCE," *Classical Philology* 116, no. 3 (July 2021): 336–68.

3. The skeptical position is summarized in Hunter, "Prison of Athens," who concludes that the prison in Athens was just another form of holding cell of the sort common to many premodern European societies. The standard reference work of nineteenth-century scholarship calls incarceration "not ordinarily a punishment" (*Real-Encyclopädie d. klassischen Altertumswissenschaft*, s.v. "Δεσμοτήριον"), and its twenty-first-century edition says prison was "not imposed as a punishment" (*Der neue Pauly*, s.v. "Desmoterion") in the Greek world.

4. Thucydides 4.38–41; Xenophon, *Hellenica* 7.4.36–38. These detentions were often done in civic buildings (δημοσία) or even quarries (Thuc. 7.86-7).

5. Cf. Herodotus 3.23, where it is treated as unremarkable that the Ethiopians have a prison (though certainly remarkable that its chains are of gold).

6. By the late fifth century, the jail (*desmotērion*) at Athens was large enough to hold at least forty inmates at once. See Thuc. 6.60 and Andoc. 1.43–48.

7. Aristotle, *Ath. Pol.* 2.2; and Plutarch, *Solon* 13.4 inter alia.

8. For the history and distinction between debt enslavement and debt bondage, see Edward M. Harris, "Did Solon Abolish Debt-Bondage?," *Classical Quarterly* 52, no. 2 (December 2002): 415–30 (which seems to overlook the role of imprisonment).

9. Cf. Antiph. 5.63.

10. Andoc. 1.92.

11. Andoc. 2.15; Lysias 6.21. Cf. Allen, "Imprisonment in Classical Athens," 123–124 and following, for more evidence of the slow evolution of imprisonment.

12. Andoc. 4.4–5. The uncertain author and date of this speech (mid- to late fourth century?) make it unreliable for determining the precise evolution of the penal practice, but it is suggestive that the prison comes into common use concurrently with the cessation of ostracism, the old paradigmatic method of checking elite ambition. The last recorded attempt at an ostracism was in 415 BCE, the same year that the forty suspects in the affair of the mysteries were confined to the prison. According to *Der neue Pauly*, s.v. "Ostrakismos (P. J. Rhodes)," the practice was neglected in favor of the more reliable, routinized process of public prosecution, especially the *graphē paranomōn*. Incarceration can, perhaps, be associated with this transition. As we will see, the association of imprisonment and ostracism draws attention to its potential as a "vertical" punishment.

13. The evolution of the prison alongside the political crises of the late fifth century is noted and discussed by Folch, "Political Prisoners." Folch

dates the emergence of the political significance of the prison to the crisis around the profanation of the mysteries (c. 415 BCE). This earlier date may very well have been important, but, as discussed below, it was the use of the prison under the Thirty that was the more powerful historical symbol.

14. Lysias 12.16, 13.44. Control of the prison was an oligarchic priority according to Aristotle, *Ath. Pol.* 35.1. Memory of the link between the Thirty and the Prison lingered, as will be seen below.

15. On communal knowledge and punishment, see Danielle Allen, *The World of Prometheus: The Politics of Punishing in Democratic Athens* (Princeton, NJ: Princeton University Press, 2000). Cf. Virginia Hunter, *Policing Athens Social Control in the Attic Lawsuits, 420–320 B.C.* (Princeton, NJ: Princeton University Press, 1994), 178ff, on "displayed" (stocks) vs. "undisplayed" corporal punishment. Hunter, "Prison of Athens," tries to suggest that the act of public arrest (being "dragged off to jail," as the texts often have it) serves the purpose of public humiliation (p. 318), but in any case, the prison is certainly qualitatively different from its predecessor, the stocks. Folch notes that the prison was very easily visited, but surely this closed, if accessible, space must be judged different from public stocks.

16. See Marie Gottschalk, *The Prison and the Gallows: The Politics of Mass Incarceration in America* (Cambridge: Cambridge University Press, 2006).

17. *Apology* 37b8–c2: "Perhaps [I should propose] prison? And why should it be necessary for me to live in jail, always enslaved to the whoever's the magistrate in office? Or should I take a fine, and be imprisoned until I pay in full? But that's the same to me, as indeed I was just was saying. For I don't have any possessions from which to pay." On "proposing" a sentence (*timēsis*) as opposed to a sentence mandated by law, see Douglas Maurice MacDowell, *The Law in Classical Athens* (Ithaca, NY: Cornell University Press, 1986), 257; and Allen, "Imprisonment in Classical Athens," 123. The Greek text of Demosthenes used here is the Loeb (ed. Vince) and the Greek text for Plato the OCT (ed. Burnet). The fact that Xenophon does not record this in his version of the *Apology* does not negate the importance of the passage. Plato did not need to be writing a true record of the speech; he only needed to be writing a *plausible* record. To judge this passage as "fictitious" (Todd, *Shape of Athenian Law*) since it is unusual is to beg the question.

18. Plato describes the imprisonment of Socrates (*Phaedo* 59b–60a, 116e–118a) and uses imprisonment as a metaphor (*Cratylus* 400c, *Gorgias* 525b) and a setting (*Crito*). For Plato's use of the prison see, inter alia, Egil A. Wyller, "Platons Gesetz Gegen Die Gottesleugner," *Hermes* 85, no. 3 (November 1, 1957): 292–314; Trevor J. Saunders, *Plato's Penal Code: Tradition, Controversy, and Reform in Greek Penology* (Oxford: Clarendon Press, 1991); Virginia Hunter, "Plato's Prisons," *Greece and Rome* 55, no. 2 (2008): 193–201.

19. For the debate, see note 2 above, Allen, "Imprisonment in Classical Athens" and Hunter, "Prison of Athens." Both suggest that it is time to ask the question of the social meaning of the prison. Allen suggests a historical shift in the role of the prison, from insignificance (early fifth century and before), to limited involvement in matters of state (and debt imprisonment, including indebtedness to the state, mid-fifth century), to more widespread usage (fourth century). She also notes the egalitarian possibilities in a punishment that, unlike a fine, would be equally burdensome for rich and for poor. Plotted diachronically, the development of the prison might map on to the development of Athenian democratic power (Allen, "Imprisonment in Classical Athens," 131-35). Concurrently, however, and using much of the same evidence, Hunter is more skeptical—of both the expansion of the prison as a "normal" sentence and of the role of the prison in anything beyond detaining inmates and signaling the displeasure of society—containment and deterrence (Hunter, "Prison of Athens," 316-19).

20. The focus on "democratic ideology" as an important precondition for understanding how and why Athenian institutions functioned (rather than reading them through the lens of critics who thought they did not) has become well established. See Josiah Ober, *Mass and Elite in Democratic Athens: Rhetoric, Ideology, and the Power of the People* (Princeton, NJ: Princeton University Press, 1989); J. Peter Euben, *Corrupting Youth: Political Education, Democratic Culture, and Political Theory* (Princeton, NJ: Princeton University Press, 1997); and for the ideology of punishment, Allen, *World of Prometheus.*

21. I borrow this language from Demetra Kasimis, *The Perpetual Immigrant and the Limits of Athenian Democracy*, Classics after Antiquity (Cambridge: Cambridge University Press, 2019), 9, who applies a similar method of discursive analysis to the study of metics in Athens.

22. The present study was written before I was aware of Folch's papers Marcus Folch, "Political Prisoners in Democratic Athens, 490-318 BCE Part I: The Athenian Inmate Population," *Classical Philology* 116, no. 3 (July 2021): 336-68, and Marcus Folch, "Political Prisoners in Democratic Athens, 490-318 BCE Part II: Narrating Incarceration in Athenian Historiography and Oratory," *Classical Philology* 116, no. 4 (October 2021): 498-514, which are now the most comprehensive historical account of the prison in democratic Athens. We share a desire to move from a positivistic, "juridical" analysis to an account of the prison within the context of democratic politics, and on most points of interpretation, our analyses concur.

23. E.g., see Foucault's reliance on a distinction between custodial and punitive punishment that originated with Ulpian and continued throughout the history of medieval and early modern law. Foucault, *Discipline and*

Punish, 118. Geltner, *Medieval Prison,* 44ff, shows that even this principle could be honored mostly in the breach.

24. Demosthenes uses the passive for people being dragged off: *es to desmotērion helkesthai.*

25. "Everything in a democracy is gentler [*praotera*]" (22.52, see below). Gentleness is taken up and elaborated by Plato in the *Laws,* with its ethic of reform and rehabilitation instead of anger and revenge. We will examine this Platonic development more closely in Chapter 2.

26. 22.52: *tēn idian oikian hekastōi desmotērion kathistē.*

27. 22.55, an identical argument to 24.167 but deployed to opposite ends, as will be seen below.

28. On the democratic virtues of gentleness and generosity, see Jacqueline de Romilly, *La douceur dans la pensée grecque* (Paris: Les Belles Lettres, 1979); Matthew R. Christ, "Demosthenes on Philanthrōpia as a Democratic Virtue," *Classical Philology* 108, no. 3 (2013): 202–22; and below.

29. 22.68. Androtion's father was a wealthy man who makes a cameo in Plato's *Protagoras* (315c) and *Gorgias* (487c, as an associate of Callicles). Amusingly, he seems to have escaped while being allowed to dance in the annual procession of the Dionysia on a sort of furlough. See Mervin R Dilts, *Scholia Demosthenica* (Leipzig: Teubner, 1986), 22.68. Of course, this does not explain why non-elites might be imprisoned (as they most certainly were).

30. This problem of the ambiguous boundary of the demos when it comes to punishment sheds light on a current debate in political theory over the meaning of word *dēmos.* It must mean, as per Josiah Ober, "The Original Meaning of 'Democracy': Capacity to Do Things, Not Majority Rule," *Constellations* 15, no. 1 (March 2008): 3–9; "the whole of the citizenry" and not the disjuncture between "*dēmos* and leading men" posited by Daniela Cammack, "The Dēmos in Dēmokratia," *Classical Quarterly* 69, no. 1 (May 2019): 42–61. If "leading men" are eo ipso outside of the demos, the tension that Timocrates and Demosthenes negotiate around how they are to be punished ceases to make sense.

31. For the former case, see the pseudo-Aristotelian *Rhetoric to Alexander,* 1423b3–4, where such behavior deserves the "greatest penalties [*megistai zēmiai*]." For similar language about the latter case (where disagreement among oligarchic ephors is said to deserve the "greatest punishment [*megistē timōria*]") see Xenophon, *Hellenica* 2.3.34. Both cases are discussed in Matthew Simonton, *Classical Greek Oligarchy: A Political History* (Princeton, NJ: Princeton University Press, 2017), 120 and 84 respectively.

32. For oligarchic exile, see Simonton, *Classical Greek Oligarchy,* 99ff; for spectacular punishments, see Simonton, 108. One cannot help but be reminded of Foucault's distinction between punishment under the ancient

regime and the "gentle way" preferred by liberalism. Simonton borrows the language of horizontal and vertical relationships in Greek states from Nick Fisher, *Hybris: A Study in the Values of Honour and Shame in Ancient Greece* (Warminster, England: Liverpool University Press, 1992).

33. Demosthenes, *Demosthenes, Speeches 20–22,* 1st ed., ed. Edward Monroe Harris, Oratory of Classical Greece, vol. 12 (Austin: University of Texas Press, 2008), 170—after all, Androtion was appointed to an embassy the next year.

34. Demosthenes's speech made a big enough impression to attract the attention of Isocrates, who seems to have responded to it, per Galen O. Rowe, "Two Responses by Isocrates to Demosthenes," *Historia: Zeitschrift Für Alte Geschichte* 51, no. 2 (2002): 149–62.

35. Given the absolute authority juries had to determine a verdict, the appeal to a form of "jury nullification" as a way to rewrite and reinterpret the legal canon was a crucial strategy in the Athenian courts. See Allen, *World of Prometheus,* 5–8.

36. At points, he says Timocrates has already made such arguments (e.g., 24.77, "presenting himself as one who … will free the prisoner") that this is the sort of argument the jury should expect to hear (e.g., the rhetorical questions "perhaps it would be shameful" at 24.125) and once that he "hears [Timocrates] is going to cite" the law on pretrial bail as precedent (24.144).

37. 24.147: "Now let these things be sufficient evidence for you that it is possible to imprison." Note that here Demosthenes seems to consider imprisonment a regular penalty (*timēma*).

38. For the knotty problem of archaic laws in classical oratory, see Adele C. Scafuro, "Identifying Solonian Laws," in *Solon of Athens*, ed. Josine Blok and André Lardinois (Leiden, Netherlands: Brill, 2006), 173–96.

39. Memories of historical shift from debt enslavement to imprisonment mentioned above may also have given Demosthenes reason to think the connection between Solon's emancipatory legislation and imprisonment would seem plausible to jurors.

40. As both Folch, "Political Prisoners," and Hunter, "Prison of Athens," agree.

41. Inscriptions have confirmed this—in some cases the punishments were even precisely correlated with each drachma of the fine corresponding to one lash for a slave. See Margaretha Debrunner Hall, "Even Dogs Have Erinyes," in *Greek Law in Its Political Setting: Justifications Not Justice* (Oxford: Oxford University Press, 1996), 73–90.

42. This distinction has been acknowledged since Latte, "Beiträge Zum Griechischen Strafrecht. II. Die Strafen." For an analysis, see Hunter, *Policing Athens,* ch. 6. It is not only that in prison a man is not his own master (John Burnet, *Euthyphro, Apology of Socrates, and Crito* [Oxford: Clarendon Press, 1990], *ad Apol.* 37c), it is the very fact of being

chained up—note the significance Plato gives to the removal of Socrates's chains in the *Phaedo* (59b, 60e).

43. 24.167, cf. 22.55.

44. Physically, imprisonment (*to dedesthai*—lit., "to be chained") seems always to have involved some physical restraint. Its "corporal" nature was never in doubt. See Hunter, *Policing Athens,* and Hunter, "Prison of Athens."

45. "When you abolish imprisonment [*ton desmon*] you will abolish corporal punishment [*to pathein*] as well" (24.119).

46. For the modern avoidance of corporal violence, and the new "political anatomy" where "the soul is the prison of the body" see Foucault, *Discipline and Punish,* 30. In practice, both modern and ancient democracies are far less squeamish about violating noncitizen bodies, but modern democracies do not necessarily experience this as an issue of the boundaries of the demos in the same way. In fact, such boundaries around violence are being steadily eroded in contemporary liberal states. Bernard E. Harcourt, *The Counterrevolution: How Our Government Went to War against Its Own Citizens* (New York: Basic Books, 2018), 63–66ff.

47. For difficulty distinguishing between slaves and citizens, Xenophon, *On the Constitution of the Athenians* 1.10; for the importance and consequences such legal distinctions, see Demosthenes's speeches *Against Eubulides* (57) and *Against Neaera* (59).

48. Cf. *Il.* 2.260–77, where Odysseus threatens to expose Thersites's shameful parts (*aidō*) and proceeds to beat him; and Mary Margaret Mackenzie, *Plato on Punishment* (Berkeley: University of California Press, 1981), 70–80.

49. See Douglas Maurice MacDowell, *Demosthenes the Orator* (Oxford: Oxford University Press, 2009); and the prosopographical data collected in John S. Traill, ed., *Persons of Ancient Athens*, 21 vols. (Toronto: University of Toronto Press, 1994).

50. Alexis (frags. K-A 131–32) gives us evidence of thieves and cheats being "hauled off" and describes the meager meals of inmates (frag. K-A 220, suggesting that inmates could be supported by a ration rather than by food brought by relatives and visitors). Intriguingly, there is also evidence of the stereotypical figure who "spends more time in jail than his own home" (see Dinarchus 2.14 and Theophrastus, *Char.* 6). Of course, that could make it even more effective as a punishment for errant politicians. Both Dinarchus 2 and Demosthenes 25, *Against Aristogeiton,* give a colorful picture of the "low characters" who inhabit the *desmotērion* (discussed in Hunter, "Prison of Athens"). Taken as a whole, passages such as those from Alexis and Aeschines (1.43, 3.150) suggest that "to drag someone off to prison" (*apagein eis to desmotērion*) could have an almost idiomatic force of "to punish." The weight of the evidence supports Allen's chronological reading and suggests that the prison's place in the

social imaginary was expanding and that the meaning of the prison for democratic elites would have been constructed against a (possibly overwhelming) social reality of non-elite incarceration.

51. The formulations used for both the physical pain and political rebuke are so similar across elite speakers as to suggest a rhetorical topos: *kakopathia*, Dem. *Ep.* 2.17 and Antiph. 5.18; *kaka tōi sōmati*, Andoc. 2.15; *oneidos* in all three authors.

52. The rhetorical appeal to ethos as well as to law suggests an important way in which Athenian democracy was emphatically not just a "procedural" democracy—it depended or saw itself as depending on a set of shared values and behaviors as much as a set of juridical practices. For the role of civic ethos in a theory of democracy based closely on ancient Athens, see Josiah Ober, *Demopolis: Democracy before Liberalism in Theory and Practice* (Cambridge: Cambridge University Press, 2017), 71–72.

53. On the "civilizing virtues" as claimed by Demosthenes for democracy, see de Romilly, *La douceur*; Christ, "Demosthenes on Philanthrōpia"; Allen, *World of Prometheus*, 177–79 (on the privileged place of "fairness" [*epieikeia*]); and, for a skeptical view, Debrunner Hall, "Even Dogs Have Erinyes." Plato is predictably biting about this democratic "gentleness" (*praotēs*), pointing out that punishment in a democracy is so lackadaisical that "people who've been condemned to death or exile under such a constitution stay on at the center of things, strolling around like the ghosts of dead heroes, without anyone staring at them or giving them a thought." *Rep.* 558a, Grube trans. Plato, *Complete Works*, ed. John M Cooper and D. S. Hutchinson (Indianapolis: Hackett, 1997).

54. The metaphor is Demosthenes's, not Pierre Bourdieu's or Robert Putnam's. See *Against Meidias* 21.101, where he speaks of "loans" (*eranoi*).

55. See *Against Aristogeiton* I 25.87–90; and Christ, "Demosthenes on Philanthrōpia," 213–17. The idea is mocked by Plato at *Rep.* 558b, with *suggnomē* standing for *homonoia*.

56. 24.190: "He will not, I suppose, spare you the argument that it would be very hard on him (*hōs deina an pathoi*) to be punished for proposing that no Athenian citizen shall be sent to prison; and that it is for the benefit more especially of the powerless (*tōn adunatōn*) that the laws should be as moderate and gentle as possible" (Vince trans., emended).

57. See Georges S. Maridakis, "Démosthène, theoricien du droit," *Revue internationale des droits de l'antiquite* 5 (1951): 155–81.

58. The argument that imprisoning the rich and powerful has an explicitly *democratic* potential is found in at least three places in Demosthenes—the pair discussed here and *On the Trierarchic Crown* (51, of contested authorship). In *On the Trierarchic Crown*, once again the comparison is made between rich trierarchs who can imprison sailors with impunity and the

corruption of the trierarchs themselves, who rarely end up in prison. "How can this appear equal and democratic?" (51.11–12).

59. 24.192–93.

60. One of the clearest historical examples of this democratic focus on the future is the "amnesty" declared after the end of the Peloponnesian war, when different factions of Athenian society agreed not to prosecute one another for the crimes of the past. For more context and interpretation in light of the reconstruction of Athenian democratic institutions see Edwin Carawan, *The Athenian Amnesty and Reconstructing the Law*, 1st ed. (Oxford: Oxford University Press, 2013).

61. Demosthenes is not entirely clear in this passage about what benefit the people derives from incarcerating people. It may be possible that this benefit is the pleasure of vengeance—certainly that is a traditional view available to Demosthenes and the jurors—but taken together with 24.116 and 24.218, it seems that an educative/habitual view of the law as improving human behavior is meant.

62. It may be right to recall here Demosthenes's outrage that those who *are* correctly habituated (*hoi sōphronōs bebiōkotes,* 24.126) should be subject to imprisonment. The idea that punishment is a form of prophylactic civic education is also found in *On the Trierarchic Crown* (51.12).

63. For a sympathetic account of this "aristocratic" moral psychology, see Bernard Williams, *Shame and Necessity* (Berkeley: University of California Press, 1993), esp. ch. 3.

64. The most famous case of this is probably Alcibiades, although he was by no means the only exile to behave in such a way. Two fourth-century sources (Plato, *Gorgias* 516e and Andoc. 4.5) mention Alcibiades in their critiques of contemporary practices of elite punishment as ineffectual, and both appeal to the practice of incarceration.

65. It seems likely that in Athens, as in Geltner's medieval prisons, prisoners paid for their own fare (the parsimonious aspects of punishment are visible in Plato's *Phaedo,* where Socrates must pay for his own poison). It was not, however, unimaginable, as Plato's *Laws* shows, that the city might provide daily rations (*Laws* 909c).

66. The value of the central location of the prison in urban space is striking in both late-medieval/republican and Enlightenment forms of incarceration, as is the acknowledgment that those being punished are an indispensable part of the civic fabric. Geltner notes this and finds in it a reflection of Durkheim's sociology of punishment. See Geltner, *Medieval Prison,* 5, 7, 107; and Michael Meranze, *Laboratories of Virtue: Punishment, Revolution, and Authority in Philadelphia, 1760–1835* (Chapel Hill: University of North Carolina Press, 1996), for similar dynamics in eighteenth-century Philadelphia.

67. Above. Benjamin Rush predicted the democratic response to released convicts would be "This our brother was lost, and is found—was dead and is alive." Rush, *Essays, Literary*, 157.

68. See Mackenzie, *Plato on Punishment*; and Saunders, *Plato's Penal Code*, for Plato's innovations vis-à-vis his more traditional predecessors.

69. He wrote the law code for the colony of Thurii and published a work that at least one fourth-century historian thought anticipated the chief claims of Plato's *Republic*. Diehls-Kranz 80 A10, A1, B6. For more, see G. B. Kerferd, *The Sophistic Movement* (Cambridge: Cambridge University Press, 1981), 42–44. Scholars since Diehls agree that the "great speech" placed in his mouth by Plato in the eponymous dialogue at least approximates some of his positions, though precisely how much is open to debate. For an extensive discussion of this question, see Farrar, *Origins of Democratic Thinking.*

70. A note on translation: I translate *timaō* as "penalize" because to translate it as "punish" would be to beg the question and miss Protagoras's (and Plato's) transvaluation of punishment as an institution (perhaps, after all, imposing penalties is neither sufficient *nor* necessary for punishing). *Kolazein* I translate as "correction" or "discipline," though sometimes in Plato *kolasis* can be treated as "punishment" itself. For terminological analysis, see Mackenzie, *Plato on Punishment*; Allen, *World of Prometheus*; and Saunders, *Plato's Penal Code.*

71. Thucydides *Hist.* II.41.1. For the fifth-century idea that there are better rational modes of education than the traditional Homeric modes, cf. Xenophanes DK 11 B10.

72. Thucydides, *Hist.* III.37–50.

73. Cf. for *euboulia* as a particularly Protagorean topos, see Paul Woodruff, "Euboulia as the Skill Protagoras Taught," in *Protagoras of Abdera: The Man, His Measure* (Leiden, Netherlands: Brill, 2013), 179–93.

74. *Hist.* III.44.3, Gagarin and Woodruff translation, adopted from Michael Gagarin and Paul Woodruff, eds., *Early Greek Political Thought from Homer to the Sophists*, Cambridge Texts in the History of Political Thought (Cambridge: Cambridge University Press, 1995).

75. Diodotus speaks of criminals "changing their minds" (*metagnōsai*) and "making an end of their error" (III.46.1). For the Protagorean/Periclean/democratic overtones of Diodotus's speech, see Harvey Yunis, *Taming Democracy: Models of Political Rhetoric in Classical Athens* (Ithaca, NY: Cornell University Press, 1996), 92–99. It is even possible that the first ship to Lesbos tarried because the democratic sailors were uneager to carry out such a retributive punishment, an "unwelcome mission" in Thucydides's words (III.49.4).

76. Edward Schiappa, *Protagoras and Logos: A Study in Greek Philosophy and Rhetoric* (Columbia: University of South Carolina Press, 1991), goes so far as to suggest that Protagoras's attitude toward contrasting arguments ("concerning everything there are two *logoi* each opposed to the other") played a role in the development of Athenian democratic institutions, a counterpoint to G. E. R. Lloyd's arguments about the influence of political practice on science. See, e.g., G. E. R. Lloyd, *Magic, Reason, and Experience: Studies in the Origin and Development of Greek Science* (Cambridge: Cambridge University Press, 1979).

77. It is interesting to note that Protagoras excludes exile as a reformative penalty, implicitly confirming the importance of localization to the process of reform. The only punishments actually mentioned in Protagoras's speech are execution and exile (325bc), which are reserved for "incurable" (*aniaton*) cases, though doxographic record may provide some evidence that as a lawgiver, Protagoras was quite an imaginative punisher—decreeing public transvestitism for deserters and pacifists. See J. V. Muir, "Protagoras and Education at Thourioi," *Greece and Rome* 29, no. 1 (1982): 17–24, 20.

78. Mary Margaret Mackenzie, *Plato on Punishment* (Berkeley: University of California Press, 1981), 222.

79. For democratic justice as the communal display of and control over anger, see Allen, *World of Prometheus,* esp. ch. 6. For Demosthenes's focus on law as a late development, see Allen, 180ff.

80. See Larsen, *Early Christians and Incarceration.*

2. PLATO'S THEORY OF INCARCERATION

1. For this context, including Socrates's possible offenses against democratic sensibilities, see Josiah Ober, "Socrates and Democratic Athens," in *The Cambridge Companion to Socrates,* ed. Donald R. Morrison, Cambridge Companions to Philosophy (Cambridge: Cambridge University Press, 2010), 138–78.

2. For the interior of the prison, see Virginia Hunter, "The Prison of Athens: A Comparative Perspective," *Phoenix* 51, no. 3/4 (October 1, 1997): 296–326, https://doi.org/10.2307/1192540; and Chapter 1.

3. The Athenian Stranger, an unnamed old man visiting the island of Crete, is the main speaker in the *Laws.* He does not necessarily speak for Plato, but he does take the lead in the philosophical investigation in the *Laws,* and as his positions are clearly in conversation with other arguments entertained by Plato in other dialogues, I treat him as the voice of an approximate Platonic position, though it should be kept in mind that Plato never endorses these in propia persona.

4. This first prison may look like the prison discussed in Chapter 1, but it can unambiguously be used to punish crimes as varied as assault (880cd), public debt (855b), violations of exile (864e), unseemly business dealing (919e–920a), and disrespect of parents (932b). Additionally, unlike the Athenian prison, even this "demotic" prison works on the principle of ordered prison terms (an apparent innovation). Cf. Virginia Hunter, "Plato's Prisons," *Greece and Rome* 55, no. 2 (2008): 193–201, 197. The sentences, one to three years in the cases above (with the possibility of extension), are shorter than those of convicts in the other prisons. As explained below, this is because incarceration as a corporal punishment performs a different form of psychic correction from rehabilitative incarceration.

5. σωφρονιστήριον, a word of Plato's coinage almost impossible to translate. It is at once a punning rejoinder to Aristophanes's mocking satire of a Socratic club (the φροντιστήριον, or "think tank," *Nub.* l. 94), and, as Klaus Schöpsdau, *Nomoi = Gesetze. Buch VIII–XII* (Göttingen: Vandenhoeck & Ruprecht, 2011), ad loc., and Egil A. Wyller, "Platons Gesetz Gegen Die Gottesleugner," *Hermes* 85, no. 3 (November 1, 1957): 292–314, note, a pun on the idea that prudence is "the salvation of the mind" or soul, according to *Crat.* 411e (again, in contrast to the first prison that "saves bodies").

6. E.g., Trevor J. Saunders, *Plato's Penal Code: Tradition, Controversy, and Reform in Greek Penology* (Oxford: Clarendon Press, 1991); and Hunter, "Plato's Prisons."

7. See E. B. England, ed., *The Laws of Plato; the Text Ed. with Introduction, Notes, Etc* (Manchester: Longmans, Green, 1921), ad loc.; and Leo Strauss, *The Argument and the Action of Plato's Laws* (Chicago: University of Chicago Press, 1975), 174.

8. I conjecture that the technical name of this prison will be Tartarus, after the lowest realm in Hades, where such impious figures of myth as Sisyphus, Tantalus, and Ixion were imprisoned, along with the Titans. Fittingly, at 701c, atheists are compared to the rebellious Titans.

9. Plato's commitments to the reformative theory of punishment remains consistent across dialogues and does not seem to depend on whether the speaker is Socrates. In this chapter, I do not rely on any particular theory or chronology of the relation between the dialogues. For broader introductions to Plato's theory of punishment, see Mary Margaret Mackenzie, *Plato on Punishment* (Berkeley: University of California Press, 1981); and Saunders, *Plato's Penal Code.*

10. For the debate over these arguments, including whether and how they are fallacious, see inter alia Gregory Vlastos, "Was Polus Refuted?," *American Journal of Philology* 88, no. 4 (1967): 454–60; Terence Irwin, *Gorgias*

(Oxford; New York: Clarendon Press; Oxford University Press, 1979), ad loc.; Gerasimos Xenophon Santas, *Socrates, Philosophy in Plato's Early Dialogues* (London: Routledge & Kegan Paul, 1979), ch. 8; Mackenzie, *Plato on Punishment,* 241–45; R. McKim, "Shame and Truth in Plato's Gorgias," in *Platonic Writings / Platonic Readings,* ed. Charles L. Griswold (New York: Routledge, 1988), 34–48; Scott Berman, "How Polus Was Refuted: Reconsidering Plato's Gorgias 474c–475c," *Ancient Philosophy* 11, no. 2 (1991): 265–84; Roslyn Weiss, *The Socratic Paradox and Its Enemies* (Chicago: University of Chicago Press, 2006), 79–119; and Georgia Sermamoglou-Soulmaidi, "The Refutation of Polus in Plato's Gorgias Revisited," *Apeiron* 50, no. 3 (2017): 277–310, https://doi.org/10.1515/apeiron-2016-0034.

11. The ability of well-connected citizens to escape punishment is implied by the offer to smuggle Socrates out of prison in the *Crito* and, more amusingly, in the account of a wealthy oligarch who danced his way out of confinement during a festival (*Schol. ad Dem.* 22.68).

12. On this myth, see especially Rachana Kamtekar, "The Soul's (After-) Life," *Ancient Philosophy* 36, no. 1 (2016): 115–32.

13. The word for punishment here is τιμάω, which I have been translating as "penalize." Here, it clearly means punish. Plato's switch to retributive language in the myth goes unexplained—perhaps it is an effort to reclaim all the words relating to punishment in the Athenian lexicon.

14. Both Radcliffe G. Edmonds, "Whip Scars on the Naked Soul: Myth and Elenchos in Plato's Gorgias," in *Platonic Myths: Status, Uses, and Functions,* ed. Collobert, Destrée, & Gonzalez (Leiden: Brill, 2012), 165–86, 183–85, and David Sedley, "Myth, Punishment, and Politics in the 'Gorgias,'" in *Plato's Myths,* ed. Catalin Partenie (Cambridge: Cambridge University Press, 2009), 51–76, 63–68, give excellent accounts of the myth as a dialectical scenario.

15. The idea of the afterlife as a sort of prison is almost a cliché in post-Christian literature, but the image is very unusual in early Greek mythography, though Prometheus is often depicted in chains, and the word for the "pit" (τὸ βάραθρον) of Tartarus was used by the Athenians to describe a form of capital punishment with which, as Plato notes at 516d9, they threatened Militiades. For the varied views of the afterlife then current in Athens, see Jan N. Bremmer, *The Rise and Fall of the Afterlife: The 1995 Read-Tuckwell Lectures at the University of Bristol* (London: Routledge, 2002); and K. J. Dover, *Greek Popular Morality in the Time of Plato and Aristotle* (Berkeley: University of California Press, 1974), 261–67.

16. Plato closes two other dialogues (the *Phaedo* and *Republic*) with extensive eschatological myths and includes shorter myths about the soul and its progress in at least two more (the *Phaedrus* and the *Meno*). It is not possible to do justice to all the relevant similarities and differences between

these myths in the current context. See Saunders, *Plato's Penal Code*, 196–211.

17. The presence of the word "incantation" (*epōidos*) is *leitwort* linking each of these myths. Plato seems to use the word to indicate something that bears repeating, regardless of its literal truth.

18. Earlier attempts to answer the charges of "institution begging' in Plato's theory of punishment, including Christopher Rowe, "The Moral Psychology of the Gorgias," in *Gorgias-Menon: Selected Papers from the Seventh Symposium Platonicum*, ed. Luc Brisson and Michael Erler (Sankt Augustin: Academia Verlag, 2007), 90–101, and J. Clark Shaw, "Punishment and Psychology in Plato's Gorgias," *Polis* 32, no. 1 (2015): 75–95, largely avoided the *Laws*. These accounts show the way in which being proven wrong is being punished, but they do not answer the problem of Callicles or Thrasymachus, interlocutors who refuse to be proven wrong. They also leave Plato open to the charge that when he constructed his most detailed penal code, he abandoned penological innovation and had recourse to traditional punishments. Saunders, *Plato's Penal Code*, 186–87, provides an ingenious attempt to defend Plato's use of corporal punishments by connecting the *Laws* to the physiological doctrines of the *Timaeus*. Saunders's arguments can be made stronger by an appeal to moral psychology.

19. For a thoughtful discussion of the dramatic context of the dialogue, see Catherine H. Zuckert, *Plato's Philosophers: The Coherence of the Dialogues* (Chicago: University of Chicago Press, 2012), 55. This is not to say that Plato does not still largely draw from the Athenian institutions he knew, as per Glenn Morrow, *Plato's Cretan City: A Historical Interpretation of the Laws* (Princeton, NJ: Princeton University Press, 1960).

20. Agreeing with Andrea Wilson Nightingale, "Plato's Lawcode in Context: Rule by Written Law in Athens and Magnesia," *Classical Quarterly* 49, no. 1 (May 1999): 100–122, 104, and George Klosko, *The Development of Plato's Political Theory* (Oxford: Oxford University Press, 2006), 221, against Susan Sauvé-Meyer, *Plato: Laws 1 and 2*, Clarendon Plato Series (Oxford: Oxford University Press, 2015).

21. For more on the link between law and reason, see Jacob Abolafia, "Solar Theology and Civil Religion in Plato's Laws," *Polis: The Journal for Ancient Greek Political Thought* 32, no. 2 (October 1, 2015): 369–92, with bibliography. The issue is also treated extensively in André Laks, *Plato's Second Republic: An Essay on the Laws* (Princeton, NJ: Princeton University Press, 2022). See, for instance, his discussion of the *Laws* as a "theo-noo-nomocracy" (19).

22. See Joshua Wilburn, "Akrasia and Self-Rule in Plato's Laws," *Oxford Studies in Ancient Philosophy* 43 (2012): 25–53.

23. Plato has not abandoned the potential of the "shame culture" he exploited in Socrates's argument with Polus. My interpretation agrees

substantially with that of Wilburn, "Akrasia and Self-Rule," 33, as opposed to what he calls the "standard interpretation," where "reasoning" is limited to what an individual "takes to be correct." The "help" (645a) that reasoning receives is not only from a person's own psychic resources but also all the persuasive power inherent in the laws and the habit of law following—in short, it is the tendency developed to listen to the voice of law and reason.

24. Meyer, *Plato*, 161 (ad 643b1), notes that the language of "stronger than" or "weaker than" is merely meant to appeal rhetorically to the interlocutors (and reader) but that Plato thinks correct behavior is a harmony between parts, not a victory of one part. My reading is an attempt to harmonize Sauvé-Meyer and Wilburn, for while virtuous behavior does require all parts to function together in and their proper and proportionate roles (see below), this sort of behavior only occurs when one sort of "training," linked to the rational law, triumphs over another, unplanned pattern of psychic life (indeed the description of these psychic patterns as different life courses [*bioi*] lends credence to this reading—see 732e–734d).

25. From several passages, including 731c–e and 860c–864a, it is clear that the *Laws* is in agreement with the *Gorgias* about both the involuntary nature of crime, the rehabilitative character of punishment, and the social context for punitive correction.

26. As is described in Joshua Wilburn, "Tripartition and the Causes of Criminal Behavior in Laws IX," *Ancient Philosophy* 33, no. 1 (2013): 111–34, the discussion of the moral causes of crime should not be taken as a commitment to a specific theory of moral psychology—it is a context-dependent guide to the points at which psychology interacts with punishment. When the Athenian writes that "anger" (*thumos*, also "passion" or "boldness") may be a "part of" (*meros*) or a "passion" (*pathos*) in the soul (863b), he hopes that his description may appeal even to adherents of different psychological theories—another intriguing clue about the "public reasoning" of law. On the partition of the soul and the moral psychology of the *Laws* see also Laks, *Plato's Second Republic*, 169–76.

27. An ambiguous sentence. I adopt Bury's emendation of the text in his Loeb edition and the suggestion of Trevor J. Saunders, "The Socratic Paradoxes in Plato's Laws: A Commentary on 859c–864b," *Hermes* 96, no. 3 (January 1, 1968): 421–34, about the meaning of κἂν σφάλληταί τι, as well as his surmise about the meaning of τὴν δὲ τοῦ ἀρίστου δόξαν, which I agree must approximate ὀρθὴ δόξα.

28. Here Plato seems to be closing off a certain understanding of the Socratic tendency toward intellectualism. Socrates's intellectualist heirs, the Stoics, go on to have great debates over whether the sage can err in anything at all. For Plato, the answer is unequivocally yes. It seems likely

that Plato has in mind the erring yet just (and possibly even wise) atheist of *Laws* X.

29. Or ugliness. See *Sophist* 227e–228d.

30. Liberal education can be further divided into traditional "chastisement" (τὸ νουθετητικὸν, 230a8) and the most effective way of deflating ignorance, dialectical refutation (ἔλεγχος). These are the two tasks of the jailers from the Nocturnal Council, discussed below.

31. The idea that the psychic pain of anger (and comparable pleasures like revenge or expectation) is analogous to the physical reaction to pleasure is one used by Plato here and at *Philebus* 40e. The logic of the comparison is controversial and is discussed, along with the parallels to the *Gorgias*, at length in Wilburn, "Tripartition and the Causes," 119–21. See also Susan Sauvé-Meyer, "Pleasure, Pain, and 'Anticipation' in Plato's Laws, Book I," in *Presocratics and Plato: A Festschrift in Honor of Charles H. Kahn*, ed. R. Patterson, V. Karasmanis, and A. Hermann (Las Vegas: Parmenides, 2012), 349–66.

32. In the *Laws* these punishments include fines, exile, and yes, incarceration, though probably in the marketplace jail—see the passage on assault (880cd) and the comment of Saunders, *Plato's Penal Code,* 274.

33. Saunders, 174, with an apt comparison to the physiological theories of the *Timaeus*.

34. This "corporal" use of incarceration is the closest thing to evidence of a link between the discourse on incarceration as a liminal punishment in fourth-century Athens (see Chapter 1) and the penology of the prison in the *Laws*.

35. The typology of atheists and their punishment is controversial, textually and philosophically. The best discussion of the prisons in the *Laws* and the punishment of Atheists remains Wyller, "Platons Gesetz," but see also Saunders, *Plato's Penal Code,* 305, and Robert Mayhew, *Plato: Laws 10* (Oxford: Clarendon Press, 2008), ad 908a.

36. Adopting the emendations and translation of Saunders, "Socratic Paradoxes," 432–33, with further emendations for continuity.

37. See Jean Roberts, "Plato on the Causes of Wrongdoing in the Laws," *Ancient Philosophy* 7 (1987): 23–37, 28, who notes that the influence between ignorance and injustice can flow both ways: "One must be careful not to confuse the ignorance implicated in injustice, the ignorance due to the corruption of reason by undisciplined appetites and emotions, with the ignorance that is a cause of wrongdoing distinct from injustice. The latter will have to be purely intellectual in origin and not due to habituation to bad pleasures."

38. On the naming of this prison, see England, *Laws of Plato,* ad 908a. Marcus Folch, "Political Prisoners in Democratic Athens, 490–318 BCE Part II: Narrating Incarceration in Athenian Historiography and Oratory," *Classical*

Philology 116, no. 4 (October 2021): 498–514, rightly draws attention to the mytho-poetic elements in the description of this prison, elements that may persist from the *Gorgias*.

39. Some have been puzzled by the penology of this prison, judging it inconsistent with the Socratic theory of punishment as improvement. Saunders, *Plato's Penal Code*, 312n68. This is the only moment in Plato's corpus where the secondary rationale for punishment—deterrence—becomes primary. Plato is at pains to adduce a punishment that makes sense both from the perspective of society and from the perspective of the punished (rightly construed). He often includes the death penalty as a punishment that deters and, understood correctly, saves the soul from becoming worse. Why not apply the death penalty here? For those atheists who do not believe in an afterlife, death might seem, as Socrates proposes in the *Apology*, to be a "gain" (*kerdos*). And, in the *Laws* itself, death is described as "the smallest of evils" (854e). For all others, like the traditionalists who have pedaled a populist picture of the gods, a more forgiving afterlife might await. The state cannot administer a penalty that the criminal would not experience as deterrent. Somewhat perversely, the model here seems to be Socrates, who was famously undeterred by the threat of death.

40. *Sophist* 230b, d (tr. White) in Plato, *Complete Works*, ed. John M Cooper and D. S. Hutchinson (Indianapolis: Hackett, 1997).

41. As we have been at pains to show, the themes and approach to punishment in the laws, up to and including dialectical examination in the prison, are fundamentally continuous with Plato's Socratic dialogues. For the Socratic character of the *Laws*, see also C. J. Rowe, "Socrates, the Laws and the Laws," in *Plato's Laws: From Theory into Practice*, ed. Luc Brisson and Samuel Scolnicov (Sankt Augustin: Academia, 2003), 87–97.

42. Though throughout the *Laws*, the necessity of propitiating blood guilt and the concern for making restitution to sib groups reminds the reader that, whatever its philosophical sophistication, Plato is legislating for a premodern city. The moral basis for the law may be one of reform, but the legal necessities of the Greek city are those of an ethic of revenge. Plato himself seems conscious of this tension. When speaking of restitution, he uses the atavistically Homeric word ἄποινα for the only time; see Schöpsdau, *Nomoi = Gesetze*, ad 862c1.

43. An idea with deep roots in the Greek poetic tradition—see C. C. W. Taylor, ed., *Protagoras* (Oxford: Clarendon Press, 1976), ad loc. An early and influential example is to be found in Hesiod's excursus on justice *Op.* ll. 170–201 and Tyrtaeus 12.39–40.

44. The major exception to this is Christina H. Tarnopolsky, *Prudes, Perverts, and Tyrants: Plato's Gorgias and the Politics of Shame* (Princeton, NJ: Princeton University Press, 2010), which explores the tension between useful shame and dangerous ("flattering") shame (p. 92) as it relates to Plato's

critique of democratic politics and contemporary democratic theory. Tarnopolsky's reading, while insightful, does not adequately account for the final moments of the *Gorgias* that suggest the failure of even "good" shame to perform its function correctly. Conversely, Jill Locke, *Democracy and the Death of Shame: Political Equality and Social Disturbance*, (Cambridge: Cambridge University Press, 2015), addresses the "decline of shame" narrative in the history of political theory but does not directly treat Plato's texts.

45. LSJ, *s.v.* αἰδῶς. For these different senses of shame and examples in Greek literature, see Douglas L. Cairns, *Aidōs: The Psychology and Ethics of Honour and Shame in Ancient Greek Literature* (Oxford: Clarendon, 1993); and David Konstan, *The Emotions of Ancient Greeks: Studies in Aristotle and Classical Literature* (Toronto: University of Toronto Press, 2006), 91–111. Shalini Satkunanandan, "Drawing Rein: Shame and Reverence in Plato's Law-Bound Polity and Ours," *Political Theory* 46, no. 3 (June 1, 2018): 331–56, interprets the role of shame in the *Laws* developmentally— following Christopher Bobonich, *Plato's Utopia Recast: His Later Ethics and Politics* (Oxford: Clarendon Press, 2002)—suggesting that it leads beyond shame itself toward "aidōs as reverence for the fragility of the law-bound polity" (p. 348). This chapter explains the relationship between the institutions of the law and the social bonds of shame the other way, because shame cannot function correctly without the support of political institutions like the prison.

46. For the central importance of sexual continence to the Greek concept of shame, see E. M. Craik, "ΑΙΔΩΣ in Euripides' Hippolytos 373–430: Review and Reinterpretation," *Journal of Hellenic Studies* 113 (November 1993): 45–59. For the increasingly important link between shame and self-control (*sōphrosunē*) over time, see Helen F. North, *Sophrosyne: Self-Knowledge and Self-Restraint in Greek Literature*, Cornell Studies in Classical Philology (Ithaca, NY: Cornell University Press, 1966); and A. W. H. Adkins's comment on Cairns, "AIDOS: The Psychology and Ethics of Honour and Shame in Ancient Greek Literature. Douglas L. Cairns," *Ethics* 105, no. 1 (October 1, 1994): 181–83.

47. Additionally, in fifth- and fourth-century Athenian usage, the aspects of *aidōs* connected to shameful behavior increasingly came to be expressed using a related word stem: *aisch-*. See Konstan, *Emotions of Ancient Greeks*, 93–98, for an account of the overlapping senses of the two words. For the purposes of the current study, the difference does not matter, particularly as Plato does not distinguish between the two. Tarnopolsky notes that the *aidōs* form does not occur in the *Gorgias* while, as we will see, it predominates in the *Laws* (*Perverts, Tyrants, and Prudes,* 11). This may be because of the "archaizing" language in and importance of a theological sensibility for the latter work.

48. *Gorgias* 494aff. Cf. Jessica Moss, "The Doctor and the Pastry Chef: Pleasure and Persuasion in Plato's Gorgias," *Ancient Philosophy* 27, no. 2 (2007): 229–49, for a view that holds that Callicles is in fact successfully shamed. This view fails to adequately explain the role of the dialogue's final myth.

49. As Sauvé-Meyer notes in her commentary ad 644b6–c3, the Athenian does not entirely endorse the "warlike" model of human behavior and may himself endorse an alternate "harmony-based" model. Whether shame helps a citizen "be stronger than herself" or merely withstand harmful passions (*pathoi,* cf. 649c) by achieving a harmonious psychic state, it is clear that Plato views shame as an important legal tool in the regime of the *Laws.* Here, as throughout the *Laws,* the Athenian is willing to compromise with traditional beliefs to reach the broadest possible audience.

50. 643d. This precise definition of citizenship is echoed by Aristotle in the *Politics.*

51. Cf., for example, the second definition of *sōphrosunē* in Plato's *Charmides,* 160e.

52. This is an elucidation of the terminology in the *Laws* 644cd. For varying interpretations of the moral psychology here, see the sources cited in Sauvé-Meyer, *Plato,* ad loc. The presentation is clearly hedonistic in character, though the meaning of this hedonism as presented, *arguendo,* is not entirely clear. R. Stalley, *An Introduction to Plato's Laws* (Indianapolis: Hackett, 1983), 88–89, suggests that the limited "utopianism" of the *Laws* recalls the work of More and Bentham. As this passage and Chapters 4 and 5 show, this affinity is deeper and more significant than has heretofore been supposed.

53. As England, *Laws of Plato,* notes (ad loc.), this passage, particularly the phrase "with the [help of the] law," makes clear that for Plato shame is a state institution.

54. For the connection between law, reason, and virtue, see Julia Annas, *Virtue and Law in Plato and Beyond* (Oxford: Oxford University Press, 2017).

55. The question of gender in the *Laws* is a vexed one. See Kenneth Royce Moore, *Sex and the Second-Best City: Sex and Society in the Laws of Plato* (London: Routledge, 2005); and Thanassis Samaras, "Family and the Question of Women in the Laws," in *Plato's Laws: A Critical Guide,* ed. Christopher Bobonich (Cambridge: Cambridge University Press, 2010), 172–96 among others. For the role of the symposium in social bonding in Athenian life around the time of the composition of the *Laws,* see James N. Davidson, *Courtesans and Fishcakes: The Consuming Passions of Classical Athens,* 1st US ed. (New York: St. Martin's, 1998), ch. 2.

56. This placement of the (Attic/Ionian) symposium against the (Dorian) martial arts of Sparta and Crete suggests another way in which the Athenian is

preferring the "harmony" between a person's behavior when drunk and sober (cf. 653b) to a "victory" of his sober self over his drunk self. The symposium is a test that will show whether shameful attitudes still hold sway even when constraints are weakened.

57. We use the term "institution" advisedly (although Bury, Sauve-Meyer, Saunders, and others freely use it to translate the Greek terms *politeia* [lit.: political arrangement], *koinonia* [lit.: communal arrangement], and even *epitedeuma* [lit.: undertaking]). Just as frequently, Plato does not even use any abstract noun to describe the things created by the laws, but for our purposes, "institution," with its varied English meanings, is appropriate. In a context close to that of the current study, Virginia Hunter, "Institutionalizing Dishonour in Plato's Laws," *Classical Quarterly* 61, no. 1 (May 2011): 134–42, writes of Plato's project of "institutionalizing dishonor" (p. 142).

58. The connection between honor, blame, and shame is both psychologically intuitive and well-established in Greek literature. In Euripides's *Hippolytus*, it is Phaedra's fear for her honor that drives her to preserve her reputation for shame through the calumny against Hippolytus. For more on dishonor in the *Laws*, see Hunter, "Institutionalizing Dishonour."

59. In his discussion of the *Laws*, Cairns mischaracterizes the role shame plays in the dialogue as being "about conformity rather than commitment" (*Aidōs*, 376). Plato's aim in the *Laws* is precisely to collapse any logical distinction between conformity and commitment. Stalley, *Introduction to Plato's Laws*, 42–44, also errs in accusing Plato of excessive coercion. Schöpsdau, *Nomoi=Gesetze*, ad 711b4–c2, is closer to the mark in his appreciation of the internal/external dynamic, as is the excellent discussion in, Annas, *Virtue and Law*, 72–119.

60. For the uniqueness of the prologues, Bobonich, *Plato's Utopia Recast*, 97–119.

61. Shame and blame do not appear in the "code" of Gortyn; nor are they brought out as "laws" in the speeches of Demosthenes and Aeschines, although orators frequently try to paint their opponents as shameful.

62. 720a.

63. At the rhetorical peak of the "prologue" to the law code, the Athenian praises self-control and wisdom as the highest forms of merit (730e), and at various points, self-control seems to stand as a sort of synecdoche for health of the soul (e.g. 743e–744a). This makes shame, as the midwife of temperance, of first importance to the project of the *Laws*. Stalley, *Introduction to Plato's Laws*, 56: "*Sophrosune* is the *raison d'etre* of the social and educational institutions described in the later books. It is as fundamental to the *Laws* as justice, *dikaiosune*, is to the Republic."

64. Literally, the regime form in the *Laws* is a "theocracy," but given that reason is divine, the distinction collapses. See Abolafia, "Solar Theology."

65. We can perhaps connect this Platonic intuition with recent attempts to argue in favor of penal technocracy as an antidote to penal populism. See Rachel Elise Barkow, *Prisoners of Politics* (Cambridge, MA: Harvard, 2021); an important version of this view is Franklin Zimring, "Populism, Democratic Government, and the Decline of Expert Authority: Some Reflections on 'Three Strikes' in California," *McGeorge Law Review* 28, no. 1 (January 1, 1996): 243–56; and the qualified defense of "continental" bureaucratic penal apparatuses against politicized American "democratic" penality in James Q. Whitman, *Harsh Justice:Criminal Punishment and the Widening Divide between America and Europe* (New York: Oxford University Press, 2005) 199–202.

66. Marcus Folch, "Is Red Figure the New Black? The Imprisonment of Women in Classical Athens," *Ramus* 50, no. 1–2 (December 2021): 45–67. Even if, in fact, most people who ended up in the prison were almost certainly poor and low status.

67. It is no coincidence that the two paradigmatic "opponents" in Plato's political dialogues, Callicles and Thrasymachus, fit squarely into this elite social category of politicians and intellectuals. Plato often writes about "punishment" in broad terms, but he is most deeply interested in the threat posed by wayward elites, not, as for Athenian democrats, because these elites threaten popular rule but rather because it is the wealthy and well-educated who are most likely to "think they know what they do not," the error that is most fundamentally at odds with epistocracy.

68. See Josiah Ober, *Mass and Elite in Democratic Athens: Rhetoric, Ideology, and the Power of the People* (Princeton, NJ: Princeton University Press, 1989).

69. 886a. There is a characteristically complex bit of Platonic wordplay here. The Athenian "fears" Atheists (*phoboumai*) but goes out of his way to clarify that he does not respect (*aidoumai*) them. This both underlines the connection between fear (*phobos*) and shame (*aidos*) and emphasizes that the atheists stand outside of normal shame relations.

70. The *Laws* does not punish the Atheists for their beliefs; it punishes them for their actions—spreading those beliefs to others. Incarceration, however, acts directly on those beliefs, undermining the distinction between belief and practice.

71. Cf. *Laws* 967e. The direct connection between believing in rational theology and rational ethical theory is addressed in Abolafia, "Solar Theology."

72. The memorable "immoralists" of Plato's other dialogues become, in the *Laws,* anonymous heterodox intellectuals. One reason for this may be analytic precision—the *Laws* recognizes that citizens may hold politically dangerous views without being ill-willed.

73. Note that this form of expectation (*elpis*) is distinct from the "expectation about the future" connected to the moral psychology of shame discussed above (644b).

74. At least one later Greek author thought that Plato himself was responsible for stemming the tide of subversive atheism (Plutarch, *Nicias* 23.4).

75. *Laws* 701a.

76. The line taken by Hunter, "Prison of Athens"; Hunter, "Plato's Prisons."

77. See the introduction.

78. For this analogical tradition, see C. Farrer, "Power to the People," in *The Origins of Democracy in Ancient Greece*, ed. Kurt A. Raaflaub, Josiah Ober, and Robert W. Wallace (Berkeley: University of California Press, 2009), 170–96; Josiah Ober, John R. Wallach, and J. Peter Euben, eds., *Athenian Political Thought and the Reconstitution of American Democracy* (Ithaca, NY: Cornell University Press, 1994); and the contributions in the latter.

79. For the affinity with later hedonistic theories, see Stalley, *Introduction to Plato's Laws*, 88–89. The central role of hedonism in later theories of incarceration is treated in Michael Ignatieff, *A Just Measure of Pain* (London: Macmillan Education UK, 1978).

3. INCARCERATION IN THOMAS MORE'S *UTOPIA*

1. As reported by his son-in-law, see Gerard Wegemer and Stephen W. Smith, eds., *A Thomas More Source Book* (Washington, DC: Catholic University of America Press, 2004), 52.

2. See, for instance, Polybius's description of a general amnesty of debtors in prison in Achaea in the lead-up to war against the Romans (38.11.10–11), a decision that succeeds in currying favor with "the many." This evidence suggests that imprisonment could still be a tool of elite politics, even if elite prisoners were no longer in question. I thank Matt Simonton for pointing this out to me.

3. For the distinction between penal slavery and penal incarceration, see Fergus Millar, "Condemnation to Hard Labour in the Roman Empire, from the Julio-Claudians to Constantine," *Papers of the British School at Rome* 52 (1984): 124–47; Joan Burdon, "Slavery as a Punishment in Roman Criminal Law," in *Slavery and Other Forms of Unfree Labour*, ed. Léonie J. Archer (London: Routledge, 1988), 68–85; and Peter Garnsey, "Why Penalties Become Harsher: The Roman Case, Late Republic to Fourth Century Empire," *American Journal of Jurisprudence* 13, no. 1 (January 1, 1968): 141–62. For an overview of incarceration in the Roman world, see Edward M. Peters, "Prison before the Prison," in *The Oxford History of the Prison*, ed. Norval Morris and David J. Rothman (Oxford: Oxford University Press, 1997), 3–47.

4. For an extensive study of the extant archaeological and epigraphic evidence concerning places of confinement in the Hellenistic and Roman worlds, see Matthew D. C. Larsen and Mark Letteney, *Ancient Mediterranean Incarceration,* University of California Press, 2023, forthcoming.

5. The old scholarly consensus, which relied largely on the sparse and often contradictory literary evidence, is that, as in the Greek world, incarceration was only rarely itself a means of punishment (*poena*) rather than a form of custody (*custodia*). See both the old *Real-Encyclopädie d. klassischen Altertumswissenschaft Band 3* (1899), s.v. "carcer"; and *Der neue Pauly,* s.v. "carcer" (Gottfried Schiemann). For a new approach seeking to recenter the place of incarceration in the Roman world and challenge a view that was overly reliant on the prejudiced reports of the jurists, see Larsen and Letteney, *Ancient Mediterranean Incarceration,* based on a large-scale reappraisal of archaeological and inscriptional data.

6. The significance of the prison for Christian writers was primarily theological rather than political, and to tease out the politics behind theological tropes of incarcerated martyrs would be far beyond the range of this study. See, however, Matthew Larsen, *Early Christians and Incarceration: A Cultural History* (New York: Oxford University Press, forthcoming).

7. See Ulpian's famous statement in the *Digest* (48.19.8.9): "Governors usually (*continendos*) sentence criminals to be confined in prison, or to be kept in chains; but they should not do this, for penalties of this kind are forbidden, as a prison should be used for the safe-keeping of men, and not for their punishment." This is not to say that incarceration was not ever used as a penalty; it clearly was (as the *Digest* itself suggests, for crimes including forced gambling (Ulp. *Dig.* 11.5.1) and misuse of the imperial image (*Dig.* 47.38), and if imperial reforms succeeded in doing away with some types of sentence (life imprisonment, as per Callistratus, *Dig.* 48.19.35), other forms clearly persisted (see Lactantius, *De mort. Persec.* 22).

8. On this fundamental ideological distinction in Roman law and punishment, see Peter Garnsey, *Social Status and Legal Privilege in the Roman Empire* (Oxford: Clarendon, 1970).

9. Though the word does appear twice more in Platonizing Christian discussions of good and evil by Eusebius (*Dem. Ev.* 4.1.4) and Gelasius Cyzicenus (*Hist. Ev.* 2.7.6), I thank Marcus Folch for these references. Ironically, Eusebius seems to use the word as a euphemism for hell, reversing the theoretical transformation from the myth of the *Gorgias* to the institution of the *Laws.* This return of the language of Platonic soul craft to the afterlife was characteristic of Christian penal thought from Tertullian ("the poets trembling before the tribunal, not of Rhadamanthus, nor of Minos, but of unexpected Christ" [*De Spec.* 30.1–4]) up to and including Dante (who includes Minos as a judge administering the principle of *contrapasso*).

Sōphronistērion would eventually return to modern Greek as the translation for "penitentiary."

10. Plato and earlier Platonic writers do appeal to this model of what Malcom Schofield calls "the assimilation thesis" of soul craft as well. Malcolm Schofield, "Callicles' Return: Gorgias 509–522 Reconsidered," *Philosophie Antique. Problèmes, Renaissances, Usages*, no. 17 (November 1, 2017): 7–30. See, e.g., *Gorgias* 510d; and the (possibly spurious) *Theages*.

11. This account was originally arranged as a sort of diptych with a description of the Essenes, another ascetic sect who Philo presumably thought represented the pinnacle of the *vita activa* (or practical virtues). Cf. *Quod omnis liber probus sit*, 71–91.

12. For Philo as an origin point for Western asceticism, see J. C. O'Neill, "The Origins of Monasticism," in *The Making of Orthodoxy: Essays in Honor of Henry Chadwick,* ed. R. Williams (Cambridge: Cambridge University Press, 1989), 270–87.

13. See D. T. Runia, *Philo in Early Christian Literature* (Leiden, Netherlands: Brill, 1993).

14. Julia Hillner, *Prison, Punishment and Penance in Late Antiquity* (Cambridge: Cambridge University Press, 2015), 351. Hillner notes that *sōphronismos* became a term for educative punishment.

15. In its entry *"Phrontistērion,"* the medieval Byzantine dictionary the Suda takes up a word coined by Aristophanes in the *Clouds* to make fun of Socrates and his dangerous, irreligious "school." (Plato was punning on this when he called his reformatory the *sōphronistērion*.) The dictionary makes no mention of Plato, or indeed of Aristophanes, but simply refers to its medieval meaning, a "holy place or monastery," using exactly the same hendiadys coined by Philo. Elsewhere, the Suda describes a monastery as a place where monks "change for the better through a sort of frenzy for moderation (*sōphroni maniai tini*)." Suda, s.v. "Phrontistērion," and s.v. "Monachos."

16. For involuntary confinement in a monastery, see Hillner, *Prison, Punishment, and Penance.* Foucault, for his part, explicitly rejected the idea that monasteries could have a genealogical relationship to the prison. Michel Foucault, *The Punitive Society: Lectures at the Collège de France, 1972–1973*, ed. Arnold I. Davidson (New York: Palgrave Macmillan, 2015), 86–92.

17. The scholarly literature on More and *Utopia* is copious. For general bibliographic introductions, see J. C. Davis, "Thomas More's Utopia: Sources, Legacy, and Interpretation," in *The Cambridge Companion to Utopian Literature* (Cambridge: Cambridge University Press, 2010), 28–50; George M. Logan, *The Meaning of More's Utopia* (Princeton, NJ: Princeton University Press, 1983); Dominic Baker-Smith, *More's Utopia,* Unwin Critical Library (London: HarperCollinsAcademic, 1991); the introduction to Thomas More, *Utopia,* ed. George M. Logan, Robert M. Adams, and Clarence H.

Miller (Cambridge: Cambridge University Press, 1995); and the collection of articles in Richard Standish Sylvester and Germain Marc'hadour, *Essential Articles for the Study of Thomas More* (Hamden, CT: Archon Books, 1977). The word for "without a place" in Greek is *atopos*. More's avoidance of this word, with its established connotations of strangeness and paradox, suggests his desire for something new. The naming of *Utopia* belongs to a late stage in its composition, as in a letter to Erasmus More still refers to it by a Latin name: *Nusquama*. For this and other details, see the introduction to what remains the standard critical edition of *Utopia*: Thomas More, *Utopia*, ed. Edward L. Surtz and J. H. Hexter, vol. 4, Yale Edition of the Complete Works of St. Thomas More (New Haven, CT: Yale University Press, 1965).

18. Aside from the general descriptions in Hugh Trevor-Roper, "The Intellectual World of Sir Thomas More," *American Scholar* 48, no. 1 (1979): 19–32, and Quentin Skinner, *Visions of Politics*, vol. 2, *Renaissance Virtues* (Cambridge: Cambridge University Press, 2002), 193ff, see J. B. Trapp, *Erasmus, Colet, and More: The Early Tudor Humanists and Their Books*, Panizzi Lectures (London: British Library, 1991).

19. The "Letter to Dorp," perhaps More's most important piece of Grecophile humanist polemic, was written at around the same time as *Utopia*. See Thomas More, *In Defense of Humanism: Letters to Dorp, Oxford, Lee, and a Monk*, ed. Daniel Kinney, vol. 15, Yale Edition of the Complete Works of St. Thomas More (New Haven, CT: Yale University Press, 1986), 19. His writing previous to *Utopia* had involved translations of the satirist Lucian and some poetic epigrams. See Thomas More, *Translations of Lucian*, ed. Craig R. Thompson, vol. 3, part 1, Yale Edition of the Complete Works of St. Thomas More (New Haven, CT: Yale University Press, 1974), 197.

20. For republican liberty, see Skinner, *Visions of Politics*, 213–34. For the Hellenists' repost, E. Nelson, "Greek Nonsense in More's Utopia," *Historical Journal* 44, no. 4 (2001): 889–917.

21. Citations to *Utopia* will refer to page numbers in More, *Utopia* (1995). For the most part, I have relied on the translation and Latin text there, with occasional emendations, and the editorial notes have been a great help.

22. Dominic Baker-Smith, "Uses of Plato by Erasmus and More," in *Platonism and the English Imagination*, ed. S. Hutton and A. Baldwin (Cambridge: Cambridge University Press, 1994), 86–99, 89, and Nelson, "Greek Nonsense," 891, suggest that Hythloday's own name is a Platonic reference to Socrates as thinker, whom the ignorant decry as a peddler of nonsense (*huthlos*, cf. *Rep.* 336d). Whether or not that is so, many of his sentiments, such as that "well and wisely trained citizens you will hardly find anywhere," are clearly Socratic, as is his unkempt appearance.

23. See Giles's poem and letter, in More, *Utopia* (1995), 19 and 25 respectively, and Busleyden's letter to More, in same, 253.

24. The books "in Aldine letters" gifted to the Utopians (183).

25. For a convincing argument that More did not rely on the Latin of Ficino, see Paul Oskar Kristeller, "Thomas More as a Renaissance Humanist," *Moreana* 17, no. 1–2 (June 1, 1980): 5–22, 10. See also Baker-Smith, "Uses of Plato," 94, who muses the entire project may have been inspired by the presence of the Aldine Plato.

26. Erasmus, who was slightly older, was closer to Ficino's neo-Platonic interpretive tradition. See Baker-Smith, "Uses of Plato." More, who unlike his older colleagues Colet, Grocyn, and Erasmus had not made the trip to Italy, took as his model Pico della Mirandola's eclecticism, which encouraged him to use Plato (and other classical texts) for their particular strengths rather than to treat them as a philosophic whole. This applied to More's use of Epicurus and Aristotle as well. See Edward Surtz, "The Setting for More's Plea for Greek in Utopia," *Philological Quarterly* 35 (1956): 353–65; Thomas I. White, "Pride and the Public Good: Thomas More's Use of Plato in Utopia," *Journal of the History of Philosophy* 20, no. 4 (1982): 329–54; and Thomas I. White, "Aristotle and Utopia," *Renaissance Quarterly* 29, no. 4 (1976): 635–75.

27. Thorsten Sellin, *Pioneering in Penology: The Amsterdam Houses of Correction in the Sixteenth and Seventeenth Centuries* (Philadelphia: University of Pennsylvania Press, 1944), 12–14.

28. R. J. Schoeck, "More, Plutarch, and King Agis: Spartan History and the Meaning of Utopia," *Philological Quarterly* 35 (1956): 366, and Nelson, "Greek Nonsense," both read the reference as fundamentally ironic and deflationary. The other way to read the passage is as a counterfactual challenge—what if Agis had succeeded?

29. This is not to say that More's relationship with Plato actually *was* unmediated. Skinner and others have shown the dependence of the northern Renaissance on the earlier scholarship of the Italians. Quentin Skinner, *The Foundations of Modern Political Thought,* vol. 1, *The Renaissance* (Cambridge: Cambridge University Press, 1978). More himself was not a "Platonist" but rather, like his hero Pico, something of an eclectic. Cf. White, "Pride and the Public," 332.

30. For a general overview of approaches, see William Nelson, ed., *Twentieth Century Interpretations of Utopia: A Collection of Critical Essays* (Englewood Cliffs, NJ: Prentice-Hall, 1968).

31. This has been amply explored above, but for what was a closer stylistic influence on More's literary Latin and sense of the dialogue form, see Cic. *Off.* (discussed below), and, for controversial opinions, his *Nat. D.*

32. White, "Pride and the Public," has the best general account. The current discussion focuses on the *Republic* and *Laws* because of their relevance to political thought. Also present in the text, however, are references to the *Timaeus* and *Critias,* which have received very little attention from

scholars (with some exceptions); see Logan, *Meaning of More's Utopia,* 104, on the relation to the *Critias* and an extensive discussion of other Platonic debts. The *Critias* was clearly in More's mind as he drafted *Utopia,* as a connection between Plato and the discoveries of the New World was, at the time, obvious and uncontroversial. As late as 1522 Alessandro Geraldini could claim that the Natives he had seen in the Caribbean were relatives of Plato's Atlanteans, and the introductory materials to the Aldine edition of Plato even mention the New World in its dedication. See Plato, *Omnia Platonis opera,* ed. Aldo Manuzio (Venetiis: Aldus, 1513). The geography of Utopia and its connection to ancient wars all suggest engagement with the Atlantis narrative in the *Critias,* while the use of war to illustrate the excellence of the Utopian society is reminiscent of the *Timaeus* (43a).

33. See White, "Pride and the Public," 329n1, for a list of culprits. In political theory there has been a particular tendency, especially among students of Leo Strauss, to pursue this connection. See, e.g., Nicholas Opanasets, "More Platonism," *Review of Politics* 51, no. 3 (1989): 412–34; J. Steintrager, "Plato and More's Utopia," *Social Research* 36, no. 3 (1969): 357–72; and Harry Neumann, "On the Platonism of More's 'Utopia,'" *Social Research* 33, no. 4 (1966): 495.

34. Cf. pp. 57 and 105 for Platonic language that also made its way into the broader early modern discourse on punishment. See Sellin, *Pioneering in Penology,* 11.

35. Colin Starnes, *The New Republic: A Commentary on Book 1 of More's "Utopia" Showing Its Relation to Plato's Republic,* Canadian Electronic Library Books Collection (Waterloo, ON: Wilfrid Laurier University Press, 1990); and now Tae-Yeoun Keum, *Plato and the Mythic Tradition in Political Thought* (Cambridge, MA: Harvard University Press, 2020), ch. 2.

36. *Rep.* 473c, cf. p. 83.

37. Some have attempted to see in the educated "tranibors," who are a sort of upper house in the Utopian government, a form of philosophical rule. Given the fact that the educated officials (cf. p. 52) must co-rule with the uneducated syphogrants (cf. p. 48), this cannot be what More meant.

38. *Laws* 738c, Saunders trans. in Plato, *Complete Works.*

39. See Desiderius Erasmus, *Adagiorum Chilias Prima,* ed. M. L. van Poll-van de Lisdonk, M. Mann Phillips, and Chr. Robinson, vol. 2, part 1, Opera omnia Desiderii Erasmi (1969–) (Amsterdam: North-Holland, 1993), *Adages* 1 and 2, 84–86. Each of the first two entries features citations from the *Laws,* suggesting that for northern Renaissance humanists (as opposed to twentieth-century anglophone scholars), the *Laws* was as potent a source for Platonic political thought as the *Republic,* if not more so. For the *Adages* of Erasmus as a fundamental stimulus for the composition of *Utopia,* see three excellent articles: John C. Olin, "Erasmus' Adagia and

More's Utopia," *Moreana* 26, no. 1 (January 1, 1989): 127–36; D. Wootton, "Friendship Portrayed: A New Account of Utopia," *History Workshop Journal* 45, no. 1 (March 1, 1998): 29–48; and David Harris Sacks, "Utopia as a Gift: More and Erasmus on the Horns of a Dilemma," *Moreana* 54, no. 2 (December 1, 2017): 157–71.

40. See J. H. Hexter, *More's Utopia: The Biography of an Idea*, History of Ideas Series (Princeton, NJ: Princeton University Press, 1952).

41. Both Logan, *Meaning of More's Utopia,* and Starnes, *New Republic,* interpret the relation of the later book 1 to the earlier book 2 as a prolegomenon. Starnes is also explicit about the critique of the *Republic* in book 1 but decides this means that book 2 must be an attempt to write a "New Republic"—an unnecessary interpretive leap. For the *Republic* as a *paradeigma*, see 592b, a passage, as we have seen, that was on More's mind.

42. That is, "*sermo tam insolens*" and "*philosophia scholastica*" respectively.

43. "*Imago*" as opposed to "*facere*," a stress taken up in the "parerga," where More insists in his letter to Giles on the reality of the island (p. 31ff), and Giles repays him by claiming (in his anonymous poem) that what Plato only accomplished in speech, Utopus accomplished in fact (p. 19).

44. This attention to the realities of human frailty may be connected to More's lifelong interest in Augustine. Cf. Davis, "Thomas More's Utopia," 33; and below.

45. See Peter A. Hall and Rosemary C. R. Taylor, "Political Science and the Three New Institutionalisms," *Political Studies* 44, no. 5 (1996): 936–57.

46. For a complete list of *institutum* and its cognate terms in Utopia, see Mary Pawlowski and Gerard Wegemer, "Utopia: Index of Latin Terms," *Thomas More Studies* 6 (2011): 1–57, 42–43. For the broad classical usage of the Latin term, cf., for instance, the first page of Cicero's *Off.* and Lactantius's *Divine Institutes.*

47. In this and following passages, I have sometimes amended Logan and Adams's translation.

48. (*quod maximum totius institutionis fundamentum est . . . qua una re . . .*)

49. See Hall and Taylor, "Political Science," 942–46.

50. First and foremost, White, "Pride and the Public." This kinship between Plato's method of behavioral control in the *Laws* through education, marriage laws, foreign trade, and religion has been noticed by a number of scholars, including Edward Surtz, *The Praise of Pleasure: Philosophy, Education, and Communism in More's Utopia*, 1957, p. 59; Logan, *Meaning of More's Utopia* (in an extended discussion of parallels, pp. 198–202); and Baker-Smith, "Uses of Plato," who links the discussion of the rationality of institutions in *Utopia*'s peroration to the rational prologues of the *Laws*.

51. Hall and Taylor, "Political Science," 946–50.

52. As we saw in Chapter 2, the heart of the idea of the penal institution as it emerged from Plato's *Laws* was the use of institutions in the broad

sense—norms, rules, organizations, and hierarchies—to interface with what was taken to be a plausible theory of human behavior. Using the image of the "puppet," pulled about on strings that correspond to pleasures, pains, and passions, Plato tried to show how "law" could be a sort of "golden string," shaping the movements of the puppet while considering its tendency to respond to the other strings. By placing an account of human behavior at the very beginning of the discussion of the *Laws* (and, indeed, at the beginning of the discussion of a particular institution, the symposium), Plato suggested that an institution that seeks a certain prosocial outcome needs to have a realistic understanding of the parts of the mind that govern choice, action, and the distinction between right and wrong.

53. Scholars have noted the similarity between this oratorical defense of hedonism and Erasmus's earlier encomium *In Praise of Folly*. See Surtz, *Praise of Pleasure,* 9–11. Surtz also notes the influence of Valla's *De voluptate*. For a recent overview of More's views on pleasure and a measured discussion of the disagreement over their sincerity, see Gerard Wegemer, "Thomas More's 'Rule' of Pleasure before, after, and in Utopia," *Moreana* 54, no. 1 (May 29, 2017): 36–56.

54. These passages are full of More's frequent and remarkable use of litotes in *Utopia*, perhaps intended to lessen the effect of radical passages, or perhaps to destabilize the possibility of any straightforward reading. See Elizabeth McCutcheon, "More's Use of the Litotes in Utopia," *Moreana* 8 (Number 31–32), no. 3–4 (November 1, 1971): 106–21.

55. p. 161.

56. *Laws* 732e–734d, cf. 644dff.

57. NE X.1, 1172a20, cf. NE VII.5, see T. I. White, "Aristotle and Utopia," 651–53.

58. Prelude is Plato's word at *Laws* 734e. NE X begins with the observation that people educate the young "by steering them in the right direction with pleasure and pain" (1172a5) and ends with the suggestion that "then perhaps as well a person who wishes to improve people . . . should try to develop a capacity for legislating" (1180b20).

59. Surtz, *Praise of Pleasure,* 78.

60. Stephen Jay Greenblatt, *Renaissance Self-Fashioning: From More to Shakespeare* (Chicago: University of Chicago Press, 1984), 50.

61. As was first noted by Leland Miles, "The Platonic Source of Utopia's 'Minimum Religion,'" *Renaissance News* 9, no. 2 (1956): 83–90. Even the identification of the god of the Utopians with the sun and with Mithras (a deity associated with the cult of the Invincible Sun in the late Roman Empire) may be related to the account of religion in the *Laws*. See Jacob Abolafia, "Solar Theology and Civil Religion in Plato's Laws," *Polis: The Journal for Ancient Greek Political Thought* 32, no. 2 (October 1, 2015): 369–92.

62. *Laws* 885b4. See Abolafia, "Solar Theology," and More, *Utopia* (1965), 585.

63. This too can be traced to the *Laws* (854e).

64. My account of punishment owes much to Greenblatt's incisive interpretation in Greenblatt, *Renaissance Self-Fashioning.* The topic has been treated only rarely since then, for instance, in the very flawed Jason Gleckman, "The Polylerite Episode in Relation to Book II of Utopia: A Preliminary Study," *Moreana* 42, no. 4 (December 1, 2005): 85–92. Gleckman's lack of understanding of the historical context of penal servitude makes his argument nonsensical. For this context, see below.

65. p. 145.

66. Analyzed in detail in Chapter 2. This relationship was also noticed by Miles, "Platonic Source."

67. For a different account of More on punishment, see McBride, *Punishment and Political Order,* 17–27, which focuses on the tension between an ideal political theory and the unpredictability of individual behavior.

68. See Harris Sacks, "Utopia as a Gift."

69. Punishment and the other issues, including expansionism and enclosure, are clearly related, but a fuller literary examination of book 1 is beyond the scope of this chapter.

70. For later such efforts, see Leon Radzinowicz, *A History of English Criminal Law and Its Administration from 1750* (London; New York: Stevens & Sons; MacMillan, 1948); and Douglas Hay, *Albion's Fatal Tree: Crime and Society in Eighteenth-Century England,* 1st American ed. (New York: Pantheon Books, 1975).

71. This formulation is the mirror of Hythloday's approbation for penal slavery in book 2. This critique is also found in Starkey's *Dialogue,* which may be echoing More on this point. See More, *Utopia* (1965), 484.

72. Tellingly, this is one of the only aspects of *Utopia* visible in More's later, public career. See John Scarisbrick, "Thomas More: The King's Good Servant," *Thought: Fordham University Quarterly* 52, no. 206 (1977): 249, 263–265.

73. As many since Hexter and Surtz's edition have noted, the rational of Polyleritean punishment, restitution, deterrence, and reform, owes much to the penology of the laws (862d–864e) discussed in Chapter 2.

74. Unlike Plato, More does not suggest anything approaching a fixed sentence.

75. It seems to be this indifference to precise mechanisms that Bentham would later criticize as typically "utopian."

76. More's contribution to the history of political economy, as with other aspects of his thought, has proved remarkably polarizing. For a good account, see James W. Park, "The Utopian Economics of Sir Thomas More," *American Journal of Economics and Sociology* 30, no. 3 (1971): 275–88; and,

more recently, Guido Giglioni, "From Thomas More to Thomas Smith: Utopian and Anti-Utopian Understandings of Economic Change in Sixteenth-Century England," in *Utopia 1516–2016: More's Eccentric Essay and Its Activist Aftermath* (Amsterdam: Amsterdam University Press, 2017).

77. My thanks to Tae Yeoun Keum for drawing my attention to this.

78. See *Utopia*, 185: "The Utopians . . . deal more harshly with their own people . . . because they had an excellent education and best of moral training."

79. For the positive exceptions to the intellectual distrust of labor, see Birgit van den Hoven, *Work in Ancient and Medieval Thought: Ancient Philosophers, Medieval Monks and Theologians and Their Concept of Work, Occupations, and Technology*, Dutch Monographs on Ancient History and Archaeology, vol. 14 (Amsterdam: JCGieben, 1996), 21–38.

80. The distinction, according to Seneca, can be traced to Posidonius, who distinguished four types of occupation. The "vulgar handicrafts are those which employ the hand and are occupied with the furnishing of life's necessities, in which there is no pretense to charm or honor" (Sen., *Ep.* 88.21).

81. Sen. *Ep.* 88.23: "liberales . . . quibus curae virtus est" and 88.2: "*virum bonum facerent.*" Seneca himself is not sure whether the liberal arts alone can make a person good.

82. For an excellent treatment of the Roman views of work, labor, and im-provement, especially those of Cicero, see Sabine MacCormack, "The Virtue of Work: An Augustinian Transformation," *Antiquité Tardive* 9 (January 1, 2002): 219–37, as well as Andrea Giardina, "Il tramonto dei valori ciceroniani (ponos ed emporia tra paganesimo e cristianesimo)," in *La parte migliore del genere umano. Aristocrazie, potere e ideologia nell'Occidente tardoantico. Antologia di storia tardoantica*, ed. Sergio Roda (Torino: Scriptorium, 1996), 141–63.

83. For the development of penal slavery in Roman law, see Joan Burdon, "Slavery as a Punishment in Roman Criminal Law," in *Slavery: And Other Forms of Unfree Labour* (London: Routledge, 1988), 68–85. For the "dual system" of punishment that differentiated between high- and low-status criminals see Garnsey, *Social Status,* part 2.

84. For the legal curriculum at Oxford and the Inns of Court in More's day, see R. J. Schoeck, "Rhetoric and Law in Sixteenth-Century England," *Studies in Philology* 50, no. 2 (1953): 110–27.

85. The best account of these punishments is Millar, "Condemnation to Hard Labour"; see esp. 126ff.

86. This language comes straight out of the Roman digests, cf. Millar, 132–35.

87. For the Platonic resonance of recalcitrant criminals as "wild beasts," see *Laws* 909a.

88. For incapacitation as the central aim of Roman penal slavery, see Burdon, "Slavery as a Punishment," 80.

89. See Jacques Le Goff, *Time, Work, and Culture in the Middle Ages* (Chicago: University of Chicago Press, 1980). I have also relied on van den Hoven, *Work in Ancient.*

90. See Lynn White Jr., *Medieval Religion and Technology: Collected Essays* (Berkeley: University of California Press, 1978), 217ff; and Joel Mokyr, *The Lever of Riches: Technological Creativity and Economic Progress* (Oxford: Oxford University Press, 1990), 203–4. See van den Hoven, 152ff.

91. More gave a well-attended lecture course on Augustine as a young man and read him closely over the course of his life. See Martin N. Raitiere, "More's Utopia and the City of God," *Studies in the Renaissance* 20 (1973): 144–68; and Dominic Baker-Smith, "Who Went to Thomas More's Lectures on St Augustine's De Civitate Dei?," *Church History and Religious Culture* 87, no. 2 (2007): 145–60.

92. *De opere monachorum* XXI.25: . . . *tanto ulique felicius quanto forties educati.* Cf. *De opera monachorum.* XXIV.32.

93. Van den Hoven, *Work in Ancient,* 243–55, finds the attitudes even in the High Middle Ages still fundamentally equivocal, suggesting a larger role for the Renaissance in this story than has heretofore been acknowledged in the literature.

94. Max Weber, *Economy and Society: An Outline of Interpretive Sociology,* ed. Guenther Roth and Claus Wittich, trans. Ephraim Fischoff, 2 vols. (Berkeley: University of California Press, 1978), 1171.

95. So the earliest biographical account, by William Roper, attests. Wegemer and Smith, *Thomas More Source Book,* 19. Some scholars have expressed doubt that this is true, but even if he was not technically a lay brother and merely associated with the Charterhouse while living nearby, More's familiarity with the Carthusian way of life is amply attested in his work. See Caroline Barron, "Thomas More, the London Charterhouse and Richard III," in *Parliament, Personalities, and Power: Papers Presented to Linda S. Clark,* Fifteenth Century 10 (Woodbridge, UK: Boydell & Brewer, 2011), 203–14, for the fullest account of More and the Carthusians and bibliography.

96. For the history and lifestyle of the English Carthusians, see Glyn Coppack and Michael Aston, *Christ's Poor Men: The Carthusians in England* (Stroud, UK: Tempus, 2002); and James Hogg, "Life in an English Charterhouse in the Fifteenth Century: Discipline and Daily Affairs," in *Studies in Carthusian Monasticism in the Late Middle Ages,* ed. Julian Luxford, Medieval Church Studies 14 (Turnhout, Belgium: Brepols, 2009), 19–60. For the Carthusian monastery as an important waypoint in the architecture of reformation, see Robin Evans, *The Fabrication of Virtue: English*

Prison Architecture; 1750–1840 (Cambridge: Cambridge University Press, 1982), 57.

97. As reported by Roper. Wegemer and Smith, *Thomas More Source Book,* 52.

98. In More's Renaissance Latin, *cubiculum* meant not only bedroom but any small room, something like a monk's cell. The Carthusian order, like other monastic orders, made use of confinement in an "ecclesiastical prison" to punish infractions.

99. For the origins of monastic incarceration, see the excellent Hillner, *Prison, Punishment, and Penance,* esp. 191.

100. Penal servitude did not survive in any meaningful sense as a form of state punishment through the Middle Ages, and More's reference is clearly to the Roman practice, not to medieval or feudal versions, which had more to do with private recompense than public law. For the historical discontinuity between ancient and medieval penal servitude, see Alice Rio, "Penal Enslavement in the Early Middle Ages," in *Global Convict Labour,* ed. Christian Giuseppe De Vito and Alex Lichtenstein, Studies in Global Social History (Leiden, Netherlands: Brill, 2015).

101. For indolence, p. 63; for pride, p. 245.

102. The idea of combining the virtues of monasticism with the moral precepts of the pagan philosophers was a shared trope in the northern Renaissance. Erasmus, who, it will be remembered, shared More's affinity for the *Laws,* ends the first of the *Adages* by connecting Platonic and Pythagorean communism with "*coenobium,* nimirum a vitae fortunarumque societate." Erasmus, *Adagiorum Chilias Prima.* 85.

103. This makes the Utopian cities similar in size to More's London (perhaps a little smaller) and Plato's Athens (excluding its slave population).

104. For the social situation of More's London, see, for instance, C. G. A. Clay, *Economic Expansion and Social Change: England 1500–1700,* vol. 1 (Cambridge: Cambridge University Press, 1984), 197ff. For the reliance on reputation and informal social trust during this period, see Craig Muldrew, *The Economy of Obligation: The Culture of Credit and Social Relations in Early Modern England* (London: Palgrave Macmillan, 1998).

105. For these "liberal" moments, see pp. 135, 68, and 223.

4. "ALL RESTRAINT OF MOTION"—INCARCERATION IN HOBBES

1. Pieter Spierenburg, *The Prison Experience: Disciplinary Institutions and Their Inmates in Early Modern Europe* (Amsterdam: Amsterdam University Press, 2007), 25.

2. Spierenburg, *Prison Experience,* 43.

3. In between More and Hobbes, a third Englishman, Robert Burton, also made a noteworthy utopian case for penal confinement. Burton was

greatly influenced by More and was read by Hobbes. For the recommendation of workhouses in his ideal society, see Robert Burton, *The Anatomy of Melancholy: What It Is, with All the Kinds Causes, Symptomes, Prognostickes, & Seuerall Cures of It. In Three Partitions, with Their Severall Sections, Members & Subsections. Philosophically, Medicinally, Historically, Opened & Cut up. By. Democritus Iunior. With a Satyricall Preface, Conducing to the Following Discourse*, 5th ed., corrected and augmented by the author, Early English Books Online (Oxford: Robert Young, Edinburgh, by Miles Flesher, London, and by Leonard Lichfield and William Turner, Oxford for Henry Cripps, 1638), 65n. See note k for the direct reference to *Utopia*.

4. The oddness of Hobbes's argument is noted by his comtemporaries John Bramhall and Edward Hyde, the Earl of Clarendon. On these criticisms see Jean Hampton, *Hobbes and the Social Contract Tradition* (Cambridge: Cambridge University Press, 1987); and Signy Gutnick Allen, "Thomas Hobbes's Theory of Crime and Punishment" (PhD diss., London, Queen Mary University of London, 2016). The modern debate began with M. Cattaneo, "Hobbes's Theory of Punishment," in *Hobbes Studies*, ed. K. C. Brown (Oxford: Blackwell, 1965), 275–97, and has continued with Alan Norrie, "Thomas Hobbes and the Philosophy of Punishment," *Law and Philosophy* 3, no. 2 (1984): 299–320; Thomas S. Schrock, "The Rights to Punish and Resist Punishment in Hobbes's *Leviathan*," *Western Political Quarterly* 44, no. 4 (December 1, 1991): 853–90; David Heyd, "Hobbes on Capital Punishment," *History of Philosophy Quarterly* 8, no. 2 (1991): 119–34; Arthur Yates, "The Right to Punish in Thomas Hobbes's *Leviathan*," *Journal of the History of Philosophy* 52, no. 2 (2014): 233–54; and Gutnick Allen, "Thomas Hobbes's Theory," among many others.

5. See Richard Tuck, *Natural Rights Theories: Their Origin and Development* (Cambridge: Cambridge University Press, 1981), ch. 5.

6. Citations to Hobbes in this chapter will take the form ([*Work*] [chapter]. [paragraph], [page] in the modern edition). The editions used were as follows: for *Elements of Law,* Thomas Hobbes, *The Elements of Law Natural and Politic,* ed. M. M. Goldsmith and Ferdinand Tonnies, 2nd ed. (London: F. Cass, 1969); for *De Cive,* Thomas Hobbes, *Hobbes: On the Citizen,* ed. Richard Tuck, trans. Michael Silverthorne (Cambridge: Cambridge University Press, 1998); and for *Leviathan,* Thomas Hobbes, *Leviathan: With Selected Variants from the Latin Edition of 1668,* ed. Edwin Curley (Indianapolis: Hackett, 1994).

7. A point first observed by Pufendorf, though see also Norrie, "Thomas Hobbes."

8. For this criticism, see Hampton, *Hobbes and the Social*; and Schrock, "Rights to Punish."

9. See, for instance, Alan Ryan, "Hobbes's Political Philosophy," in *The Cambridge Companion to Hobbes*, ed. Tom Sorell, Cambridge Companions to

Philosophy (Cambridge: Cambridge University Press, 1996), 208–45; and Susanne Sreedhar, *Hobbes on Resistance: Defying the Leviathan* (Cambridge: Cambridge University Press, 2010).

10. Yates, "Right to Punish," 238. For Hobbes on the sovereign as constrained by law, see *L* XXI.19, 143.

11. Yates, 247.

12. Gutnick Allen, "Thomas Hobbes's Theory," 84.

13. See Heyd, "Hobbes on Capital Punishment," 124; and, on the rationality of resistance, Claire Finkelstein, "A Puzzle about Hobbes's Right of Self-Defense," *Pacific Philosophical Quarterly* 82, no. 3–4 (2001): 332–61.

14. This cost-benefit approach to crime is expressed most clearly in *De Cive* (XIII.16, 151): "Now deliberation is simply weighing up the advantages and disadvantages of the action we are addressing (as on a pair of scales). . . . If the penalty which a legislator attaches to a crime is too small to make fear weigh more heavily than greed, the legislator, i.e. sovereign is responsible." This approach would later be taken up more systematically by utilitarians, including Bentham and Gary Becker.

15. *De Cive* (VI.4, 78): "The wickedness of human character is evident to all. . . . Hence security is to be assured not by *agreements* but by *penalties*; and the assurance is adequate only when the penalties for particular wrongs have been set so high that the consequences of doing them are manifestly worse than of not doing them."

16. Gutnick Allen, "Thomas Hobbes's Theory," 169. This should remind us of Mackenzie, *Plato on Punishment*, and her analytic category of "institution begging" (positing an institution that solves a philosophical problem without explaining how)—Hobbes, like Plato, takes measures to avoid this potential pitfall.

17. Cf. Adrian Blau, "Hobbes's Practical Politics: Political, Sociological and Economistic Ways of Avoiding a State of Nature," *Hobbes Studies* 33, no. 2 (November 11, 2019): 109–34. While critics tend to focus on the deterrent role for Hobbes, Hobbes always lists reform before deterrence in his discussions of the aim of punishment.

18. Cf. the variant from the Latin *Leviathan*: "Because the commonwealth wills that public words, i.e., laws, count for more with citizens than the words of a private citizen . . . it holds that those who cannot even tolerate words are the most cowardly of all men" (variant of XXVII.20, 196, Curley trans.).

19. As Samuel Zeitlin pointed out to me, there may be a sixth form of punishment hidden within Hobbes's laws of nature (*L* XV.18, 96): "A sixth law of nature is this *that upon caution of the future time, a man ought to pardon the offences past of them that, repenting, desire it.*" The idea of pardon as the "prince's part" and a legal strategy preferable to punishment has its origins in Hobbes's mentor Francis Bacon, who thought that the aim of

revenge (and punishment was) "making the party repent" (Bacon, "Of Revenge"). Hobbes does say that "[crimes] that concern the Commonwealth only may without breach of equity be pardoned" (XXX.15, 226), but pardons, for Hobbes, are only given "upon security of the future time" (XV.19, 96), that is to say, when the pardoner is certain of the forthcoming change in behavior. Had Hobbes intended pardons to play a role within his system, one would expect the mechanism for this security to have been made clear. Additionally, Hobbes notes (XXVII.14, 194) that pardons are one of the ways the rich hope to avoid punishment, making them, like fines, as much a danger as a boon. Lastly, as Rosemarie Wagner suggested to me, the idea of pardons in place of the maximum punishment set out by law runs counter to Hobbes's belief that punishments must be "determined and prescribed," not "indeterminate, that is to say . . . arbitrary" (XXVIII.10, 205). Part of shaping criminal behavior is making use of prudential "foresight"—a pardon that cannot be foreseen is of no use to the criminal law as a whole. Bacon's use of the prerogative power of pardon is thus somewhat at odds with Hobbes's approach to the rationalization of punishment.

20. Heyd, "Hobbes on Capital Punishment," 131.

21. *De jure belli ac pacis,* book 2, chapter 7, section 3, p. 965 (Liberty Fund edition). For Hobbes's familiarity with and use of Grotius's text, see Richard Tuck, *Philosophy and Government 1572–1651*, Ideas in Context (Cambridge: Cambridge University Press, 1993); and Curley's note ad *L* XXVIII.1.

22. Hobbes's comment at *L* IVX.8 that wounds are equivalent to death "both because there is no benefit consequent to such patience (as there is to the patience of suffering another to be wounded or imprisoned), as also because a man cannot tell, when he seeth men proceed against him by violence, whether they intend his death or not" is ambiguous. It may be that wounding and imprisonment gain their power from their association with death, and a removal of the death penalty would remove much of their force.

23. Grotius, like More before him, is not coy about his debts to Plato. He explicitly cites the arguments of the *Gorgias* as an authority in support of his future-directed theory of punishment (cf. *De jure belli ac pacis.* p. 405).

24. For this debate, see Robert Zaller, "The Debate on Capital Punishment during the English Revolution," *American Journal of Legal History* 31, no. 2 (1987): 126–44; and Christopher Hill, *The World Turned upside down: Radical Ideas during the English Revolution* (London: Temple Smith, 1973), ch. 12.

25. See Zaller, "Debate on Capital Punishment"; Paul Griffiths, "Introduction: Punishing the English," in *Penal Practice and Culture: Punishing the English, 1500–1900* (London: Palgrave Macmillan, 2004), 1–36; and J. M. Beattie, *Policing and Punishment in London, 1660–1750* (Oxford: Oxford University Press, 2001).

26. Chains are listed as both a corporal punishment and a form of imprisonment. Perhaps Hobbes is thinking of stocks and other forms of temporary immobilization.

27. Griffiths, "Introduction," 23.

28. See Joanna Innes, "Prisons for the Poor: English Bridewells 1555–1800," in *Labour, Law, and Crime: An Historical Perspective* (London: Tavistock, 1988), 42–122; Spierenburg, *Prison Experience*; Griffiths, "Introduction."

29. For the equivalence of capital punishment and incarceration, see, e.g., *L* IVX.29, 87.

30. For the role of labor in English bridewells, the Dutch *Rasphuis,* and French galleys during Hobbes's lifetime, see Spierenburg, *Prison Experience.*

31. It is tempting, though impossible, to suggest a relationship. See Gerrard Winstanley, *The Law of Freedom, and Other Writings,* ed. Christopher Hill, Past and Present Publications (Cambridge: Cambridge University Press, 2006).

32. "A New Year's Gift for the Parliament and Army" in Winstanley, *Law of Freedom,* 180.

33. "Poor Oppressed People of England" in Winstanley, 102. We might explain the powerful presence of the prison in Winstanley's rhetoric by his interest in and attention to precisely those "marginalized" aspects of seventeenth-century society who were most likely to encounter a bridewell or "house of correction." As he writes elsewhere, "England is a prison; the variety of subtleties in the laws preserved by the sword are bolts, bars and doors of the prison; the lawyers are jailors, and poor men are the prisoners." Winstanley, 170.

34. "The True Levellers' Standard Advanced" in Winstanley, 86.

35. For Hobbes's theory of slavery and its debts, see Daniel Luban, "Hobbesian Slavery," *Political Theory* 46, no. 5 (October 1, 2018): 726–48 (who rightly highlights the relationship between Hobbes's theory of punishment and his theory of slavery); Tuck, *Natural Rights Theories*; and Annabel S. Brett, *Liberty, Right, and Nature: Individual Rights in Later Scholastic Thought,* Ideas in Context (Cambridge: Cambridge University Press, 2003).

36. Gutnick Allen, "Thomas Hobbes's Theory," 274, expresses this most clearly.

37. We have been referring to Hobbes as a reformative theorist of punishment. This is not a term that Hobbes himself used, and some have worried that it does not accurately reflect the aims of punishment in Hobbes. Gutncik Allen, 179n459. But if we keep in mind that Hobbes should not be read teleologically, as a predecessor of the "corrective" tradition that emerged in the wake of Beccaria and Bentham in the late eighteenth century, the term more or less accurately reflects Hobbes's own thinking.

McBride, *Punishment and Political Order,* 53, is correct in suggesting that Hobbesian punishment is related to other forms of carceral soul craft or even, to use Wendy Brown's terminology, "subject formation."

38. Cf. the seventh law of nature in chapter 15 of *Leviathan.*

39. Hobbes even tries to muster scripture to support this position (and here too reform, *emendatio,* comes before deterrence, *DCiv* IV.9, 61).

40. Even deterrence, for Hobbes, is directed not at the avoidance of a particular crime but at "deterring of them from doing disservice to [the Commonwealth]" (XVIII.14, 114).

41. "For by this authority, given him by every particular man in the Commonwealth, he hath the use of so much power and strength conferred on him that, by terror thereof, he is enabled to form the wills of them all" (*L* XVII.13, 109).

42. For the prevalence of the passions and desires associated with them in motivating human activity, see, e.g., *L* XIV.31, 87.

43. See Adrian Blau, "Reason, Deliberation, and the Passions," in *The Oxford Handbook of Hobbes,* ed. Al P. Martinich and Kinch Hoekstra (Oxford University Press, 2016), 195–220; and for a dissenting view, Arash Abizadeh, "Hobbes on Mind: Practical Deliberation, Reasoning, and Language," *Journal of the History of Philosophy* 55, no. 1 (2017): 1–34.

44. Unlike, for instance, for the ancient Athenians.

45. Blau, "Reason, Deliberation."

46. The suggestion in Gutnick Allen, "Thomas Hobbes's Theory," 179, that Hobbes cannot be a theorist of reform because mere prudence does not rise to the level of affecting judgment is as far as I can see unsupported.

47. This passage is one of the sources for a recent attempt at a radically expanded reading of the right of resistance in Hobbes. Sreedhar, *Hobbes on Resistance.*

48. This sort of criminal is related to Hobbes's famous "foole" who has said in his heart there is no justice, and the example draws on the great immoralists of Greek and Roman history. See Kinch Hoekstra, "Hobbes and the Foole," *Political Theory* 25, no. 5 (1997): 620–54.

49. This makes the criminals Hobbes is concerned with directly parallel to the Platonic criminals of the *Laws.* See Chapter 2.

50. For *doxosophia* as the fundamental characteristic of the dangerous intellectuals in the *Laws,* see Seth Benardete, *Plato's "Laws": The Discovery of Being* (Chicago: University of Chicago Press, 2000), 268–71. For Hobbes's Machiavellianism, see David Wootton, "Thomas Hobbes's Machiavellian Moments," in *The Historical Imagination in Early Modern Britain: History, Rhetoric, and Fiction, 1500–1800,* ed. David Harris Sacks and Donald R. Kelley, Woodrow Wilson Center Press (Cambridge: Cambridge University Press, 1997), 210–42.

51. On the Utopian as opposed to the "Republican" tradition of Machia-velli, see J. C. Davis, *Utopia and the Ideal Society: A Study of English Utopian Writing; 1516–1700* (Cambridge: Cambridge University Press, 1981).

52. This reading of Hobbes was pioneered by Keith Thomas in Keith Thomas, "The Social Origins of Hobbes's Political Thought," in *Hobbes Studies*, ed. K. C. Brown (Oxford: Oxford University Press, 1965), 185–236. Thomas is responding to the well-known interpretation of C. B. MacPherson, among others.

53. For the role of shame and shame culture in theories of punishment, see Chapter 2.

54. As discussed in *Leviathan*, chapter 10. See Quentin Skinner, "Hobbes and the Social Control of Unsociability," in *The Oxford Handbook of Hobbes*, ed. Al P. Martinich and Kinch Hoekstra (Oxford University Press, 2016), 432–50.

55. Latin variant of XXVII.20, 196, Curley trans.

56. Cf. *L* IVX.33 and compare with the role of oaths in Plato's *Laws*.

57. See the debate between Tuck and Hoekstra: Richard Tuck, "Hobbes and Democracy," and Kinch Hoekstra, "A Lion in the House: Hobbes and Democracy," both in *Rethinking the Foundations of Modern Political Thought*, ed. Annabel Brett and James Tully (Cambridge University Press, 2006), 171–218.

58. Cf. Hoekstra, "Lion in the House," 211n103.

59. Tommie Shelby, *Dark Ghettos: Injustice, Dissent, and Reform* (Cambridge, MA: Belknap Press of Harvard University Press, 2016).

60. R. A. Duff and S. E. Marshall, "Civic Punishment," in *Democratic Theory and Mass Incarceration*, ed. Albert Dzur, Ian Loader, and Richard Sparks (Oxford: Oxford University Press, 2016), 33–59; Ramsay, "Democratic Theory of Imprisonment."

5 BENTHAM'S PANOPTICON—BETWEEN PLATO AND THE CARCERAL STATE

1. Bentham wrote under the pseudonym "Hermes." *Gazetteer and New Daily Advertiser*, July 26, 1776. For the context of the exchange, see Yiftah Elazar, "Liberty as a Caricature: Bentham's Antidote to Republicanism," *Journal of the History of Ideas* 76, no. 3 (2015): 417–39.

2. For studies that highlight the role of Bentham's Panopticon in the history of the prison, see Michael Ignatieff, *A Just Measure of Pain* (London: Macmillan Education UK, 1978); Norval Morris and David J. Rothman, eds., *The Oxford History of the Prison: The Practice of Punishment in Western Society* (New York: Oxford University Press, 1997); Michel Foucault, *Discipline and Punish: The Birth of the Prison* (New York: Pantheon Books, 1977); Robin Evans, *The Fabrication of Virtue: English Prison Architecture; 1750–1840*

(Cambridge: Cambridge University Press, 1982); and Dario Melossi and Massimo Pavarini, *The Prison and the Factory: Origins of the Penitentiary System* (London: Macmillan, 1981), among others. For three of the most important studies of Bentham's Panopticon, see Gertrude Himmelfarb, "Bentham's Utopia: The National Charity Company," *Journal of British Studies* 10, no. 1 (November 1, 1970): 80–125, https://doi.org/10.1086/385602; Charles F. Bahmueller, *The National Charity Company: Jeremy Bentham's Silent Revolution* (Berkeley: University of California Press, 1981); and Janet Semple, *Bentham's Prison: A Study of the Panopticon Penitentiary* (Oxford: Clarendon Press, 1993).

3. For the development of Bentham's political theory, see Philip Schofield, *Utility and Democracy: The Political Thought of Jeremy Bentham* (Oxford: Oxford University Press, 2009). And, for a slightly different interpretation, David Lieberman, "Bentham's Democracy," *Oxford Journal of Legal Studies* 28, no. 3 (2008): 605–26.

4. Bentham intended for both architectural transparency and the financial transparency of public corporations to hold this despotic power in check. These checks are not, however, democratic in nature. It should be noted that the bulk of Bentham's prison theory dates from before his radical democratic turn, but to the end of his life, Bentham never disavowed the Panopticon. For the works of Jeremy Bentham, I have tried to cite the most recent edition available, especially when that edition has been published in the collected works (1968–present). When I have made reference to the earlier, Bowring edition of Bentham's work, *The Works of Jeremy Bentham*, ed. John Bowring (Edinburgh; London: W. Tait; Simpkin, Marshall, 1843), available at https://oll.libertyfund.org/title/bentham-works-of-jeremy-bentham-11-vols, I use the form B *[volume, in Roman numerals].[page, in Arabic numerals]*; and when referring directly to Bentham's manuscripts, I have followed the convention *[Library–UC= University College, BL= British Library] [box number].[folio number]*.

5. For an indispensable treatment of the French influence on the young Bentham, see Emmanuelle De Champs, *Enlightenment and Utility: Bentham in French, Bentham in France,* Ideas in Context (Cambridge: Cambridge University Press, 2015), esp. 41ff.

6. See De Champs, *Enlightenment and Utility,* 23–24. Bentham himself traced the origins of the principle of utility, perhaps fancifully, to his youthful reading of *Telemachus* (see B x.10). For a discussion of the role of French thought among other influences on the emergence of Bentham's utility principle, see Schofield, *Utility and Democracy,* 28ff.

7. Cesare Beccaria, *Beccaria: On Crimes and Punishments and Other Writings,* ed. Richard Bellamy, trans. Richard Davies (Cambridge: Cambridge University Press, 1995), 122.

8. Jeremy Bentham, *The Correspondence of Jeremy Bentham*, vol. 2, *1777–80*, ed. T. L. S. Sprigge, Collected Works of Jeremy Bentham (London: Athlone, 1968), 140–141. Chastellux was a "fellow disciple" of the archmaterialist Helvetius, perhaps the most important French model for Bentham. See De Champs, *Enlightenment and Utility*, 42–45.

9. In the original "Panopticon Letters," he refers to the Panopticon as "my own utopia" (B.iv.49). He more than once refers to the pauper Panopticon as a "utopia" as well, although more ambivalently, sometimes affirming and sometimes denying the label. See Jeremy Bentham, *The Correspondence of Jeremy Bentham*, vol. 5, *January 1794 to December 1797*, ed. Alexander Taylor Milne, Collected Works of Jeremy Bentham (London: Athlone, 1981), 377; and Jeremy Bentham, *Writings on the Poor Laws*, 2 vols., ed. Michael Quinn, Collected Works of Jeremy Bentham (Oxford; New York: Clarendon Press; Oxford University Press, 2010), 2:653n. See also Emmanuelle De Champs, "From 'Utopia' to 'Programme': Building a Panopticon in Geneva," in *Beyond Foucault: New Perspectives on Bentham's Panopticon* (Burlington, VT: Ashgate, 2012), 63–78; and the balanced assessment of Bentham and More in Semple, *Bentham's Prison*, 297ff.

10. See for instance, Bentham, *Writings on the Poor Laws*, 2:374n2.

11. Jeremy Bentham, *Official Aptitude Maximized, Expense Minimized*, ed. by Philip Schofield (Oxford: Clarendon Press, 1993), 37. For a similar formulation about the Panopticon, see below.

12. For a sophisticated explication of Bentham's utilitarianism against the background of his epistemological skepticism, see Michael Quinn, "Post-Modern Moments in the Application of Empirical Principles: Power, Knowledge, and Discourse in the Thought of Jeremy Bentham vs. Michel Foucault," *Revue d'études Benthamiennes*, no. 8 (May 1, 2011).

13. Jeremy Bentham, *An Introduction to the Principles of Morals and Legislation*, ed. J. H. Burns and H. L. A. Hart, Bentham, Jeremy, 1748–1832. Works. 1983. (Oxford; New York: Clarendon Press; Oxford University Press, 1996), henceforth IPML. Cf. IPML, 11–12. George Kateb, "Punishment and the Spirit of Democracy," *Social Research* 74, no. 2 (2007): 269–306, cites this as a principle of the democratic spirit of punishment, though, in the Athenian tradition, there can be democratic harshness, but it must be directed at the appropriate party. Bentham's principle of leniency, on the other hand, does not have any obviously democratic effects.

14. Given that punishment is a fictitious entity, its meaning in language can vary. Bentham sometimes refers to it as something like a person being "punished" by stubbing her toe on an object she did not see (B viii.197; cf. B viii.219n, on discipline and punishment). The looseness of punishment as a concept is discussed below.

15. The cases are where no mischief was perpetrated, where the mischief in question would be outweighed by the mischief of the punishment, where deterrence is impossible, and where a nonevil (such as instruction) would do just as well. See IPML, 159–64.

16. Of course, in a sense, it is precisely the absolute control of the Panopticon that allows this frugal relation to emerge.

17. Bentham makes this point against Beccaria in the *Rationale of Punishment* (see below; B i.399). More than a few scholars have noted that it is precisely in his "economic" understanding that Bentham advanced beyond earlier thinkers. H. L. A. Hart, "Bentham and Beccaria," in *Essays on Bentham* (Oxford: Oxford University Press, 1982), 46; and especially Anthony J. Draper, "Punishment, Proportionality, and the Economic Analysis of Crime," *Journal of Bentham Studies* 11, no. 1 (January 1, 2009): 1–32. Gary Becker himself credited Bentham with a fundamental anticipation of elements of his argument about crime as a question of minimizing the loss of aggregate income. Gary S. Becker, "Crime and Punishment: An Economic Approach," in *Economic Analysis of the Law*, ed. Donald A. Wittman (Oxford: Blackwell, 2004), 255–65; see also Richard A. Posner, *Frontiers of Legal Theory* (Cambridge: Harvard University Press, 2004), 52–61.

18. A fourth, subsidiary element is compensation or restoration.

19. This is the position taken by some Bentham scholars who claim that incarceration was merely a "penal device," not central to Bentham's philosophical ideas. This wording is from Anthony J. Draper, "An Introduction to Jeremy Bentham's Theory of Punishment," *Journal of Bentham Studies* 5, no. 1 (January 1, 2002): 1–17, 1; but could equally apply to F. Rosen, "Crime, Punishment and Liberty," *History of Political Thought* 20, no. 1 (January 1, 1999): 173–85.

20. *The Theory of Punishment* does not exist as an integral text. The manuscript drafts were used by Dumont to produce his French recensions of Bentham (*Traités de législation civile et pénale* [1802] and *Théorie des peines et des recompenses* [1811]). Parts of this were then translated back into English by Richard Smith as *The Rationale of Punishment* and included in the Bowring edition. For more textual history see IPML, xxxiii; and Hugo Bedau, "Bentham's Theory of Punishment: Origin and Content," *Journal of Bentham Studies* 7, no. 1 (January 1, 2004): 1–15, https://doi.org/10.14324/111.2045 -757X.023, 1–3. Strictly speaking, it is not clear how much of the Bowring edition texts represent Bentham rather than Dumont or Smith. (Dumont only rarely makes his intervention clear; Smith, never.) Some Bentham scholars use this as a reason for excluding *The Rationale of Punishment* and other texts from a discussion of Bentham's theory. See Draper, "Introduction to Jeremy Bentham's Theory." Manuscript evidence suggests, however, that at least the subject matter of the material in *The Rationale of*

Punishment maps, more or less, on to Bentham's plan for the work (see UC 99.2–6), published in Bedau, "Bentham's Theory of Punishment," 14. The contents of that plan guide this chapter's use of the works printed in the Bowring edition.

21. I avoid direct quotation of words that cannot be verified as Bentham's own, but this distinction is well attested in the manuscripts.

22. This is not dissimilar to Plato's discussion of "expectation" in the *Laws* or More's careful hedonism in *Utopia*. One crucial difference, of course, is that Bentham's hedonism is not merely pragmatic and is advanced in propia persona.

23. See Ross Harrison, *Bentham* (London: Routledge & Kegan Paul, 1983), 137.

24. Jeremy Bentham, *Deontology; Together with A Table of the Springs of Action; and the Article on Utilitarianism,* ed. Amnon Goldworth (Oxford; New York: Clarendon Press; Oxford University Press, 1983), 91.

25. From the manuscript draft of *Indirect Legislation* (UC 96.260). Note the interchangeability of "artificial interest" and "artificial consequence." Interests are, psychologically, a function of consequences. Neither Plato nor More, even at their most hedonistic, makes this leap from consequence to interest. This is because each has an understanding of an agent-independent good (i.e., a good independent of all agents).

26. See UC 140.60: "The Law has to do with Pain as a means: with Pleasure, as a means and as an end."

27. Recent scholarship has begun to draw the obvious parallels between Bentham's project and that of "behavioral economics," particularly the "libertarian paternalism" of Sunstein and Thaler. See Malik Bozzo-Rey, Anne Brunon-Ernst, and Michael Quinn, "Editors' Introduction," *History of European Ideas* 43, no. 1 (January 2, 2017): 1–10; Michael Quinn, "Jeremy Bentham, Choice Architect: Law, Indirect Legislation, and the Context of Choice," *History of European Ideas* 43, no. 1 (January 2, 2017): 11–33; Malik Bozzo-Rey, "Indirect Legislation: It Is Just a Question of Time," *History of European Ideas* 43, no. 1 (January 2, 2017): 106–21; Anne Brunon-Ernst, "Nudges and the Limits of Appropriate Interference: Reading Backwards from J. S. Mill's Harm Principle to Jeremy Bentham's Indirect Legislation," *History of European Ideas* 43, no. 1 (January 2, 2017): 53–69; Stephen Engelmann, "Nudging Bentham: Indirect Legislation and (Neo-)Liberal Politics," *History of European Ideas* 43, no. 1 (January 2, 2017): 70–82.

28. Relying on Quinn, "Jeremy Bentham, Choice Architect," 14–16.

29. Cf. B i.394, where taxation is a "concomitant."

30. This slipperiness was also noticed by Hart, in his introduction to IPML. H. L. A. Hart, "Bentham's Principle of Utility and Theory of Penal Law," in *Introduction to the Principles of Morals and Legislation* (Oxford: Oxford

University Press, 1996), cvii. Hart does think that there may be a defensible distinction between "criminal" punishments in Bentham and other punishments.

31. Bentham's metaphor, (B i.557). See Christian Laval, "'The Invisible Chain': Jeremy Bentham and Neo-Liberalism," *History of European Ideas* 43, no. 1 (January 2, 2017): 34–52.

32. Jeremy Bentham, *Of the Limits of the Penal Branch of Jurisprudence,* ed. Philip Schofield, Collected Works of Jeremy Bentham (Oxford: Clarendon Press, 2010), 233.

33. Dumont's editorial footnotes, which put these pages in the context of the Panopticon, give some reason to be confident of their authenticity.

34. Bentham's scheme has several striking similarities to the system proposed by Plato in the *Laws* (see Chapter 2). The first prison, to be painted white, is for debtors and conforms to the jails of Bentham's own day. The second, to be painted gray, "is designed for correction as well as for example" and inflicts "solitude, darkness and spare diet." The last, to be painted black, does not release its inmates, who are to be made "as miserable" as they can be.

35. Bentham would have known about efforts to employ convicts in dredging projects on canals and rivers.

36. See especially Ignatieff, *Just Measure of Pain,* 44–142.

37. *A View of the Hard Labour Bill* (B iv.6) was the text Bentham sent off to the French thinkers he admired most, including Morellet and Chastellux, and it was thus this text that reminded Chastellux of More.

38. See Erving Goffman, *Asylums: Essays on the Social Situation of Mental Patients and Other Inmates,* 1st ed. (Garden City, NY: Anchor Books, 1961), xiii: "A total institution may be defined as a place of residence and work where a large number of like-situated individuals, cut off from the wider society for an appreciable period of time, together lead an enclosed, formally administered round of life."

39. For the "asylum" as a total institution not limited to one functional form, see also David J. Rothman, *The Discovery of the Asylum: Social Order and Disorder in the New Republic* (Boston: Little, Brown, 1990); and Norbert Finzsch and Robert Jütte, eds., *Institutions of Confinement: Hospitals, Asylums, and Prisons in Western Europe and North America, 1500–1950,* Publications of the German Historical Institute (Washington, DC; Cambridge: German Historical Institute; Cambridge University Press, 1996).

40. *Panopticon; or The Inspection House* (B iv.58–66).

41. Besides the prison, pauper, and school Panopticons discussed below, Anne Brunon-Ernst, "Deconstructing Panopticism into the Plural Panopticons," in *Beyond Foucault* (Burlington, VT: Ashgate, 2012), 17–42, includes the panoptic situation of certain structures in the design of the administrative buildings in Bentham's *Constitutional Code.* This is also

noted in F. Rosen, *Jeremy Bentham and Representative Democracy: A Study of the Constitutional Code* (Oxford: Clarendon Press, 1983), 114.

42. For the structure of the Panopticon, see Evans, *Fabrication of Virtue*; for its history, see L. J. Hume, "Bentham's Panopticon: An Administrative History—I," *Historical Studies* 15, no. 61 (October 1, 1973): 703–21; and L. J. Hume, "Bentham's Panopticon: An Administrative History—II," *Historical Studies* 16, no. 62 (April 1, 1974): 36–54; and for the best all-around account of the design, history, and theory behind the prison, see Semple, *Bentham's Prison*.

43. As with the penal Panopticon, scholarly opinion has been divided as to whether Bentham's plan to bring the indigent poor into a system of Panopticon workhouses was admirably reform minded (given that the alternative may have been Malthusian pessimism and starvation) or deeply despotic in aim and method. For the former case, see J. R. Poynter, *Society and Pauperism: English Ideas on Poor Relief, 1795–1834,* Studies in Social History (London; Toronto: Routledge & Paul; University of Toronto Press, 1969), 106–44; and Warren Roberts, "Bentham's Poor Law Proposals," *Bentham Newsletter* 10, no. 3 (December 1, 1979): 28; for the latter, Himmelfarb, "Bentham's Utopia"; and, most comprehensively, Bahmueller, *National Charity Company*, who writes of the "pervasive, soul destroying repressiveness" of Bentham's plan. The question must be taken up again in light of the important new edition of Bentham's Poor Law writings: Jeremy Bentham, *Writings on the Poor Laws,* ed. Michael Quinn, 2 vols., Collected Works of Jeremy Bentham (Oxford; New York: Clarendon Press; Oxford University Press, 2001, 2010).

44. Bentham, *Writings on the Poor Laws,* vol. 1, 3.

45. Bentham, 6–7. Note this strange use of "punish."

46. Bentham, 19.

47. From Bentham's perspective, social equality is preferable, *ceteris paribus,* but it is still more "frugal" to confine and feed the poor than it would be to redistribute wealth from the rich, because of the expectation the wealthy have to enjoy their property, as discussed below and in P. J. Kelly, *Utilitarianism and Distributive Justice: Jeremy Bentham and the Civil Law* (Oxford; New York: Clarendon Press; Oxford University Press, 1990).

48. Bentham, *Writings on the Poor Laws,* vol. 1, 68.

49. Bentham, 207.

50. Bentham, 212.

51. Bentham, 288. The eligibility of poverty is a great worry to Bentham, who may not have had the language of free riding but was ever fearful of "hangers-on."

52. Bentham, 66. The coinage seems to be Bentham's own—one of a number of striking coinages to emerge from Bentham's *nachlass,* including the first recorded English uses of "capitalist" and "rationalize."

53. For the uses of this centralized institutional network, see Bentham, *Writings on the Poor Laws,* vol. 1, 69–140.

54. For Bentham's reading on this topic, see L. J. Hume, *Bentham and Bureaucracy,* Cambridge Studies in the History and Theory of Politics (Cambridge: Cambridge University Press, 1981). See also Michel Foucault, *Security, Territory, Population: Lectures at the Collège de France, 1977–78* (Basingstoke; Paris: Palgrave Macmillan; République Française, 2007), 311ff. Like the authors in Brunon-Ernt's *Beyond Foucault* (especially Christian Laval) and the authors in the special issue of the *History of European Ideas* (particularly Michael Quinn), this chapter finds Foucault's later writing on governmentality and "the conduct of conduct" equally, if not more, useful for thinking about Bentham's work than *Discipline and Punish.* As much as the Panopticon is a metaphor for disciplinary power, it is also a site for the production of statistical data, a site for the perfection of frugality.

55. See Bentham, *Writings on the Poor Laws,* vol. 1, 285.

56. See Elissa S. Itzkin, "Bentham's Chrestomathia: Utilitarian Legacy to English Education," *Journal of the History of Ideas* 39, no. 2 (1978): 303–16; and the editorial material in the new edition of Jeremy Bentham, *Chrestomathia,* ed. M. J. Smith and W. H. Burston (Oxford; New York: Clarendon Press; Oxford University Press, 1983).

57. Bentham, *Chrestomathia,* 106.

58. From *Panopticon,* though in the section describing its use as a school.

59. Bentham, *Writings on the Poor Laws,* vol 2, 225.

60. Initially Bentham, following Howard, saw solitary confinement as essential for reform. He soon changed his mind, however, and the reformatory aspects of incarceration were limited to the role of forced labor. See B iv.71–73.

61. The actual principles of panoptic management (beyond those mentioned above, such as the interest-duty principle and the earn-first principle) have been adequately treated elsewhere. See Bentham, *Writings on the Poor Laws,* 2010, 112–35. There are good discussions in Bahmueller, *National Charity Company,* 186ff; and Hume, *Bentham and Bureaucracy,* which brilliantly describes the broad development of management as a theme in Bentham's work; see also Marco E. L. Guidi, "'My Own Utopia': The Economics of Bentham's Panopticon," *European Journal of the History of Economic Thought* 11, no. 3 (September 1, 2004): 405–31; and Spencer J. Weinreich, "Panopticon, Inc.: Jeremy Bentham, Contract Management, and (Neo)Liberal Penality," *Punishment and Society* 23, no. 4 (October 1, 2021): 497–514, on the reception (or lack thereof) of this aspect of Bentham.

62. Very late in his life, Bentham still rued that he had not been given management of the contract for the prison: but for the conspiracies of sinister

interest, "all the prisoners in England would, years ago, have been under my management. . . . All the paupers in the country would, long ago, have been under my management" (B xi.96–97).

63. This contractor need not have been one person. In the case of the pauper Panopticon, Bentham explicitly envisioned a joint stock company (on the model of the East India Company) that would run the entire "network" of institutions and sell shares at a low enough price that the middle classes could afford to invest small sums.

64. See B iv.125ff; Bentham, *Writings on the Poor Laws,* vol. 2, 322.

65. For the theme of Bentham, transparency, and mistrust, see Jonathan R. Bruno, "Vigilance and Confidence: Jeremy Bentham, Publicity, and the Dialectic of Political Trust and Distrust," *American Political Science Review* 111, no. 2 (May 2017): 295–307. Bentham spent considerable effort designing and considering the administrative details and methods of bookkeeping, which were as important to the Panopticon as the brick-and-mortar architecture. For a discussion, see Hume, *Bentham and Bureaucracy.*

66. Bentham, *Writings on the Poor Laws,* vol. 2, 373.

67. Hume, *Bentham and Bureaucracy,* 17–54.

68. Bentham, *Writings on the Poor Laws,* vol. 1, 278. Smith notes the tendency of tax farmers to combine to avoid competition, to extract profit at the cost of the general good, and any number of other failures of public/private partnership. Smith, *Wealth of Nations,* V.2.218.

69. Bentham, *Writings on the Poor Laws,* vol. 2, 373.

70. Bentham, 521, cf. 558.

71. *Panopticon versus New South Wales* (B iv.185n).

72. See, e.g., Werner Stark, *Jeremy Bentham's Economic Writings: Volume One* (London: Taylor and Francis, 2013), 143. For Bentham's account of egoism and interest, IPML, 11–14; and, e.g., Jeremy Bentham, *Securities against Misrule and Other Constitutional Writings for Tripoli and Greece* (Oxford; New York: Clarendon Press; Oxford University Press, 1990), 265: "If the result depended upon himself each individual would give expression and effect to such will as in his judgment would in the highest degree be conducive to his own greatest happiness, whatsoever became of the happiness of others, and consequently on most if not all occasions at the expense of the happiness of all others."

73. Scholars have long been interested in the possibility of a conflict between the individual's calculation of interest and the interests of the "greatest number." See the debate over David Lyons, *In the Interest of the Governed: A Study in Bentham's Philosophy of Utility and Law,* rev. ed. (Oxford; New York: Clarendon Press; Oxford University Press, 1991), with contributions including F. Rosen, "Individual Sacrifice and the Greatest Happiness: Bentham on Utility and Rights," *Utilitas* 10, no. 2 (July 1998): 129–43; and

Gerald J. Postema, "Bentham's Equality-Sensitive Utilitarianism: Gerald J. Postema," *Utilitas* 10, no. 2 (1998): 144–58.

74. Bentham, *Securities against Misrule*, 219n4. Ultimately, Bentham's democratic theory relies on a precise, almost Rousseauian sifting out of individual from general ("universal") interests. See Gerald J. Postema, "Interests, Universal and Particular: Bentham's Utilitarian Theory of Value," *Utilitas* 18, no. 2 (June 2006): 109–33.

75. Bentham, *Writings on the Poor Laws*, vol. 1, 66–92.

76. See Bentham, *Writings on the Poor Laws*, vol. 2, 582–89, "Frugality assisted." Many of these ideas (as with Bentham's proposal for universal health records) would not find wider expression in public policy for another two centuries, but they reflect an approach to poverty alleviation that is strikingly similar to modern, market-based efforts to encourage microfinance, savings, and accessible urban banking in the developing world and impoverished communities.

77. Bentham, *Writings on the Poor Laws*, vol. 1, 45.

78. Bentham, *Writings on the Poor Laws*, vol. 2, 201–2. For more on the behavioristic project of the Panopticon, see Bahmueller, *National Charity Company*, 164–200. Bahmueller describes Bentham's project as the inculcation of what Max Weber dubbed "worldly asceticism." The Panopticon becomes an iron cage in a doubled sense.

79. With apologies to Laval, "'The Invisible Chain,'" who uses the phrase "fabric of certainty" to describe this feature of the Panopticon (Laval is himself punning on Bentham's interest in the "fabric of security," IPML, 11). For Bentham's experimentalism, see B iv.64–65 and B viii.424–428 (reprinted in Bentham, *Writings on the Poor Laws*, vol. 2). "In this point of view, at least, Bacon . . . would not have regarded [the Panopticon] with indifference."

80. For the former formulation, see Allison Dube, *The Theme of Acquisitiveness in Bentham's Political Thought*, Political Theory and Political Philosophy (New York: Garland, 1991), 316ff. For the latter, Laval, "The Invisible Chain," first published in French as Christian Laval, "'La chaîne invisible'. Jeremy Bentham et le néo-libéralisme," *Revue d'études benthamiennes*, no. 1 (September 1, 2006). Laval was among the first to explore the connection between Bentham's work on frugality, indirect legislation, and punishment. Bentham as a theorist of "subject formation" brings him even closer to a leading position in the history of neoliberalism. Weinreich, "Panopticon, Inc."

81. Bentham seems to use "economy" as a narrower subset of the broader "frugality." For Bentham's use of the terms, see Anne Brunon-Ernst, *Utilitarian Biopolitics: Bentham, Foucault and Modern Power* (London: Pickering and Chatto, 2012), 113–20, as well as Anne Brunon-Ernst, "Le Vocabulaire Benthamien Dans Le Lexique Français et Anglais: Couple

Langue-Culture Fusionnel?," in *Langue et Culture, Un Mariage de Raison?*, ed. R. Greenstein (Paris: Presses de la Sorbonne, 2009), 95–118.

82. IPML, 282.

83. IPML, 263n. See the discussion of Hobbes in Chapter 4.

84. IPML, 287.

85. Bentham, *Writings on the Poor Laws,* vol. 2, 46.

86. Bentham acknowledges the traditional aspects of "family responsibility" that had accompanied poor laws since Elizabethan times, but he does not rely on it. He would be just as happy to have the necessary "human capital" produced within the panoptic system. In this, Bentham differs from Gary Becker and others who relied on the family to produce the productive, rational actor. See Melinda Cooper, *Family Values: Between Neoliberalism and the New Social Conservatism*, Near Futures (New York: Zone Books, 2017).

87. Here Bentham also accepts service in the East India Company. See Semple, *Bentham's Prison*, 177–80. Semple writes that these policies are due to the fine levied on the contractor in cases of recidivism that Bentham proposed to encourage reform.

88. Bentham notes that because of his limited employability, the wages of such a Metasylum man can be low.

89. Bentham, *Writings on the Poor Laws,* vol. 2, 217–18.

90. Bentham, 139.

91. See Semple, *Bentham's Prison*, 288–90.

92. Bentham, *Writings on the Poor Laws,* vol. 1, 191.

93. Bentham, 191. In Bentham's defense, he was not the only reformer at the time concerned or skeptical about the fate of discharged convicts. His friend and interlocutor Patrick Colquhoun wrote: "That man will deserve a statue to his memory who shall devise and carry into effect a plan for the employment of *Discharged Convicts*, who may be desirous of laboring for their subsistence in an honest way." Similar sentiments were surely on Bentham's mind. See Patrick Colquhoun, *A Treatise on the Police of the Metropolis: Explaining the Various Crimes and Misdemeanors Which at Present Are Felt as a Pressure Upon the Community; and Suggesting Remedies for Their Prevention* (H. Fry, 1796), 89–92.

94. More, *Utopia*, 75.

95. Bentham, *Writings on the Poor Laws,* vol. 2, 12, 23; cf. Bentham, *Writings on the Poor Laws,* vol. 1, 284.

96. Bentham, *Writings on the Poor Laws,* vol. 2, 23–60. Bentham's language here could be read as strictly a comment on enlarging the labor force (creating the "docile bodies" necessary for industrial labor), but Bentham is equally interested in *what kind* of laborer will exist. The Panopticon is designed to take the place of the entire educational-familial

apparatus that trains and prepares a worker. Bentham is approaching the territory of Becker's "human capital."

97. For the complete listing of the categories of unused labor, see the chart printed by Bentham in the "Annals of Agriculture" and published in Bentham, *Writings on the Poor Laws,* vol. 1, lvii.

98. See Bentham, *Writings on the Poor Laws,* vol. 2, 334. It will be remembered that in the penal Panopticons, the limited monopoly on labor power will provide sufficient margins for profit. Many readers of the Poor Law writings have found the nadir of the scheme's depredations in the dependence on child labor. See Bahmueller, *National Charity Company*; and Himmelfarb, "Bentham's Utopia." Others have noted conditions for poor children were not necessarily more eligible than this. See Poynter, *Society and Pauperism.*

99. For Bentham's attempt to wrestle with the ultimately untenable Royal Society numbers, see Bentham, *Writings on the Poor Laws,* vol. 2, 442ff; and the editorial introduction to same, lxxxii–lxxxiv. For the table, see Bentham, 470.

100. Bentham, *Writings on the Poor Laws,* vol. 1, 39; cf. B i.310-312.

101. Bentham, 39.

102. Bentham, *Writings on the Poor Laws,* vol. 2, 66–67.

103. Bentham, 236-37.

104. Bentham, 56.

105. UC 29.6, from a bruillion with the heading "Civil Reforms."

106. See Kelly, *Utilitarianism and Distributive Justice,* 83–94; and Michael Quinn, "A Failure to Reconcile the Irreconcilable? Security, Subsistence and Equality in Bentham's Writings on the Civil Code and on the Poor Laws," *History of Political Thought* 29, no. 2 (January 1, 2008): 320–43, 335–41.

107. Bentham, *Writings on the Poor Laws,* vol. 2, 168, 169. It is worth noting, given the loaded meanings of the term "class," that it is Bentham's own preferred term, both in terms of the "class of person maintained by their own labor" (above) and in terms of the "gentlefolk" versus the "the Poor." Bentham, 167-68.

108. In a note to the initial "Panopticon Letters," Bentham conceded, "Nor do I imagine [Rousseau] would have put his *Emilius* into an inspection-house; but I think he would have been glad of such a school for [the unfaithful] Sophia" (B iv.64).

109. Bentham, *Writings on the Poor Laws,* vol. 1, 213.

110. Bentham, *Writings on the Poor Laws,* vol. 2, 180; cf. 171–79.

111. Bentham, 180.

112. Bentham, 267. Quinn, "A Failure to Reconcile the Irreconcilable?," aptly describes the tension between Bentham's moral egalitarianism and hierarchical social theory.

113. For the first, Bentham, *Writings on the Poor Laws,* vol. 1, 195; for the second, Bentham, *Writings on the Poor Laws,* vol. 2, 168.

114. See B iv.74.

115. Bentham, *Writings on the Poor Laws,* vol. 2, 49.

116. Bentham, 49.

117. Bentham, 49.

118. Bentham, 49.

119. Bentham, *Writings on the Poor Laws,* vol. 1, 202.

120. Bentham, 203. For the incarceration of the accused before trial in both types of Panopticon, see B iv.59 (prison) and Bentham, 96–98 (pauper Panopticon). For the untenability of Bentham's attempt to distinguish between modes of intervention on the basis of "time," see Bozzo-Rey, "Indirect Legislation."

121. Bentham, 49–50. Bentham's suspicion of "liberty" was intense. "I would no more use the word liberty in my conversation . . . than I would brandy in my diet . . . both cloud the understanding and inflame the passions" (UC 100.70). Bentham's preferred term for what is often called "negative liberty" was "security."

122. See the introduction. For the abolitionist case against jails as well as prisons see Angela Y. Davis, Gina Dent, Erica R. Meiners, and Beth E. Richie, *Abolition. Feminism. Now.,* Abolitionist Papers Series (Chicago: Haymarket Books, 2022). For the relationship between changes in the welfare state and changes in the late modern prison, see, inter alia, David Garland, *The Culture of Control: Crime and Social Order in Contemporary Society* (Oxford: Oxford University Press, 2002); Michael Cavadino and James Dignan, *Penal Systems: A Comparative Approach* (Los Angeles: Sage, 2006); Jonathan Simon, *Governing through Crime: How the War on Crime Transformed American Democracy and Created a Culture of Fear* (New York: Oxford University Press, 2007); Loïc J. D. Wacquant, *Punishing the Poor: The Neoliberal Government of Social Insecurity,* English language ed., Politics, History, and Culture (Durham, NC: Duke University Press, 2009).

123. See Michel Foucault, *Wrong-Doing, Truth-Telling: The Function of Avowal in Justice* (Chicago; Louvain-la-Neuve, France: University of Chicago Press; Presses Universitaires de Louvain, 2014), 254.

124. From the *Principles of the Civil Code,* B i.302.

125. BL Add. MS 33550, folio 125, from 1828, late into Bentham's "radical" period.

126. See B i.314; Kelly, *Utilitarianism and Distributive Justice,* 71–136; and Quinn, "A Failure to Reconcile the Irreconcilable?," both of whom examine the security/equality/property relationship and Bentham's squeamishness about redistribution.

127. The interwoven questions of economic and penal intervention are, to a great extent, the thesis of Bernard E. Harcourt, *The Illusion of Free Markets*

(Cambridge, MA: Harvard University Press, 2011), 48–52, with which this chapter is in substantial agreement. For the contradiction of Bentham's intervention in one sphere and abstention in another, see especially pp. 103–20. Michel Foucault's use of the Panopticon as a metaphor for industrial modernity had the effect of both universalizing Bentham's prison writings and, conversely, limiting their importance for the study of contemporary prisons. If the point of the Panopticon is only to create disciplined, docile bodies, then Bentham's theory would seem to be obsolete in the age of "penal post-modernity," when prisoners are warehoused rather than reformed. This point is echoed by Weinreich, "Panopticon, Inc."

128. See Malik Bozzo-Rey, Anne Brunon-Ernst, and Michael Quinn, "Editors' Introduction," *History of European Ideas* 43, no. 1 (January 2, 2017): 1–10, 1. This chapter shares their ambition to more closely connect Bentham to the history of what Foucault called "neo-liberalism."

129. Bentham, *Panopticon versus New South Wales* (B iv.185n).

130. Bentham, *Writings on the Poor Laws,* vol. 2, 201–2.

CONCLUSION

1. This transition is discussed at greater length in the introduction. For the transition to a postpanoptic era of punishment, see Malcolm M. Feeley and Jonathan Simon, "The New Penology: Notes on the Emerging Strategy of Corrections and Its Implications," *Criminology* 30, no. 4 (1992): 449–74; and David Garland, *The Culture of Control: Crime and Social Order in Contemporary Society* (Oxford: Oxford University Press, 2002).

2. For recent abolitionist arguments see, inter alia, Allegra M. McLeod, "Envisioning Abolition Democracy," *Harvard Law Review* 132, no. 6 (April 2019): 1613–49. And Angela Y. Davis, Gina Dent, Erica R. Meiners, and Beth E. Richie, *Abolition. Feminism. Now.,* Abolitionist Papers Series (Chicago: Haymarket Books, 2022). For a recent reformist rejoinder, see Tommie Shelby, *The Idea of Prison Abolition* (Princeton, NJ: Princeton University Press, 2022).

3. For the historical background, see the introduction. For an account of the decline of reformism in the United States, see Francis A. Allen, *The Decline of the Rehabilitative Ideal: Penal Policy and Social Purpose* (New Haven, CT: Yale University Press, 1981).

4. See, for instance, Peter Ramsay, "A Democratic Theory of Imprisonment," in *Democratic Theory and Mass Incarceration,* ed. Albert Dzur, Ian Loader, and Richard Sparks (Oxford: Oxford University Press, 2016), 84–107.

5. Mary Margaret Mackenzie, *Plato on Punishment* (Berkeley: University of California Press, 1981), 222.

6. Even noncarceral proposals like those of the restorative justice movement must confront the Platonic challenge that the institutional means

contribute to the theoretical ends. It is not easy to assist criminals in becoming "people who will not cause harm again." Danielle Sered, *Until We
Reckon: Violence, Mass Incarceration, and a Road to Repair* (New York: New Press,
2019), 246. To fully explore the contemporary alternatives to Platonic techniques of punishment would be the task of another book, but some advocates for forms of restorative justice have made powerful cases for commu-
nity-based techniques of criminal rehabilitation. See Sered, *Until We Reckon.*
However, not all forms of restorative justice pass the Platonic test of envisioning the social fabric as a whole. See Bernard E. Harcourt, "Placing
Shame in Context: A Response to Thomas Scheff on Community Confer-
ences and Therapeutic Jurisprudence (Response to Thomas J. Scheff, *Revista
Juridica de La Universidad de Puerto Rico,* vol. 67, p. 95, 1998)," *Revista Juridica de
La Universidad de Puerto Rico* 67, no. 3 (1998): 627–34, for a skeptical review of
such efforts. The most effective and least invasive forms of behavioral reform might take place before a trial or even before an arrest. See Danielle
Sered and Amanda Alexander, "Making Communities Safe, without the
Police," *Boston Review,* November 1, 2021, https://www.bostonreview.net
/articles/making-communities-safe-without-the-police/, but such efforts
are no longer recognizable as punishment, in the strict philosophical sense.

7. George Kateb, "Punishment and the Spirit of Democracy," *Social Research* 74,
no. 2 (2007): 269–306; and Ramsay, "Democratic Theory of Imprisonment."

8. For the harshness of contemporary incarceration, see, inter alia, Michelle Alexander, *The New Jim Crow: Mass Incarceration in the Age of Colorblindness,* rev. ed. (New York: New Press, 2011); Jonathan Simon, *Governing
through Crime: How the War on Crime Transformed American Democracy and
Created a Culture of Fear* (New York: Oxford University Press, 2007); Angela Y. Davis, *Are Prisons Obsolete?* (New York: Seven Stories, 2003).

9. See Loïc J. D. Wacquant, *Punishing the Poor: The Neoliberal Government of
Social Insecurity,* English language ed., Politics, History, and Culture
(Durham, NC: Duke University Press, 2009); and, more generally, John
Pratt, *Penal Populism: Key Ideas in Criminology,* Key Ideas in Criminology
(London: Routledge, Taylor & Francis, 2007).

10. Of course, some liberal theorists, among them Jeremy Bentham, will insist
that the popularly authorized tradition errs in assigning a lower importance to crimes against property, because property is the real foundation
of a stable social order. This higher-order disagreement is beyond the
scope of this study.

11. For this value in the context of ancient democracies, see Josiah Ober,
"The Original Meaning of 'Democracy': Capacity to Do Things, Not Ma-
jority Rule," *Constellations* 15, no. 1 (March 2008): 3–9; and, as values at
the heart of the American liberal-democratic project, Danielle S. Allen,
*Our Declaration: A Reading of the Declaration of Independence in Defense of
Equality,* 1st ed. (New York: Liveright, 2014).

ACKNOWLEDGMENTS

A first book is also a ledger of one's debts. I have accrued many of those over the eight or so years that I have been writing this book (and the ten or so years since I first became interested in Plato's odd passage about a prison for atheists in the *Laws*). First, to the advisors I've had over the years, from Steven Smith to David Sedley and finally to Danielle Allen, I have been fortunate to be blessed with teachers who have continually broadened my sense of what a scholar should be and what rigorous scholarship looks like. This book is also the product of long-running conversations with Richard Tuck and Bernard Harcourt. I continue to marvel at the way in which the impact of these conversations on my work has only increased with time.

I have also had the pleasure of a lengthy period of *Wanderjahre*—three post-doctoral fellowships without which I am sure this book would not have been written (at least not this decade). I am immensely grateful to Hanoch Dagan and the Edmond J. Safra Center for Ethics at Tel Aviv University; Shai Lavi, Director of the Van Leer Institute and doyen of the

Polonsky Academy; and Josiah Ober of the Stanford Civics Initiative. Not only did these fellowships give me the support to write and opportunities to share my work, but their directors are also exceptional examples of scholarly generosity. Double thanks are due to Josh, for his help putting together a manuscript workshop (as well as offering much helpful advice along the way, whether about Greek history or about grizzly bears). Thanks as well to the Zephyr Institute for sponsoring the workshop.

I have had the good fortune to present versions of this book's chapters to many audiences—at Harvard, the American Political Science Association, the Midwest Political Science Association, both Safra Centers for Ethics, the West Coast Plato Workshop, and the Hebrew University in Jerusalem– experiences that improved it immeasurably. Special thanks are due to commenters on the manuscript in whole or in part: Julie Cooper, Marcus Folch, Dimitrios Halikias, Demetra Kasimis, Tae-Yeoun Keum, Matt Landauer, Jill Locke, Jeremy Reid, Rosie Wagner, Sam Zeitlin; and to the readers from the manuscript workshop: Matthew Larsen, Alison McQueen, Jonathan Simon, and Matt Simonton. Deep thanks are also due to the anonymous reviewers for Harvard University Press who saved me from many errors, and helped me think through exactly what I was saying, and why I was saying it. I would not have had such excellent reviewers, and indeed, might not have had a text worth reviewing, were it not for my editor, Sam Stark, whose faith in this book from the beginning helped me bring it to its conclusion.

An even longer list of debts goes to the friends and family who have given me joy and ideas for decades, but especially while writing this book. As I've learned from Plato and More, friends do hold all things in common, so this work is theirs as much as it is mine. My thanks to Adam Kroopnick, James Kennedy, Raphael Magarik, Yedidya Naveh, Charles Clavey, Jon Gould, Becca Goldstein, Shira Telushkin, Leah Downey, Josh Simons, Sydney Levine, Yoav Schaefer, Jonah Fisher, and Zach Fenster. The difference between a complete "final" manuscript and a book is a subtle thing, but in my case it involved becoming part of a community, cenobitic in a special sense, in Jaffa. My deep thanks to Chana Dulin, Nora El-Zokm, Miriam Fisher, and Noa Yammer for making these years joyful; and to Maya Rosen, Danny Weininger, Alan Abbey, Sheryl Adler, Peter Cole, and Adina Hoffman, likewise, in Jerusalem. Lastly, thanks are due to the congenial colleagues who have welcomed me to the Department of Philosophy at Ben-Gurion University of the Negev in Be'er Sheva.

It was my fate and fortune to complete this book in partnership with Bella Ryb, my best friend and my best editor. It is because of her that this book found its critical voice, and it is to her sense and standard of justice that I measure my work, now and always.

Finally, I dedicate this book to my family—to my sister, Aliza, and most of all to my parents, Mitch and Amy Abolafia, who have always nurtured in me both a sense of what is right and a desire to find things out. Without them, nothing.

INDEX

Agis IV of Sparta, 81
Alexander the Great, 70
Alexandria, 78
Alighieri, Dante, 52
American Friends Service
    Committee, 17
American Revolutionary
    War, 136
Amsterdam, 102
Analogy: between ancient and
    modern prisons, 71–72; of the soul
    as a puppet in the *Laws*, 53, 67
Androtion, 30–31, 33, 35–36, 38
Archebius, 25
Aristotle, 66, 80, 87, 95
Atheism: in More's *Utopia*, 87, 89–90,
    100; in Plato's *Laws*, 47, 58, 60,
    69, 72
Athens: Athenian democracy, 5–7,
    159; democratic ideology of,

31–32, 37–39, 41, 43–44, 48, 77;
    jail in, 7, 27–28, 32–33, 45–46,
    71–73; origins of the prison in,
    3, 7, 9–10, 26–27, 69–70, 73;
    punishment and incarceration in,
    8, 26–29, 33–40, 43–45, 66, 70, 102,
    161; slave/free distinction in,
    9, 44; sovereignty of the *demos* in,
    21, 26
Augustine of Hippo, 97, 100–101,
    201n44, 205n91; *De opera
    monachorum*, 97

Battle of Hastings. *See* "Norman
    conquest"
Battle of the Milvian Bridge, 82
Beccaria, Cesare, 128–129, 134,
    215n17
Behavioral control, 11–12, 72, 86,
    145, 201n50

Bentham, Jeremy: *Constitutional Code*, 137, 217n41; inspection principle, 12, 137, 140; *Introduction to the Principles of Morals and Legislation*, 129–131; moral psychology, 129, 131–133; *Pauper Management Improved*, 150–151; part of the Platonic reformative tradition, 7, 12, 20, 127, 134–135; and poor relief, 133, 138, 144, 149, 153, 218n43; principles of institutional design, 20, 116, 128, 136, 142, 158; response to the Penitentiary Act, 136; social thought of, 138, 145, 151, 155–6; theory of class, 127, 143, 151; theory of interventions, 145, 154–156; theory of penal labor, 11, 127, 136, 138, 144, 148–149; theory of property as security, 138, 154, 161; *The Theory of Punishment* (work), 131; theory of soul craft, 127; utilitarianism, 11, 126; utopianism and, 126–129, 137; *A View of the Hard Labour Bill*, 136. *See also* contract management; legislation

Bentham's theory of punishment, 131, 141; as artificial consequence, 132–133; definition of punishment as evil, 129; distinction between custody and punishment, 4, 152–153; frugality in punishment, 130, 134, 141, 144, 153–154; punishment as intervention, 131–135, 140, 144–146, 152–156

Bielfeld, Jakob Friedrich von, 139
Bridewells, 110
Brockway, Zebulon, 113

Callicles, 49–51, 58, 61, 63, 68–69
Capitalism, 3, 20
Capital punishment: compared or contrasted with incarceration, 26, 43, 90, 93, 103, 111, 159; criticisms of, 91, 109–110; historical status of, 76, 91; Hobbes' defense of, 109–110; Plato's use of, 59; replaced by incarceration, 3; severs the

social contract, 8, 113, 123
Cardinal Morton, 91
Carthusian order, 76, 79, 97
Chastellux, François Jean de Beauvoir de, 128–129, 217n37
Choice architecture, 133
Christianity, 43, 77, 82, 98–100, 155. *See also* Jewish and Christian Platonism
Cicero, Marcus Tullius, 82, 85, 88, 90, 92, 96–97
Class, 44, 71, 128, 145–156; classism, 17, 44; lower class, 12, 150; middle class, 12, 127, 149, 154; upper class, 150, 153
Cleon, 42
Communism, 83, 101, 206n102
Constantine, 82
Contract management, 141–142
Corporal punishment, 56–59, 76, 107, 109; incarceration a form of, 28, 34–35, 43, 47, 58; incarceration not a form of, 117, 141; replaced by incarceration, 3, 72, 93; severs the social contract, 8, 113
Crete, 53
Crime, 10, 15–16, 21–23, 26, 40–41, 89; material causes of, 100, 119–121, 132, 138; psychological causes of, 19, 49, 55–60, 72, 91, 116–117, 155; public crimes, 38, 40
Criminality, 17
Criminal psychology, 46, 56, 116
Criminals: classifications of, 54–59, 136; excluded from society, 17, 26; incurables, 60, 158; as members of society, 2, 11, 26, 40, 63, 127; versus rebels, 106–107
Criminology, 17, 72–73, 136
Crito (character), 71

Davis, Angela, 18
Death penalty. *See* Capital punishment
Debtors, incarceration of, 27, 33, 35, 76
Decarceration, 14

Declaration of Independence, 13
Declaration of the Rights of
Man, 150
Democracy, 3, 8, 24, 28, 31–32, 39,
70–72, 160; democratic boundary
of, 66; future-directed punishment
and, 40, 61; incarceration and, 13,
20–22, 33, 36–37, 44. *See also*
Athens: Athenian democracy;
Theories of the prison
Demosthenes, 1, 4, 8, 22, 28–29,
43, 124; against elites, 66, 68,
70, 100; attack on incarceration,
31; defense of democratic
incarceration, 26, 33–40, 66–68,
70–71; Speech *Against Androtion,*
29–32; Speech *Against Timocrates,*
28–39; theory of democratic
punishment, 26, 38–39, 72, 103,
159–161
Deterrence. *See* Theories of
punishment
Dialectical examination, 11, 58, 61,
158, 189n30
Diggers, 110, 113–114
Diodorus, 30, 32–33
Diodotus, 41–42
Discursive site, prison as a, 4–6, 29,
33, 76

Education, 51, 53–54, 57, 63,
85, 89, 118, 139–140, 150–152;
analogy for reform in the
Platonic tradition, 40–42, 61–62,
70, 77, 90–93, 100, 128; liberal
education/*education*/*paideia*, 56, 88,
95, 135
elenchus. See Dialectical examination
Elites, 6, 11, 29, 68–69, 100, 119; as
threats to democratic rule, 23,
31–32, 37, 39, 66, 159–160
Elmira system, 19
Enclosure, 119–120
England, 71, 81, 91, 93–94, 99,
103–104, 110
Enlightenment, 3, 72, 128
Epistocracy, 67
Equality. *See* Formal equality

Erasmus, Desiderius, 80, 84;
Adages, 84
Euctemon, 26, 33
Execution. *See* Capital punishment
Exile, 59, 76–77, 89, 107–108;
compared or contrasted with
incarceration, 7, 26, 39, 43; as
oligarchic punishment, 32
Expectation, 53, 58, 63–64, 72, 127,
150–154
Expulsion. *See* Exile

Fear, 53, 55, 63–64, 117–118, 131
Fenelon, 128
Fines, 56, 59, 108, 141
Folch, Marcus, 29, 68
Formal equality/Equality before the
law, 6, 14, 22, 31–32, 39–40, 71–72,
124, 156, 160
Foucault, Michel, 6, 14–15, 17, 67,
135, 149, 155; on Bentham's
Panopticon, 140–141
France, 71
Freedom, 9, 26, 39, 44, 94. *See also*
Hobbes, Thomas
Frugality. *See* Bentham's theory of
punishment

Genealogy, 73, 79, 98, 148–149
Gentleness in punishing, 8, 22–23,
39–40
Goffman, Erving, 135, 137
Governmentality, 149, 219n54
Graphē paranomōn, 8, 175n12
Grotius, Hugo, 109, 111
Groupe d'information sur les prisons
(GIS), 17
Gutnick Allen, Signy, 106

Hadrian, 77
Hale, Matthew, 110
Hamburg, 102
Hanway, Jonas, 136
Harshness in punishing, 21–24,
37–38, 40, 44, 92, 107, 129,
159–161
Hedonism. *See* Pleasure and pain
Hillner, Julia, 78

Hobbes, Thomas: *De Cive*, 107,
111–112, 118, 124; definition of
freedom/liberty, 112–114, 122–125,
159; *Leviathan*, 104–108, 110–113,
121, 124; moral psychology of,
115–119; popular authorization
theory of incarceration and, 6,
20–21, 124–125, 159–160; on
punishing the powerful, 22,
119–122; right of resistance in, 104,
111, 125; theory of punishment, 8,
22, 103–110, 114–116; theory of
incarceration, 9, 20–21, 103,
110–115, 122–124. *See also* Freedom
Homer, 36, 62
Honor, 36, 39, 51, 56–57, 65, 90, 95,
99, 108
Horizontal punishment. *See*
Punishment
Howard, John, 136
Hythloday, Raphael, 80, 82–84

Ignorance, 55–56, 58–60, 116
Impiety, 40, 47, 58
Imprisonment and prisons, 1–5, 19,
24, 26, 72, 101, 158; history of, 5–6,
13–16, 19, 103, 110; justifications
for, 2, 8, 14–18, 38, 156, 158. *See
also* Theories of the prison
Incapacitation. *See* Theories of
punishment
Incarceration. *See* Imprisonment and
prisons; Punitive incarceration
Industrial society, 12, 15, 99, 127, 152
Inequality, 23, 39
"Institution begging," 42, 48, 91, 93,
95, 158
Institutions, 3, 11–12, 20, 29, 82, 155;
More's institutionalism, 83–86,
88–89; Plato's use of, 46–47, 50,
53–54, 67–68, 71. *See also* Total
institutions
Interests, 11, 64, 68, 85; Bentham's
theory of, 132–133, 141–144, 148, 153
Isocrates, 30

Jail, 3, 47, 57, 61, 76. *See also* Prison/
jail distinction

Jewish and Christian Platonism, 5,
10, 77, 155
Juries, 7–8, 22, 35, 43, 48, 67–68
Justice, 36, 38, 55–56, 61–66, 91, 160

Kasimis, Demetra, 29
Kateb, George, 21–22

Labor/hard work: ancient attitudes
toward, 95–97; characteristic of
social order, 94, 100, 149; as
interest formation, 136–138,
142–146; socially beneficial, 94,
148, 149; source of wealth, 127,
138, 149; technique of penal
reform, 11, 19, 76, 79, 92–95,
101–102, 111
Law, 15, 22–23, 27, 33–35, 77, 135,
145; Demosthenes' theory of, 38; in
Hobbes, 103, 106, 108, 112–118,
122; as "invisible chain," 153; in
Plato's *Laws*, 53–54, 63–67. *See also*
Legislation, direct and indirect
Legislation, direct and indirect,
133–135, 138, 140, 145, 151
Less eligibility, principle of, 93,
139, 149
Levellers, 110
Liberal(-democratic) state, 14, 16, 40,
72, 94, 123–125, 159–161
Liberalism, 20, 23, 105, 155, 159–160
Liberty. *See* Freedom
Lind, John, 127
London, 81, 99, 102
Lucian, 80
Lysitheides, 26

Machiavelli, Niccolò, 71, 121
Masses, 6, 11, 49, 119, 121
Mass incarceration, 2, 5, 14–15,
17–18, 21, 157
Materialism, 11, 72–73, 89–90,
128–129
Mausolus, 25, 33
McCabe, Margaret Mary
(Mackenzie), 42, 53, 158
Medicine, as analogy for reform, 10,
49, 77

Metasylum, 147, 153
Moderation, 62, 66, 78
Monasticism/Asceticism, 11, 43, 75, 78, 79, 97–98
Montesquieu, 128
Moral psychology, 10–11, 42, 53–59, 64, 86–90, 115–119, 131, 135
More, Thomas, 4, 7, 75, 100–101; Bentham's relationship to, 102, 119–121, 126–130, 134–136, 145; and the Platonic/reformative tradition of incarceration, 11, 79, 86, 89–91, 93, 99–100, 156, 158; and Renaissance Platonism, 76, 79–81, 84, 98; *Utopia*, 11, 75, 79–86, 89–91, 93, 96, 99, 100
Myth, 10, 50–53, 60–61, 64

Naucratis, 25
Neckar, Jacques, 139
New York system, 19
Nietzsche, Friedrich, 41
Nocturnal Council, 47, 60, 66, 68, 73
Nordic model, 19–20
Norfolk system, 19
"Norman conquest," 114
"Nothing works," 17, 53
Nudging. *See* Choice architecture

Oligarchy, and incarceration, 28, 68; oligarchic punishment, 31–33
Ostracism, 7, 27, 39

Panopticon, 12, 127, 135, 137, 140–144, 147–156; chrestomathic panopticon, 140; joint stock company, 12, 141–143; paedotrophion/baby panopticon, 147; pauper panopticon/industry house, 12, 138–139, 143, 146–154
Paradox of popularly authorized punishment. *See* Theories of the prison
Passions, 53, 55–60, 116–118, 120, 132
Paternalism, 15, 17, 60, 158
Patterson, Orlando, 147
Peloponnesian War, 27, 43

Penitentiary, 3–4, 13–14, 19, 40, 46, 73, 137; Penitentiary Act, 136
Pennsylvania system, 19
Pericles, 40–42, 54
Persian War, 53
Philo of Alexandria, 77–78
Philosophy, 4–5, 15, 46, 52, 54, 88, 123
Plato, 7, 10–11, 28, 47–48, 66–74, 77–79, 93, 158; *Apology*, 28; *Crito* (dialogue), 71; *Gorgias*, 48, 50–54, 56, 60–63, 78, 81; inspiration for Thomas More, 79–87, 99–101; *Laws*, 53–60, 63, 65–69, 77, 85–86, 156; Penal theory of, 19–20, 40, 46–49; *Phaedo*, 45, 51–52; prisons in, 10, 42, 47–48, 60–61; *Republic*, 52–53, 55, 64, 66, 68, 72, 83–84; *Sophist*, 56–58, 60–61; *Stateman*, 67. *See also* Myth; Punishment; Theories of the prison
Platonic/reformative tradition. *See* Theories of the prison
Pleasure and pain, 11, 49; in Bentham's utilitarianism, 129–130, 141–142; in More's *Utopia*, 85–89, 94, 100–101; in Plato's Laws, 53–61, 63–64
Police, 139
Polus, 48, 50, 54, 63–64
Polylerites, 92–93, 96, 98
Poor relief, 108, 133, 138, 144, 153
Poverty, 11, 91, 93, 138–139, 151, 160
"Power/knowledge," 67, 73
Praise and blame, 65
Pretrial detention, 4, 153
Pride, 88, 91, 97–98, 100–101
Prison abolition, 18, 24, 37, 158, 161
Prison/jail distinction, 4, 33, 76, 153
Prison reform, 13, 40
Prisons. *See* Imprisonment and prisons
Property, 83–85, 127, 138, 146, 150, 154, 161
Prostitution. *See* Sex work
Protagoras of Abdera, 24, 40–42, 54, 61–62, 64–65, 69, 145

Psychology. *See* Criminal psychology;
  Moral psychology
Punishment, 2, 5–6, 10, 14–15, 20–24,
  46–48, 66–67, 72–73, 91–95,
  99–100, 158–161; horizonal, 26, 32,
  38–40, 72, 159–160; as legislative
  intervention, 131–140, 152–154;
  Socratic, 48–53; vertical, 26, 32,
  38–39, 72, 159–160. *See also*
  Theories of punishment
Punitive incarceration, 4, 3–5, 1–19,
  19, 33, 76, 166n1

Racism, 17, 44
Reason, 10, 46, 53–60, 65–69, 73,
  87–90, 120, 156
Reasoning, practical, 116–118, 132,
  144, 151
Reform. *See* Prison reform; Theories
  of punishment
Reformatory. *See* Penitentiary
Reformatory (prison in the *Laws*). *See*
  Sōphronistērion
Refutation. *See* Dialectical
  examination
Rehabilitation. *See* Theories of
  punishment
Rehabilitative ideal, 128, 169n25
Reintegration, 2, 19, 32, 146
Renaissance, 81, 91–92, 98–99, 121;
  Renaissance Platonism, 5, 11, 76,
  79, 81–82
Retributivism. *See* Theories of
  punishment
Roman law, 77, 96, 98, 114
Rousseau, Jean-Jacques, 151
Rule of Benedict, 98
Rush, Benjamin, 13

Schoeck, R. J., 81
Schooling, 12, 81, 95, 137, 139–140,
  153. *See also* Education
Security, 8, 20, 138–139, 150, 152, 154
Seneca, Lucius Annaeus, 81, 97
Sentencing, 3, 15, 36, 96
Sex work, 110, 148
Shame, 36–39, 48–50, 56–57, 62–66,
  69–70, 86, 151–152; shame-based

punishments, 106–108, 122; shame
  culture, 89, 99, 122, 155
Shelby, Tommie, 125
Simonton, Matthew, 32
Slavery, 27, 34, 76–77, 114, 147;
  incarceration reminiscent of,
  20–21, 27, 37, 39; penal slavery, 90,
  92–93, 96
Smith, Adam, 142, 151
Social contract, 6, 105; incarceration
  violates, 8, 20, 22, 103–106,
  112–115, 121–123, 159–160
Social control, 27, 72, 88, 122, 145
Socrates, 28, 46–47, 50, 72
Solon, 27, 34
Sōphronistērion, 47, 58, 60, 68
Sōphrosunē, 63, 69, 78. *See also*
  Moderation
Soul craft, 14, 17, 103, 127; in later
  Platonism, 76–79; Plato's
  technique of, 46–47, 57, 61, 70
Sovereign, 8–9, 20–22, 103–107,
  112–115, 119–124, 145, 159–160;
  demos as, 46
Sparta, 27, 53, 63, 81
Statistical information, 73, 148–149
Symposia, 64–65

Tartarus (prison), 47, 50, 59–61, 68
Technique of punishment, 7, 14,
  19–20, 24, 107, 115, 158; Platonic
  tradition's interest in, 42, 50, 53,
  67, 86, 95, 128
Theories of punishment: Deterrence,
  15, 60, 115, 131, 133, 155; Future-
  directed, 11, 18–19, 39–43, 61, 90,
  115; reformative/rehabilitative/
  correctional, 10, 18–19, 40–42, 57,
  62–63, 111, 116, 156; retributivist, 2,
  15, 18–19, 41–42, 99; incapacitation,
  2, 15, 131–132, 155, 205n80
Theories of the prison: Ancient
  theory of the prison, 16, 18, 29, 71,
  73, 78, 119; contemporary/
  postmodern theory of the prison,
  4, 15–16, 23; modern theory of the
  prison, 2–4, 13–18, 23, 40, 67, 72–73,
  76, 127; Platonic/correctional

tradition, 6–7, 9–13, 18–20, 79, 95–96, 127–128, 156, 158; popular authorization tradition, 2, 6–9, 13–16, 20–24, 43–44, 103–104, 123–125, 159–161

Thirty Tyrants, 27, 30–33, 43

Thucydides, 41

Timocrates, 33–39, 46–47

Tocqueville, Alexis de, 13

Total institutions, 128, 135, 137–139, 142, 145

United States of America, 1–2, 13–14, 16–19, 21, 23, 160–161

Utility, 12, 88, 96, 100, 128, 133–134, 144–146, 148, 155; class and, 150–151, 154; principle of, 129, 131

Utopianism, 12, 126–129, 136, 147

Utopians, 80, 82–90, 99–100

Utopus, 89, 94

Vertical punishment. *See* Punishment

Virtue, 40–41, 62–63, 66, 69, 90, 95–97, 100, 130

Wealth, 7, 23, 66, 70, 85, 88, 120, 123, 149–151; punishing the wealthy, 22–24, 37, 39–40, 125, 160–161

Weber, Max, 97

Winstanley, Gerrard, 113–114

Women, 94

Yates, Arthur, 106